POSITIVE
pushing

POSITIVE
pushing

HOW TO RAISE A SUCCESSFUL
AND HAPPY CHILD

JIM TAYLOR, PH.D.

NEW YORK

Library of Congress Cataloging-in-Publication Data has been requested.

ISBN: 0-7868-8850-4

Book design by Oksana Kushnir

Hyperion books are available for special promotions and premiums. For details contact
Hyperion Special Markets, 77 West 66th Street, 11th Floor, New York, New York, 10023, or
call 212-456-0133.

FIRST TRADE PAPERBACK EDITION

10 9 8 7 6 5 4 3 2 1

CONTENTS

PART II: OWNERSHIP   81

PART III: EMOTIONAL MASTERY   171

SPECIAL THANKS TO . . .

Gerald Sindell of Thought Leaders International, my manager, mentor, and friend. If you weren't there, I wouldn't be here.

Jim Levine, my agent, for "getting me" fifteen minutes after receiving my manuscript. Gerry Sindell told me then that you would change my life . . . and you have.

Mary Ellen "MEO" O'Neill, my editor at Hyperion, for giving me a dose of my own medicine by *pushing* me to find and express my voice clearly and completely.

Everyone at Hyperion, including Ellen Archer, Will Schwalbe, Katie Long, Jane Comins, Carrie Covert, and Shana Alstaetter, for helping make my vision a reality.

The many young achievers, parents, teachers, coaches, and instructors with whom I have worked over the past seventeen years. What I know I have learned from you.

Finally, my parents, Shel and Ceci Taylor, for setting my first example of how to raise a successful achiever.

POSITIVE PUSHING

What do kids really need to be successful and happy people? Parents, educators, and society as a whole couldn't ask a more important question. How you answer this question will determine how you will raise your child, what lessons your child will learn, what values he will adopt, and, ultimately, what kind of adult he will become.

The question of what kids really need to become successful and happy people has been asked since the Enlightenment. The answers have been many and diverse, ranging from "spare the rod, spoil the child" to "let them find their own way." As with such issues, the answer to this question likely lies somewhere between those two extremes. People have a tendency to oversimplify these matters because it makes a complex issue easier to deal with. But it also probably makes the answer inadequate.

My answer to this question reflects back on what parents did well and where they may have erred during the past fifty years of child rearing. It also looks at the present to understand what is unique about our society during this period in our history that makes child rearing such a challenge. And my answer attempts to gaze into the future to better understand our society and where child rearing may be going.

My response to the question "What do kids really need?" is a two-part answer. The first part of my answer focuses on the "what" of the question, namely, the essential qualities that every child needs to become a successful and happy adult. The second part of my answer addresses the "how" of the question, specifically, how you can help your child to develop those qualities. Ultimately, my answer is intended to empower you to act on your values and beliefs, and to become a positive, active, and purposeful force in your child's life.

THREE PILLARS OF SUCCESSFUL ACHIEVERS

Parents who want their children to achieve something called "success" may find that this goal conflicts with their desire for their children to also become happy. Achieving success, as frequently defined by our society, emphasizes wealth and social status and is often at odds with experiencing satisfaction, contentment, and happiness. A perusal of the psychology section of any bookstore shows that the goal of achieving success by itself is inadequate. As Dr. Jack Wetter, a Los Angeles clinical psychologist, observes, "On the one side, you've got books on how to raise achieving, successful children. And across from that, you've got books for adults on how to overcome your depression and increase your self-esteem."

The purpose—and the theme—of *Positive Pushing* is to guide you in raising your child to be a *successful achiever*. Successful achievers are distinguished from those who simply achieve success in that, for successful achievers, success and happiness are synonymous. Not only do they not view success and happiness as mutually exclusive, parents of successful achievers see them as necessarily mutually inclusive. *Success without happiness is not success at all.*

Implicit in the notion of successful achievers is that a necessary part of success and happiness is the internalization by children of universally held values such as respect, consideration, kindness, generosity, fairness, altruism, integrity, honesty, interdependence, and compassion. Children cannot become successful achievers unless they adopt and live by these essential life-enriching values.

The development of successful achievers comes from fostering the Three Pillars of Successful Achievers: self-esteem, ownership, and emotional mastery. These three areas provide the foundation for raising children who are successful, happy, and possess life-affirming values. The goal of *Positive Pushing* is to show you how to raise your child with these three pillars so that his or her childhood development will lead to a life of success and happiness.

FIRST PILLAR: SELF-ESTEEM

Self-esteem has been perhaps the most misunderstood and poorly used developmental area in recent generations. In the last few decades, parents were led to believe that self-esteem developed if a child felt loved and valued. This belief caused parents to shower their children with love, encouragement, and support regardless of what their children actually did.

Yet this "unconditional love" is only one half of the self-esteem equation. The second part is that children need to develop a sense of competence and mastery over their world. Most basically, children must learn that their actions matter, that their actions have consequences. Since the 1970s, parents have often neglected to provide their children with this essential component of self-esteem.

Your child will develop high self-esteem from receiving appropriate love, encouragement, and support, but also from the sense of competence he develops from opportunities you give him to learn and use skills in the pursuit of achievement. High self-esteem also acts as the foundation for the other two pillars that form the essence of successful achievers.

SECOND PILLAR: OWNERSHIP

Another mistake that parents can make in trying to develop high self-esteem in their children is to provide them with *too much* love, encouragement, and support. By investing so much of their own self-esteem in their child's efforts, parents, in effect, assume ownership of their child's achievements. Though these efforts are often well-intentioned, the result is that children feel no sense of connectedness and responsibility for their efforts. The children end up being unable to say, "I'm doing this because I want to."

Children need to gain a sense of ownership of their life's interests, efforts, and achievements. This ownership means that they engage in an activity out of an enduring love for it and an internally derived determination to do their very best. This ownership also provides them with an immense source of gratification and joy from their efforts that further motivates them to strive higher in their achievement activities.

THIRD PILLAR: EMOTIONAL MASTERY

The third pillar of successful achievers, emotional mastery, is perhaps the most neglected aspect of a child's development. Parents have been led to believe that letting their children experience negative emotions such as frustration, anger, and sadness will harm them. Based on this belief, parents have felt the need to protect their children from feeling bad. They rationalize failure, distract children from experiencing emotions deeply, try to placate negative emotions, and create artificial positive emotions.

Yet, parents who protect their children from their emotions are actually interfering with their children's emotional growth. These children end up never learning how to deal effectively with their emotions and enter adulthood ill-equipped for its emotional demands. Only by being allowed to experience emotions are children able to figure out what emotions they are feeling, what the emotions mean to them, and how they can manage them effectively.

This third pillar explains that you will want to give your child opportunities to experience emotions fully—both positive *and* negative—and provide her with guidance to understand and gain mastery over her emotional life. Children who do not develop emotionally can still achieve success, but the price they pay is often discontentment and unhappiness in their successes. Emotional mastery enables children to not only become successful, but also to find satisfaction and joy in their efforts.

WHY CHILDREN NEED TO BE PUSHED

Many children are creatures of inertia (as are many adults). They will remain in their current state—for example, lying on the couch all day watching TV—unless you exert a force on them. If you do not push your child, she will be greatly hindered in her learning to walk and talk. She will not want to work very hard or strive to do very much. At best, without pushing, she will do things more slowly or less well than she is capable.

Children do not like discomfort. When they first try something new, they will often put forth effort until it gets difficult or uncomfortable. Then they will look to others—most often to you—to see whether they have gone far enough. If you say, "Great job. You can stop if you want," they often will. By stopping, your child will never find out what he is capable of and will miss out on the satisfaction of moving out of his comfort zone and pushing his limits. If you push him to try harder and persist longer, "Good job so far, but we bet you can do even better," he is more likely to face his discomfort and attain a higher level of achievement and satisfaction. As *Boston Globe* writer John Powers observes, "A funny thing happens when you raise the bar. People find a way to get over it, once they realize it's expected. Human beings can do amazing things—if they're asked to."

A powerful metaphor is that of the mother bird and the baby bird in the nest. The time has arrived for the baby bird to learn to fly. But the baby doesn't know it. If left to its own devices, it might remain in the warmth, comfort, and safety of the nest forever. The mother knows the time has come for the baby bird to leave the nest. The mother knows that any earlier the baby would have been unprepared to fly and might have fallen to the ground. And the mother knows that any later and the baby would resist leaving the nest. So, with a firm nudge, the mother bird pushes the baby bird out of the nest, having complete faith her baby is ready. And the baby bird does fly!

The best way to illustrate why pushing your child is so essential is to describe the qualities that make successful achievers both successful and happy. Successful achievers have ingrained essential values that enable them to be productive, caring, and thoughtful people. These values, in turn, allow them to take risks and to explore, test, and realize their fullest abilities. These experiences teach successful achievers about the connection between their efforts and their results, and strengthen their sense of control over their lives. In the course of their efforts, successful achievers experience both success and failure, and learn the valuable lessons of each. These experiences provide them with great satisfaction and fulfillment in giving their best effort, regardless of whether they succeed or fail. The culmination of this process results in successful achievers understanding what makes them happiest, helps them to find their life's passion, and impels them to pursue their dreams to their fullest extent.

If you don't push your child, she will have a much more difficult time developing these essential elements of becoming a successful achiever. Some people have described pushing children as a form of child abuse (and it can be), but not pushing your child may be a form of neglect that can be equally destructive. Like the mother bird with her baby bird, you need to be willing to push your child so that she will learn to fly and to soar to her greatest heights.

WHY PUSHING HAS GOTTEN A BAD RAP

The popular view of pushing holds that parents need to force their children to do things that they do not want to do, like cleaning their rooms, doing their homework, or practicing on the piano. Today's parents have been told that pushing will make their children angry and resentful, reduce their desire to achieve, and leave permanent emotional scars that will handicap them for life. There appears to be some truth to that notion of pushing. The University of Massachusetts researchers Ena and Ronald Nuttall found that parents who pushed too hard, in the form of rigid and angry control, actually reduced their children's motivation to achieve. Unfortunately, misunderstanding of research of this type and some parents' own experiences have led many to back away from pushing their children altogether rather than to learn how to push in a healthy and appropriate way.

Many baby boomers apparently have unhappy memories of their upbringings. I often hear parents say something like: "I don't want to raise my child the way my parents raised me." When I ask these parents about their childhoods, they describe their own upbringings as "oppressive, cold, restrictive, or controlling." Drs. Don Dinkmeyer and Gary D. McKay, the authors of *Raising a Responsible Child*, observe that "our autocratic tradition, emphasizing punishment and reward, has trained us to prod and nag rather than encourage. Often our language merely echoes the comments our own parents made to us."

What the above research and this quote tell us is that pushing is destructive when it is negative, angry, controlling, and demeaning. This type of pushing causes children to feel threatened. Children are inherently motivated to avoid threats and will, if threatened, avoid trying to achieve anything. Because many parents seem to have been raised with this negative kind of pushing, they fear pushing in general to be something that will hurt their children. Because of this negative view of pushing, many parents aren't able to see that the problem is *how* they push, not *whether* they push. This is a great loss to their children. As Ena and Ronald Nuttall have found, parents who are more accepting and encouraging, and less hostile, raise children who are hardworking, competent, and ambitious. Positive pushing works.

This current generation of parents seems to be reflecting on how they were raised and then choosing to raise their own children in a very different manner. Unfortunately, to correct the perceived mistakes of their parents' child-rearing methods, many new parents are going to the opposite end of the child-rearing spectrum, using a laissez-faire approach that offers children little direction in all aspects of their lives. The University of Georgia researchers Rex Forehand and Britton McKinney traced the disciplinary practices of parents over the past forty years and found four primary trends that have fostered this overreaction and resistance to pushing: (1) a shift from strict to lax discipline that gives children mixed messages, (2) guidance on discipline moving from Puritan religious beliefs to "experts" in fields such as psychology, (3) legislative changes aimed at strengthening children's rights, and (4) a diminished role of fathers in child rearing and discipline.

It seems clear that many parents of the last generation pushed too hard, too unrelentingly and inappropriately, and many children suffered because of it. You might be one of them. The current dominant child-rearing philosophy appears to be a well-intentioned reaction to correct these mistakes. Unfortunately, this overreaction has taken away from parents an essential parenting tool.

PUSHING IS A MORAL IMPERATIVE

I believe that you should push your child. Not only is it okay, it is your right, responsibility, and your absolute moral imperative as a parent. I am going to attempt to show you why you need to push your child. I will describe what I consider to be the dangers of not pushing your child. And I am going to try to show you how to push your child so that, instead of the very real possibility of your contributing to the raising of an unhappy and unproductive person, your child will have a much greater opportunity to become a successful achiever.

I hope to change the way you think about pushing your child by broadening the definition of what pushing means and describing the right and wrong ways to push. I am going to give you permission to do what you have wanted to do for a very long time, but were too afraid to do—push your child to become the most successful and happiest person she can be.

THE POWER OF POSITIVE PUSHING

Positive pushing is aimed at motivating your child to action. It encourages growth in your child. Positive pushing impels your child to move out of her comfort zone, to explore, and to take risks. It fosters achievement and success. So far, positive pushing may not seem much different from pushing as you know it. What separates positive pushing from old-style pushing is that, as the term would suggest, it is positive and encouraging. Positive pushing always demonstrates the love, respect, and value you hold for your child. Positive pushing allows your child to feel in control of her achievement efforts. It is also flexible and responsive to your child's needs. By the very nature of positive pushing, your child sees that your pushing is intended to be in her best interests.

Positive pushing involves exerting a powerful influence over the values, beliefs, and attitudes you want your child to internalize. There are three ways you can "push" your child. First, you influence your child through *modeling*, in which your child observes your emotional expressions, problem-solving strategies, and coping behaviors. Positive pushing involves "walking the walk" on your beliefs, attitudes, and values. "Do as I say, not as I do" just doesn't cut it with positive pushing. You need to live and act on what you believe. Second, you *teach or coach* your child, providing direct information, instruction, and guidance on values, beliefs, and behavior. It includes talking to your child about what you value in life and sharing your perspectives on life, family, career, and other areas. Third, you *manage your child's environment and activities*—peer interactions, achievement activities, cultural experiences, leisure pursuits—in ways that reflect the values, attitudes, and behaviors that you want your child to adopt. Positive pushing means actively creating an environment at home, in school, and in your community that will foster success and happiness.

Positive pushing emphasizes creating options for children from which they can choose a direction, and stressing that *doing nothing is not an option*. It requires that children try different things before they make judgments about them. Positive pushing demands that you push your children to go beyond what they believe are their limits. Encouraging your children, providing emotional, practical, financial, and other types of support, offering guidance and feedback, and giving them love and attention are also forms of positive pushing.

Yes, positive pushing also means occasionally strongly directing your child to do things he doesn't want to do. You will be able to push your child in this way because you believe it is in his best interest. You should hold your child to certain expectations that reflect your values and beliefs, for example, sustained effort, responsibility, consideration, and cooperation. These values will be reflected in schoolwork, household chores, and helping others. Only by requiring your child to adhere to these values will he be exposed to them, learn them, and, eventually, internalize them. Moreover, if your child is actually engaged in activities that employ the values that you deem important, he is more likely to adopt them as his own.

This kind of positive pushing is especially important in helping your child to learn to make informed decisions. Too often, a child makes a decision about something that might be of benefit to her without having tried it. Perhaps she has some preconceived notions about it, has heard about it from friends, or it just doesn't seem particularly appealing at face value. In these situations, you should strongly encourage—push—your child to actually experience it, whatever the "it" is, so that she can make an informed decision about its value and interest, and whether to continue the activity. This is particularly important because most things of value in life cause some discomfort when they are first experienced. For example, the monotony of homework, the repetition of practicing a musical instrument, or the physical demands of learning a sport can all be initially discouraging. If your child is allowed to stop before she has reached a point where she can experience some of the rewards of an activity, she will miss out on two essentials of life. Your child will not learn the value of commitment to achieving success and happiness, and she will not experience the satisfaction and pure joy of achievement.

THE PURPOSE OF POSITIVE PUSHING

What do you value in raising your child? What is important to you in his development and his progress toward adulthood? What qualities do you want to instill in him? Do you want him to be achieving or happy, driven or content, successful or satisfied, or all of these? These are fundamental questions that you need to ask yourself when your child is young. The answers to these questions will have a profound impact on which path your child chooses and what kind of person your child becomes.

The answers you find to these questions reflect your view of the meaning of life and the values that you derive from this perspective. How you value family, faith, education, social justice, health, achievement, happiness, and lifestyle will influence how you raise your child. Whether you do so consciously or not, you communicate your values to your child through the life you lead and the choices you make. As Calvin Trillin, the author of *Messages from My Father*, observes, "It seems to me that upbringings have themes. The parents set the theme, either explicitly or implicitly, and the children pick it up, sometimes accurately and sometimes not so accurately." Positive pushing is how you can forward your theme. It is the way you deliberately choose, communicate, and instill those values and perspectives in your child.

The Art of Positive Pushing

Positive pushing is not an exact science in which clear rules can be given to you about how and when to push your child. Rather, positive pushing is an art that takes thought, sensitivity, and experimentation to find out the type and intensity of pushing that will be most effective with your particular child. Some parents push their child relentlessly without considering the impact that this oppressive force has on him. Other parents give their child complete free rein to do whatever he wants with no accounting for how this unrestricted freedom affects him. The art of positive pushing involves finding a healthy balance between these two extremes.

The art of positive pushing requires that you temper your expectations of success with love of your child. Everything you do with your child is an expression of the degree of control (pushing) and acceptance (love) you express. Parents who are low in control and low in acceptance produce children who are the most troubled because they receive little from their parents in terms of love *or* boundaries. These children tend to be unhappy, undisciplined, unfocused, and emotionally immature. Parents who are low in control and high in acceptance raise children who are spoiled, impulsive, irresponsible, and dependent. Parents who are high in control and low in acceptance have children with low self-esteem who are socially unskilled, feel unloved, and are angry at and resentful of their parents. The ideal combination of these attributes is parents who are high in both control and acceptance. The children who have had the benefit of this kind of parenting tend to have high self-esteem, are emotionally mature, and are high achievers. As Dr. Mary Pipher, the author of *Reviving Ophelia*, suggests, these latter parents find "a balance between security and freedom, conformity to family values and autonomy . . . protection and challenges . . . affection and structure. [Children] hear the message 'I love you, but I have expectations.' In these homes, parents set firm guidelines and communicate high hopes."

The art of positive pushing involves learning when you are pushing too hard. Pushing too hard can produce short-term results seen as improved effort and greater achievement. Children who are less mature or less able to express their feelings toward their parents will, for a time, respond to their parents' unrelenting pushing out of fear of loss of their parents' love with strong effort and high achievement. These initial benefits can mislead parents into believing that their forceful pushing works. But excessive pushing will always come back to haunt both parents and their children. Though these children may be high achievers for some time, they will also be very unhappy because of the tremendous pressure they feel from their parents. At some point, these children will reach a level of maturity or the burden from their parents will become so great that they will push back in some destructive way to relieve the pressure. What results are children who are both unsuccessful and unhappy.

Children often have difficulty telling their parents directly that they are pushing too hard for fear that their parents will be disappointed in them. Instead, children communicate to their parents that they are feeling too much pressure initially in subtle—and often unclear—ways, such as not trying as hard, breaking or losing equipment or materials, or sabotaging their achievement efforts. Unfortunately, parents misinterpret this behavior as a lack of motivation and appreciation. Rather than considering what message their children are trying to convey, parents often have a knee-jerk reaction of anger and assume a "How ungrateful after all I have done for you" attitude that further increases the pressure on their children. These conflicting reactions produce a vicious cycle of anger and resistance, and a destructive tug-of-war for control over the child's life. If this battle of wills continues, children may communicate their messages more "loudly" by using more destructive "language," such as overt rebellion, disruptive behavior, or substance abuse.

Children have a great ability to communicate to their parents that they are being pushed too hard. Unfortunately, they often speak to their parents in a language in which their parents are not fluent. The art of positive pushing means being sensitive to how your child is responding to your pushing. An essential part of sensitivity is learning to speak your child's language. This understanding also involves deliberately considering the message your child is trying to communicate—which often your child doesn't even know consciously—and responding in a way that conveys to your child that you hear what she is saying. By learning your child's language, you can accurately interpret her messages and act in her best interests.

Two forces are required to engage in a pushing match. If you push too hard, your child will push back harder to resist the force. If you ease your pressure, your child will also let up. What parents often don't realize is that sometimes less is more—if you back off from pushing, it allows your child to continue in the direction he (and you) want to go. By backing off, you increase the likelihood that your child will regain his motivation, return to his high level of achievement, and actually have fun again in the achievement activity.

As John Gray, Ph.D., the author of *Children Are from Heaven*, observes, "When children resist a parent, it is often because they are wanting something else and they assume that if you just understood, you would want to support their want, wish, or need. . . . The power of understanding your children's resistance is that it immediately minimizes resistance. When children get the message that you understand what they want and how important it is to them, then their resistance level changes."

POSITIVE PUSHING MEANS PUSHING YOURSELF

Positive pushing doesn't just refer to your doing or not doing things to your child. In order to push your child appropriately, *you must first push yourself.* In my years of work with young achievers, I have come across *no* truly mean or ill-intentioned parents. I meet parents who are often misguided, sometimes confused, and occasionally disturbed. Mostly, though, I find parents who love their children and want the best for them, but either they don't know what is best for them or they carry so much emotional "baggage" from their own upbringings that they aren't able to act on what is best for their children. I have found that when most parents are guided to understand what is in their children's best interests, parents will try to do whatever they can to provide what is best for them.

Whether a child becomes successful and happy does not necessarily depend on how "good" or "bad" you are as a parent or what kinds of mistakes you make in raising your child. Rather, how your child ultimately turns out depends on your openness to doing things or making changes that are in the best interests of your child. If you are willing to do what is best for your child—which may include making changes yourself and supporting change in your child—the possibilities for your child's future are good. If you are not willing or able to do what is best for your child or you can't change yourself or foster change in your child, your child will have a lesser likelihood of a richly developed adulthood.

I have come across two types of problem parents in my work with young achievers. The most difficult parent is one who is unwilling or incapable of acting in his child's best interests or making changes that will help his child. This parent is so rigid in his belief that he is doing the right thing or he carries so much emotional baggage that he simply lacks the capacity to respond to his child's needs or to make necessary changes in himself. This parent is unable to consider that he has made mistakes in raising his child and is threatened by the suggestion that he must change in order to help his child. If this child is left to deal with her unsupportive parent on her own, her chances of becoming a successful achiever are slim. If this child is fortunate enough to receive support from, for example, her other parent, a psychotherapist, teacher, coach, or instructor, she has a chance, but it will be an uphill battle because she must resist the powerful and ever-present influence of her unsupportive parent in an unhealthy family environment.

The second type of parent is one who may also carry emotional baggage and may also have made mistakes, but somehow finds the courage to recognize the harm she is doing to her child, face her problems, and support changes in her child. This parent will often seek professional treatment and will provide her child with similar opportunities. With this parent's willingness to change, her child has a new environment that can encourage rather than inhibit his achievement and happiness, and the odds are in favor of his becoming productive and well-adjusted. I have immense respect for this parent who puts her child's needs ahead of her own, faces her own personal demons, and often experiences great pain in order to help her child. This kind of parent's selflessness, courage, and strength is remarkable.

For example, Michelle was a promising violinist whose father, Howard, had devoted the past ten years to her musical career. As Michelle improved and showed great promise, Howard increasingly exerted more pressure on her to practice and perform, and his anger, which had been present for most of his life, became a part of her daily regimen. When Michelle was thirteen, problems arose. She would have panic attacks before her recitals, causing her to perform poorly. Howard couldn't see that he was causing his daughter's problems and hired a psychologist to work with her. In a short time, it became clear to the psychologist that Howard was the problem. The psychologist quickly learned that Howard had been clinically depressed most of his life and was expressing his depression through anger. At the recommendation of the psychologist, Howard began seeing a psychiatrist and was put on antidepressant medication. The rapid change in Howard was remarkable. His anger subsided and he was able to step back from Michelle's music. Michelle's behavior changed dramatically too. As if a huge weight had been lifted off her shoulders, Michelle found joy in her violin again.

Positive pushing means pushing yourself to understand what is best for your child. It also involves "looking in the mirror" and seeing what in yourself might interfere with making the right choices and doing the right thing for your child. Finally, positive pushing means having the courage to make the changes that will allow your child to become a successful achiever.

LAYING THE FOUNDATION FOR SUCCESSFUL ACHIEVERS

DEFINING SUCCESS AND FAILURE

How your child comes to view success and failure can have a dramatic impact on how much success and happiness he ultimately attains. The difference between simply achieving success and becoming a successful achiever is based on whether your child is pursuing goals that have been forced on him by you or by society, or whether he fully embraces his goals as a reflection of who he is and what he wants. Imagine your child having to pursue goals that he really doesn't want to achieve. The emotional value of success in attaining those goals would be negligible.

Now imagine your child setting and achieving goals that come from *his* most basic values and beliefs about what is important. The value of that success would be one of profound fulfillment and joy.

Unfortunately, a healthy outlook on success and failure is difficult to develop in children. Our society offers definitions and views on success and failure that are narrow, limiting, and that can ultimately inhibit the growth of successful achievers. American culture often defines success simplistically in terms of "winning." This shallowness conveys the notion that in any sports competition, artistic performance, or school exam, only one winner is possible. Everyone else, then, is shunted off into the category of "losers." Our society also places great emphasis on wealth, status, physical appearance, and popularity as indicators of success—the more money and power you have and the more attractive and popular you are, the more successful you are. For most children raised by these definitions, success will be largely unattainable. At the same time, society has made losing even more intolerable to contemplate for children—being poor, powerless, unattractive, and unpopular is unacceptable. With these restrictive definitions, children perceive that they are caught in the untenable situation of *having little opportunity for success and great chance of failure.*

Blindly accepting society's narrow definitions of success and failure takes away your and your child's power to decide how to define success and failure. By buying into these narrow definitions of success and broad definitions of failure rather than choosing definitions based on your own values, your child is unlikely to become a successful achiever because she will not be choosing a path of achievement that is truly hers. Rather, your child is being forced down a path that may bring what might appear to others to be success, but may not be success to her.

In attempting to reframe success in a way that will encourage the development of a successful achiever, the new perspective should be grounded in who your child is and what she most values. Success then can be defined as setting and achieving goals that express and affirm the values that your child has chosen. Conversely, failure can be seen as not achieving those self-affirming goals. Or failure can mean achieving goals that are not consistent with your child's values, even if achieving those goals makes her successful in other people's eyes. With these new definitions, your child can now succeed without winning and lose without failing. For example, a young flutist worked extremely hard to be named to the wind section of her school's orchestra. Though she will never be a principal performer, she is a success because she set and achieved a goal that was important to her.

Defining success and failure in a positive and healthy way is only the first step in encouraging your child to be a successful achiever. These new definitions offer your child goals to strive for, but they don't show her how to attain those goals. The second essential step that provides your child with the tools to reach her goals involves the process of *achieving*. Without the ability to achieve—how your child gets to her goals—your child will never find the success she seeks. Achieving is grounded in important skills that you can teach your child and will lead to success—determination, effort, patience, and perseverance, to name a few. The process of achieving will also teach your child how to gain great satisfaction and joy in the efforts she makes as she pursues her goals. This combination of qualities will result in successful achievers realizing true success based on who they are and what they value. Your emphasis then should be on raising an *achieving and happy* child. If you can instill positive values, provide these skills, and offer these experiences, your child will be a success—however she defines it.

Some children may grow up to achieve extraordinary success in their chosen achievement activity and perhaps become famous for their success, for example, Beverly Sills, Anthony Hopkins, and Dorothy Hamill. Other children may not attain such lofty success or become famous, yet they may be no less successful. Success can be defined by the ownership, commitment, effort, and quality that your child puts into the achievement activity and the satisfaction, affirmation, and joy your child gets out of it. Success can also be defined in terms of compassion, consideration, generosity, and love. A successful achiever can be a cardiac surgeon, mathematician, concert pianist, or Olympic champion. A successful achiever can also be a teacher, artist, carpenter, or parent.

If you have done everything right and your child still doesn't reach a high level of traditional success, he may simply not be cut out for that definition of success—due to temperament, capability, or interest. But he can still be a successful achiever. You will have succeeded as a parent when you provide your child with the guidance and freedom to find his own definition of being a successful achiever and then allow him to pursue that goal with all of his heart.

WHAT MAKES YOUR CHILD HAPPY?

A great deal of *Positive Pushing* is devoted to showing you how to push your child to develop the three pillars of successful achieving and become successful. However, the definition of what a successful achiever is involves not only being successful, but also being happy in those efforts. An indispensable part of positive pushing involves pushing your child to seek happiness in his life as well.

I suggest throughout this book that a great deal of a successful achiever's happiness comes from the enjoyment and satisfaction gained from his achievement efforts. Recent research bears out my view by demonstrating that three areas that are essential for achievement—and which are central to this book—are also crucial for happiness: self-esteem, competence, and autonomy. People who have high self-esteem, who feel capable in their activities, and whose activities are of their own choosing rate themselves as happiest. Surprisingly, two of the most popularly cited and sought-after sources of happiness in our society—wealth and popularity—were unrelated to happiness or even appeared to have a negative effect on happiness.

However, happiness is not inextricably linked to achievement. Rather, happiness can stand alone and have many sources besides achievement. I will speak at length about how overinvestment in a single activity to the exclusion of other meaningful activities may lead to success, but will often not be accompanied by happiness. An essential element of what makes a child a successful achiever, unlike those children who achieve only success, is her parents' ability to create *balance in their child's life*. Much as a child should have experiences other than her achievement activity that offer meaning and affirmation, so too should a child have sources of happiness outside her achievement efforts.

A primary emphasis in my work with young achievers involves helping them understand exactly what makes them happy and identifying their most significant sources of happiness, both within and outside of their achievement activities. I also assist them in knowing what gives them balance in their lives—for example, family time, religious faith, and hobbies—and guide them in proactively creating this *balance within the imbalance*. This notion means that even when children are dedicated to one achievement activity and devote most of their time to that activity, they can still create small amounts of balance within their otherwise unbalanced lifestyles.

By engaging your child in the process of finding what makes him happy, he will be better able to recognize what makes him happy and how he can actively seek out experiences that make him happy. You can help your child gain a better understanding of what makes him happy by, first, asking him questions about what activities he enjoys and why he enjoys them. You can also observe him so that you can identify the activities that bring him the most pleasure. Then, you can encourage him to participate in these activities by setting aside time, providing resources, and sharing the experience with him.

This balance is essential for successful achievers because achieving is not always an enjoyable and rewarding process. Trying to achieve will inevitably cause your child to experience disappointment and unhappiness periodically. The process of achievement can be boring and frustrating. By having other resources from which she can gain happiness, your child will be better able to maintain a healthy perspective on the role the achievement activity plays in her life, take the inevitable ups and downs in stride, and master the demanding achievement experiences, rather than having them disrupt her progress toward her goals.

Because of his significant commitment to his achievement activity, your child needs to be able to find *happiness in its process*. Successful achievers describe gaining happiness from the process of their achievement activity quite apart from the benefits they gain from success, social interactions, or other rewards. They appreciate the minutiae of their participation. For example, the cellist who loves to restring and tune her cello. The soccer player who loves to watch professional games live and on television. The chess player who loves to talk about chess theory with his father. The math whiz who loves to study the history of mathematics. All of these practices demonstrate that the achievement activity is a great source of joy and happiness to these successful achievers. Just being involved in any way in their achievement activity is sufficient to make successful achievers happy.

This happiness occurs at many levels. Sure, they love to perform to the best of their ability and succeed, but that is not the overriding reason for their involvement. Being challenged, seeing progress in their development, and reaching their goals are tremendous sources of happiness. Becoming more skilled, seeing improved performance, and having success make successful achievers happy. What I learned from successful achievers is that they revel in all aspects and at all levels of their achievement activity, and being totally absorbed in their achievement efforts makes them both successful and happy.

Successful achievers also derive happiness from *personal time away* from their achievement activities. Most successful achievers are involved in other activities and hobbies that give them additional fulfillment. A dancer might participate in extracurricular school activities. An athlete might pursue her religious devotion and church activities. A serious student might volunteer at a homeless shelter. These experiences balance the narrowness and self-absorption that can be a part of intense achievement participation and provide a healthy perspective on the achievement activity's importance in their lives. Their personal time is their opportunity to escape from the intensity of their achievement activity, to laugh and have "meaningless fun" or "meaningful experiences." Many successful achievers find that it is this personal time that "keeps them sane" when the intense demands of their achievement participation is driving them crazy.

Many successful achievers come to learn that achieving can be a lonely and isolating pursuit. Imagine the computer student who must sit at his computer alone for hours on end. Or the figure skater who gets up at 5 A.M. every morning to go to a cold and dark rink before school. Or the percussionist who must spend three hours after school practicing alone. Because of this solitude that is so often part of achievement and personal growth, successful achievers *value their relationships with others.* The opportunity to give and receive love, friendship, and support from family and friends is essential to their happiness. Much like the person who becomes famished and, thus, celebrates his next meal, successful achievers become hungry for the interactions of meaningful relationships. They savor the simple joys of communication, sharing, laughter, and connecting with others. The "happiness" research I mentioned earlier also bears out this view. Relatedness—feeling close to others—was the final need that was most associated with happiness; people who felt connected with others viewed themselves as most happy.

Successful achievers are, by definition, children who work hard and accomplish a great deal because their achievement activities require considerable time and effort to reach their goals. Because so much of a high achiever's life is devoted to action and accomplishment, successful achievers have a *great appreciation for simply being*. Being involves engaging in activities that serve no purpose beyond simple joy—reading, watching movies, eating, walking, writing. Having the time to "just be" grounds successful achievers in who they are as people instead of what they accomplish as achievers, and provides them with an escape from the intensity of achievement.

This foundation of happiness provides successful achievers with a healthy perspective from which to pursue their achievement goals. It also enables them to maintain balance in lives that are often anything but stable. Finally, this grounding in happiness and balance allows successful achievers to commit to a rigorous path in pursuit of achievement that ultimately leads to both success and happiness.

THE GOAL OF POSITIVE PUSHING

An essential message I want to convey in *Positive Pushing* is the need for you to play a deliberate and vigorous role in raising your child. This emphasis requires that you actively guide your child in ways that will encourage his positive development. This message means that you need to thoughtfully explore the values, beliefs, and attitudes that guide your life and make a conscious decision of how you want to raise your child.

You can communicate this message effectively only if you do so in a positive, confident, and loving way. Your child needs to sense that whatever you do—whether rewarding a job well done or punishing bad behavior—you are doing it out of love and the belief that it is best for your child.

The ability of your child to become a successful achiever will be grounded in essential beliefs that you must foster in him or her. Drs. Aubrey Fine and Michael Sachs, the authors of *Total Sports Experience for Kids*, offer a valuable summary of those beliefs (I have added numbers 1 and 7, and the parenthetical comments):

1. I am loved (sense of value)
2. I am capable (sense of competence)
3. It is important to try (value of effort)
4. I am responsible for my day (sense of ownership)
5. It is okay to make mistakes (accept imperfections)
6. I can handle things when they go wrong (responding to adversity)
7. I enjoy what I do (value of passion and happiness)
8. I can change (being a master).

Positive Pushing is devoted to instilling these fundamental beliefs in your child. I encourage you to post these eight beliefs on your refrigerator as a constant reminder of what all of your parenting efforts are directed toward and what beliefs you most want to instill in your child.

The philosophy and approach that I advocate in *Positive Pushing* are aimed at helping you fulfill three essential goals. Everything you do with your child needs to be in his or her best interests; needs to help promote his or her achievement, happiness, and healthy growth into a joyful and vital adult; and finally, needs to foster a strong and loving relationship between you and your child.

For the sake of simplicity, I have alternated the use of "he" and "she," "him" and "her," throughout *Positive Pushing*.

PART I

SELF-ESTEEM

In the seventies, eighties, and nineties, "building self-esteem" was the catchphrase among parenting experts and the central focus in parents' efforts to raise their children. Authorities on child rearing spoke emphatically about the dangers of low self-esteem. Many of the woes among our society's youth—violence, substance abuse, suicide—were blamed on low self-esteem. Initiatives were created and programs were developed specifically to build self-esteem in children. "The 'experts' advised parents to direct their efforts toward building self-esteem," says John Rosemond, a family psychologist and the author of *Teen-Proofing*.

Parents became fearful of doing anything that might harm their children's self-esteem. They came to believe that any failure or a child's feeling bad would damage self-esteem. It became a national imperative to protect children from failure and any experiences that might cause children to think less of themselves. Standards and expectations changed. "Instead of setting exacting standards and challenging ourselves to meet them, we've created fuzzy ones with which we get to grade ourselves and proclaim ourselves winners. . . . Once upon a time, those verdicts were handed down by others. You passed or you failed. . . . If your ego was bruised . . . then you buckled down and you made it the next time and felt good about yourself," reflects the *Boston Globe* writer John Powers.

Reflective of this change in attitude, schools changed grading systems so children wouldn't feel like failures if they received a low grade. For example, when I was in sixth grade, our town's school board eliminated F's and replaced them with NI's (Needs Improvement), ostensibly to ensure that students didn't feel like failures for doing poorly in school. Youth sports programs began to deemphasize competition because losing might hurt children's self-esteem. Score was not kept and winners were not declared. Parents stopped pushing their children for fear that not achieving goals and not living up to expectations might scar their children for life.

According to parenting experts at the time, children needed to feel loved and valued by their parents and to always feel good about themselves in order to build self-esteem. Parents heaped love and caring on their children regardless of how children behaved or what they actually achieved. Parents rewarded their children to make sure their children always believed that they had succeeded, *even if they hadn't*.

Sadly, this approach has frequently had the exact opposite effect. "A generation or so ago, the experts began telling parents that high self-esteem would lead to better grades, better behavior, and less drug and alcohol use. Unfortunately, it just hasn't turned out that way. The whole notion of building self-esteem in children has backfired, big time. . . . Increasingly, however, it's looking as if well-intentioned efforts to make children feel good about themselves at any cost have resulted in an epidemic of undisciplined brats," argues John Rosemond. What began as a well-meaning attempt to soften the harsh parenting beliefs of post–World War II America became a parental lovefest that resulted in parents' taking away the very things that actually build self-esteem. Parents began to believe that achievement—the idea that children need to have specific areas in which they become deeply involved and that they attempt to master—might not be a good thing because of this misunderstanding of self-esteem.

The psychological problems that arose from inappropriately pushing children to try to achieve something really did exist. Many children perceived the idea of trying to succeed at something as threatening because they believed that their parents' love might depend on whether they succeeded or failed. These children were placed under the weight of unrealistic expectations and burdensome pressure. Children were often taught unhealthily narrow and rigid definitions of success and failure that severely limited their chances of success (which we've already discussed at length). They also often weren't given the necessary tools to succeed.

Instead of addressing these problems related to achievement, parents came to believe that achievement was dangerous and destructive. Rather than understanding why achievement was often associated with childhood problems, achievement as a whole was condemned. Youth sports stopped declaring winners, children received awards just for showing up, the goal of excellence was replaced by one of not doing poorly. A child's life was placed on a sliding scale so every child would feel like a success.

Taking achievement away from children was never a good solution. Achievement was, and is, the solution to the problem. Our society is highly achievement oriented. If children don't learn to respond to the challenges of achievement in a positive way, they're going to have difficulty when they enter our society as adults. To protect children from learning how to achieve is to stunt their development, limit their ability to succeed, and ensure lives of dissatisfaction and unhappiness. The goal is not to avoid achievement, but rather to prepare children for achievement. "Let us treat self-esteem as the valuable quality that it is. Let us view it as a rarified compound consisting of attitude, character, conscience, and hard work. It most certainly is not free for the taking. It is, however, within reach of anyone willing to pay the price. Let us help our students gain their self-esteem in an old-fashioned way. Let us help them earn it," offers Malcolm Gauld, the president of the Hyde Schools, New England preparatory boarding schools that emphasize character development and personal growth.

CHAPTER 1

Aren't I Good Enough for You?
Security vs. Competence

When I ask parents to define self-esteem in children, most say something like, "It's how kids feel about themselves. Kids with high self-esteem feel good about themselves and they feel loved and appreciated by their parents. Kids with low self-esteem don't feel love from their parents and don't really like themselves." This, however, is only half the definition of self-esteem.

Self-esteem is made up of two essential components. The first part of self-esteem, which has been emphasized over the past thirty years, is children's need to feel that they are loved, valued, and appreciated by their parents. The sense of security that comes from these feelings acts as the foundation for self-esteem. Children with this sense of security know that, regardless of what they do or what happens, they will still be loved and valued. This sense of security assures children that their parents will love them even if they fail in their achievement efforts.

Children also know that there are people to whom they can turn to protect them when they are at risk or feeling vulnerable. This "anchor" encourages children to confidently move away from that safe haven and begin to explore their world, take risks, and test their limits. Knowing that they are loved regardless of the outcome of their achievement efforts and that their parents will protect them from harm acts as the foundation for children's comfort and motivation to pursue achievement. "Kids are caught between a need for independence and a need for security. They need to know parents are around—not hovering over their every move, but there in the background," says psychologist Nancy Drake. This sense of security alone is not, however, sufficient to build self-esteem in children.

Where the self-esteem movement over the last few decades has missed out is in neglecting the second essential component of self-esteem—the sense of competence and mastery over one's life. Ann Masten and J. Douglas Coatsworth, researchers at the University of Minnesota and University of Miami, respectively, found that competence can be defined in two ways: broadly in terms of children's successfully achieving developmental milestones (for example, toilet training, language acquisition, and social skills), and more narrowly in terms of specific areas of achievement, such as academics and athletics. This sense of competence is based on several things. In its most basic form, competence derives from children's belief that their *actions matter*, in other words, when they act, certain outcomes result (when children do good things, good things happen; when they do bad things, bad things happen; when they do nothing, nothing happens). A sense of competence develops when children believe that they have the capabilities necessary to be successful. The development of this sense of competence is so fundamental because, as Drs. Masten and Coatsworth further show, children's perceptions of their ability and control, and their confidence in their capabilities, directly affect their future behavior.

By being overly protective, parents can take away essential opportunities for a child to gain competence in areas such as emotional maturity—awareness, understanding, and control of emotions. The lack of emotional competence severely limits a child's ability to achieve because she will not be emotionally capable of managing the inevitable obstacles and setbacks of achievement. Drs. Masten and Coatsworth discovered that low emotional confidence was related to numerous childhood, adolescent, and adult difficulties, including anxiety, aggression, poor social skills, and low achievement.

This is where the self-esteem movement failed. To protect their children's self-esteem, parents took away the very things that build self-esteem. Children were not allowed to learn that their actions matter. Parents also took away children's consequences of and responsibility for their actions. By taking away success and failure (for example, winning and losing, being evaluated and graded), parents took away children's ability to learn that their efforts lead to outcomes and consequences. For example, if parents reward their children for finishing half of their homework because that is better than none at all, they "lower the bar" for their children and demonstrate that a minimal amount of achievement is good enough.

In addition to what parents who don't understand both parts of self-esteem take away from their children, they also don't give them what they most need. Building self-esteem involves giving children the sense of security that comes from knowing that they are loved whether they succeed or fail. It also means providing children with opportunities to become competent people possessing the skills to master the challenges of achievement. Having this foundation of genuine, deeply rooted self-esteem gives children the confidence to continue to challenge themselves, to find satisfaction and validation in their efforts, and to push the limits of their capabilities. This combination of the grounding in feeling loved and secure, with the desire to explore their abilities that comes from a strong sense of competence, acts as the true source of self-esteem. Says Jean Illsley Clarke, the author of *Self-Esteem: A Family Affair*, "Positive self-esteem is important because when people experience it, they feel good and look good, they are effective and productive, and they respond to other people and themselves in healthy, positive, growing ways. People who have positive self-esteem know that they are lovable and capable, and they care about themselves and other people."

RED FLAGS

In each chapter of *Positive Pushing*, I describe "red flags" that can help you to recognize early signs of difficulties that your child may be experiencing and which may lead to more problems in the future. If any of these red flags are *your* red flags, then you will be able to look deeper and understand the underlying problems, their causes, and how you can help your child to overcome these difficulties.

As the most fundamental contributor to the development of children, every warning sign discussed in *Positive Pushing* that arises in children can be traced back to problems with self-esteem. For example, perfectionists depend on their next success to sustain their self-esteem. Children who experience performance anxiety lack a sense of competence and expect to fail. Children who express inappropriate emotions or have no emotional control feel incapable of managing the achievement situation with which they are faced. Children who suffer from more severe psychiatric disorders, such as substance abuse and eating disorders, are showing a consequence of low self-esteem.

DEVELOPING YOUR CHILD'S SENSE OF SECURITY

"For many people, what is most deeply desired is to have been seen and accepted in the family for who they are, a desire to have been treated with kindness, compassion, understanding, and respect; to have been accorded freedom, safety, and privacy, and a sense of belonging," write Myla and Jon Kabat-Zinn, the authors of *Everyday Blessings*. This requires love and a sense of security.

Children who learn that their parents' love for them is dependent on whether they succeed or fail will be threatened by the challenge of achievement. This threat arises out of their perception that every experience of achievement puts their parents' love for them on the line.

The possibility of success may motivate children to achieve in order to gain their parents' love. The possibility of failure, however, puts them in a state of constant fear at the prospect of losing their parents' love. This insecurity will inhibit children's motivation to explore, take risks, and achieve their best.

For your child to develop this sense of security, you need to express your love for your child regardless of whether he succeeds or fails. "The . . . message that children need to hear is 'You are important and lovable just because you exist.' This self-esteem building block is a gift that the child does not have to earn," observes Jean Illsley Clarke. This sounds self-evident and natural for parents to do. Yet, most achieving problems are due to some form of "conditional love." For example, there is a big difference to a child between his parents' saying that he could have tried harder in a way that he understands is for his benefit ("Honey, you won't reach your goals unless you give your best effort") and his parents' expressing their disappointment in him in response to their own needs ("You really let us down when you didn't win today"). Parents who communicate the message of lack of effort in a calm, positive, and supportive way encourage and challenge their child to work harder. Parents who take their child's lack of effort personally and convey disappointment with anger and hurt cause their child to become fearful of achieving because she will fear losing her parents' love.

The second important element of the sense of security is your child's need to feel safe and protected. This aspect of security gives children the confidence to explore their world, take risks, and pursue achievement. To your child, the world is a large and fascinating playground in which to explore. It can also be a chaotic, uncontrollable, and scary place where hidden dangers lurk. Children realize that they have limitations and that they don't know a lot about the world. Giving your child freedom without this sense of security may cause him to feel vulnerable and afraid. You can communicate to your child that you are someone who is stronger than he is and on whom he can rely to protect him when needed. This knowledge reinforces your child's sense of security—he always has a safe haven to which he can return—and gives him the confidence to seek out challenges and to develop his sense of competence.

These feelings of security will also be strengthened when you set boundaries within which your child must stay. A world without boundaries is one that can be overwhelming and threatening to your child. Because she has little experience from which to determine what is safe and what is not, your child is unable to judge how far is far enough. Instead, your child's natural curiosity may propel her into situations beyond her capabilities. Boundaries act as a safety zone to protect your child from experiences for which she is not yet ready. If you do not establish boundaries for your child at an early age, she will likely encounter inappropriate challenges for which she is unprepared. These experiences will be scary, and your child may come to view her world as fearsome and beyond control. This perception of danger will discourage future exploration and inhibit her willingness to take risks and to achieve. Notes psychiatrist David Fassler, "Kids need, want, and benefit from clear, predictable boundaries." Setting boundaries does not mean locking your child in her room and never letting her experience risks or failure. Rather, boundaries mean understanding the risks and dangers your child may encounter, being sensitive to age-appropriate exposure to those risks, and ensuring that your child has the practical, physical, psychological, and emotional skills to successfully respond to a reasonable level of challenge. For example, while visiting the zoo, a father gives his young son money to buy some ice cream at a vendor a short distance away. The boy thought he was on his own, but his father shadowed his son's journey to ensure his safety. The boy felt that he had successfully ventured out on his own and the experience gave him confidence in his ability to explore further.

As your child becomes comfortable with her current boundaries and gains greater confidence and skills that enable her to explore further, you need to constantly reexamine the boundaries to allow greater latitude, thus providing additional opportunities for your child to obtain more experience and skills. When your child reaches a certain level of maturity, the power to establish boundaries should be given to her. For example, in the early years of your child's life, you establish clear physical boundaries of where she can play. At first, the boundaries may encompass the living room, where you can keep an eye on her. Then, her boundaries might expand to the entire first floor of your home, where you can hear her playing. Next, the boundaries could include your fenced-in backyard, where you check up on her periodically. As your child grows, these boundaries could continue to increase to include the block you live on and the neighborhood park. At some later point in your child's life, you could simply ask her to tell you where she is going and trust that she is ready to take on the responsibilities of maintaining her own boundaries.

This gradual extension of boundaries offers several meaningful benefits. The ever-expanding boundaries ensure that your child is allowed to explore beyond what is comfortable and easy, knowing that there are still limits to how far she can go. Boundaries offer your child the opportunity to gain experience and more skills in increasingly challenging situations that will enhance her sense of competence. Boundaries provide children with a safe harbor to which she knows she can return when she reaches the comfortable limits of her explorations. Finally, extending the boundaries and then ceding them to your child allows her to progressively internalize the sense of security that you provided when she was young. It also enables your child to find that feeling of being loved and safe within herself which will contribute to your child's ability to strengthen her sense of competence and foster her independence.

DEVELOPING YOUR CHILD'S SENSE OF COMPETENCE

Henry Ford once said, "If you do or don't think you can do something, you're right." This simple statement goes to the heart of understanding your child's ability to achieve his goals. Most children have the intellectual, technical, or physical capabilities to achieve some level of success in the activities they choose to pursue. Yet, when they do not succeed, it is often because the one thing they lack is a sense of competence in themselves and their abilities.

A child's belief that he can succeed is critical because it allows him to do more than just use his abilities to perform at his current level, but rather it allows him to challenge himself to find the limits of his capabilities. This sense of competence begins with the conviction that a child's efforts will likely be rewarded with success. This belief in his competence and the likelihood of success counters worry and anxiety about failure and the pressure that a child may feel when the thought of failure is threatening. This confidence enables a child to push himself beyond his comfort zone to a level that could not be reached otherwise. It allows a child to take risks in his efforts, which enables him to further raise his level of achievement. Finally, this attitude girds him against the inevitable setbacks, plateaus, and valleys he will face as he strives higher.

There are two aspects of the sense of competence that are necessary to enable children to become successful achievers: *global belief* and *specific belief.* Global belief is a child's basic confidence that her actions matter and that she has the capacity to successfully overcome a range of challenges. Specific belief involves how competent a child feels to succeed in a particular achievement activity. What both of these beliefs have in common is that children learn that they can influence their world and that their actions can produce desired outcomes. For example, a child learns that if he works hard in school then he will earn good grades. Conversely, if he doesn't work hard, he will earn poor grades. Without this fundamental belief in their competence, children will doubt their ability to succeed and, not surprisingly, demonstrate little effort toward achieving their goals.

GLOBAL BELIEF

The development of this general sense of competence comes from your child learning the relationship between her actions and her outcomes—if your child does good things, good things will come from it; if she does bad things (or nothing), no good will come. Early experiences should foster your child's belief that her actions matter.

This relationship is perhaps the most important lesson children can learn to facilitate their development into successful achievers. It is grounded in the connection between effort and outcome. If children learn that when they act appropriately they achieve the outcomes they want, they will come to see that they have control over their lives. Psychologists refer to this perception as an *internal locus of control,* in which children believe that their efforts and actions are responsible for the results that they produce.

Children who recognize this connection between effort and outcome have a sense of control over their achievements because they have learned that when they expend effort they will be successful and when they don't they won't be successful. Children who internalize this relationship say things like "I was successful because I worked hard" and "I earned this."

Conversely, a danger is that children never learn that their actions matter. Either they get what they want no matter what they do (the spoiled or entitled child) or they never get what they want no matter what they do (the neglected or frustrated child). Either way, these children show little motivation to act or achieve because they have learned that their efforts don't matter—there is no relationship between their efforts and outcomes. The absence of the effort-outcome connection is exemplified with statements like "I didn't do anything to achieve this" and "Nothing I do seems to make a difference." Psychologists call this perception an *external locus of control,* where children feel that external circumstances or things outside their control—other people or luck—are responsible for their successes or failures.

Another harmful cause-and-effect distortion can occur when, instead of a connection between effort and outcome, children develop the perception that ability is linked to outcomes. The problem is that children have no control over their abilities (e.g., intelligence, creative talent, athletic prowess); they either have them or they don't. When children attribute their successes to innate abilities, they may have no sense of ownership of their achievements because their success didn't come from anything they did. This relationship is most often found with children who demonstrate early promise in an achievement activity. They have early success because of certain natural abilities rather than their efforts (they are often successful with little or no effort at all). For example, the gifted student who gets straight A's without studying or the talented athlete who wins consistently with little practice. Statements such as "It wasn't me" and "But I didn't do anything" illustrate the lack of connection between themselves and their achievements.

This ability-outcome connection is most detrimental to children because talent only goes so far. At some point, these children will reach a level of achievement at which the demands of achievement surpass their abilities, or everyone else at this level has similar talent (e.g., the big fish in the small pond who moves to a bigger pond), so it is no longer ability that determines success. At this point, talent becomes a liability rather than an asset because they never learned the importance and value of effort, so they are not able to apply their abilities with increased effort. The most successful children are those who combine their innate talents with commitment and hard work.

Children who understand the relationship between effort and outcome, regardless of their natural abilities, are assured of reaching some level of success because they will make full use of whatever innate abilities they possess. Children who don't demonstrate exceptional abilities at an early age, but do display great determination, are often characterized as overachievers because they become more successful than expected. But, as the legendary UCLA basketball coach John Wooden suggests, "There's no such thing as an overachiever. People achieve the things they are capable of achieving." In other words, children will fully realize whatever inborn abilities they have by working hard.

Dr. Susan Harter, a leading researcher in parenting and self-esteem at the University of Denver, found that parents exercise the greatest impact on their children's sense of competence by the type of feedback they give their children in response to successes and failures in achievement activities. If children receive consistent and positive feedback for their efforts and their results, they develop affirming beliefs about their capabilities and their ability to have control over future efforts. This sense of competence, Harter found, raises self-esteem and motivation, and lowers performance anxiety. This belief in their abilities also has a positive and direct impact on their level of achievement.

Say Dr. Foster Cline and Jim Fay, the authors of *Parenting with Love and Logic,* "As parents, we play an integral part in the building of a positive self-concept in our children. In our words and in our actions, in how we encourage and how we model—the messages we give to our kids shape the way they feel about themselves. . . . 'You are capable' is an important message to offer children at every age." This message is communicated in several ways. Foremost, you need to provide your child with the belief that she is loved regardless of whether she succeeds or fails and a safe haven from which she can feel comfortable exploring and testing her abilities. This belief is fostered by communicating with your child in a calm and positive way that conveys that you are there to help her meet her needs and achieve her goals.

With this foundation of love and security in place, your child is ready to develop her sense of competence. You need to give your child opportunities to act on the world and to see that her actions matter.

This can be accomplished by connecting your child's actions with either positive or negative outcomes. For example, the parents of a girl who does not put forth the effort required to be named to her school's orchestra can gently but firmly point out that her lack of effort was the reason. They can back this up with examples of how she skipped lessons or shortened her practices. Her parents can then be supportive and encouraging by telling her that she can earn a place in the orchestra next year by working harder and improving her playing, and by communicating that the choice is hers. In contrast, if her parents tell her that it was the fault of the selection committee and that she is better than other musicians who were named to the orchestra, their daughter will not take responsibility for her outcome, she will not see the connection between her lack of effort and the decision, and she probably will not be motivated to work on her playing in the future.

You should provide your child with a wide variety of opportunities in which she can be successful (and experience some failure) so she can develop a broad sense of competence. A global sense of competence that is built on many experiences in a wide range of activities is stronger and more resilient than a belief built on a limited number of experiences in a few activities.

You also influence the development of your child's sense of competence by the very beliefs that *you* hold about your child's capabilities. The University of Michigan researchers Pamela Frome and Jacquelynne Eccles discovered that parents' perceptions of their children's academic competence influenced their children's own perceptions of competence, perceptions of the difficulty of achievement tasks, and expectations of success. Moreover, Frome and Eccles found that parental perceptions had a greater effect on their child than his own past performance. Says Dr. Wayne Dyer, the author of *What Do You Really Want for Your Children*, "If you see and treat your child as worthy, important, and attractive, then your child will generally come to believe the same things about himself; thus the early seeds of self-worth are planted." You should ask yourself what perceptions you hold about your child's general competence and his competence in his specific achievement activities. You should also consider what messages you are communicating to your child about your perceptions of his competence. Are you communicating that you believe he is competent or are you sending the message that you believe he is incapable?

SPECIFIC BELIEF

Specific belief involves how children feel about their competence in a particular achievement activity. Capabilities in which children may have a specific belief can range from the technical execution of playing a musical instrument to the cognitive abilities of solving a mathematical problem to the physical abilities of mastering a sport. "People's beliefs about their abilities have a profound effect on those abilities. People who have a sense of self-efficacy bounce back from failures; they approach things in terms of how to handle them rather than worrying about what can go wrong," observes Dr. Daniel Goleman, the author of *Emotional Intelligence.*

For children to become successful achievers, specific confidence in themselves must come out of a general sense of competence. Children who perceive themselves to be globally competent more easily translate this general sense of competence to particular achievement activities. With a global sense of competence in place, you can encourage the development of specific belief by providing your child with the opportunity to develop the necessary skills to master the achievement activity. This skill development typically comes in the form of professional instruction, practice and performance experiences, opportunities to observe skilled performers, and self-instructional tools such as books and videos. These methods foster self-belief by providing your child with the cognitive, technical, physical, social, or psychological skills to succeed on which specific belief can be reasonably founded. They also offer your child opportunities to experience and to master setbacks, obstacles, and adversity that affirm his ability to overcome the most demanding aspects of the achievement activity. These strategies also give your child the practical, technical, and emotional support he needs to gain competence in the activity and confidence in his capabilities. For example, a young dancer receives ballet instruction from a qualified teacher, practices five times a week, performs in monthly recitals, attends performances of her city's professional dance company, and reads books about famous dancers. Finally, these opportunities enable your child to experience success—from mastering new skills to achieving a major goal—which is the ultimate validation of his specific belief.

To some extent, this sense of competence needs to evolve by leaving children to their own devices in their achievement efforts. Parents often want to help too much. For example, when a child is having difficulty with her homework, she often goes to her parents for assistance. Sometimes, parents end up doing the work for the child. However well intentioned, this practice hurts the child by not letting her overcome the obstacles herself and learn the skills associated with the achievement activity. As a result, she doesn't gain the competence or the specific belief in her ability to be successful at the task.

Not allowing your child to take responsibility for his work undermines the healthy development of his self-esteem by communicating to him that you don't believe he is capable of doing the work on his own. If this message is adopted, then self-doubt rather than self-confidence will underlie all of your child's efforts and he may come to view himself as incompetent and unworthy. Only by allowing your child to experience fully all aspects of achievement—obstacles, setbacks, mistakes, successes, failures, frustration, and satisfaction—will he learn to master its challenges and gain a strong belief in his ability to succeed at the activity in the future. Dr. Sylvia Rimm, the author of *How to Parent So Children Will Learn*, suggests that "children cannot become competent and confident by taking the easy road. When they meet a challenge, they can begin to understand the relationship between good habits and satisfying results. . . . If they come running to you every five minutes asking for help, you have to encourage them to problem-solve on their own. . . . There's no incentive for children to perform tasks on their own if their parents do everything for them."

You should support and guide your child, but your child should always do the work. You can best assist her when she gets stuck by helping her to understand what the obstacle is, reduce it to a manageable problem, and ascertain how it can be solved. You can teach your child how to restate a problem—"What is another way of describing the problem?" You can show your child how to take complex challenges and reduce them to more manageable pieces—"Can you break down the problem into smaller ones?" You can then guide her in solving the small problems, which will lead to a solution to the big problem. Homework presents a great opportunity for you to be supportive and to teach your child general problem-solving skills so that she can find solutions to difficult problems on her own. Once your child internalizes these skills and knows how to attack difficult problems, then she will be truly self-empowered and her specific belief in her ability in the achievement activity will grow. Also, never speak about how "we" understand the problem and "we" figured out the solution. This wording shares responsibility for the activity with you and takes ownership away from your child. Like a silent partner, you should help in the process, but you should get none of the credit.

You should use the "four E's" in assisting your child to develop confidence in a particular area. First, you need to expose your child to *experiences* that will foster specific belief in a variety of settings, such as education, the arts, sports, and hobbies. The more activities in which your child gains competence, the stronger his specific beliefs will become. Second, you should set high *expectations* toward which your child must strive. These expectations should always be within his control. The tone of your expectations should be positive, loving, and should demonstrate your confidence in his ability to attain them. Third, you should convey the essential value of *effort* in achieving success in any endeavor. Most of your comments about his work should communicate that hard work, patience, and persistence are most important to achieving his goals. Finally, you need to provide regular *encouragement* to your child to help him overcome obstacles and affirm the relationship between his efforts and meeting the expectations. Your child will often look to you to decide if he is capable. If you convey your faith in him with encouragement, he will likely internalize that confidence in himself. Part of this encouragement should help your child relate his efforts and his results with feelings of excitement, satisfaction, and happiness. John Buri, a researcher at St. Thomas College in Minnesota, further suggests that parents who are clear in their expectations and firmly push their children but, at the same time, emphasize reason, flexibility, and communication are more likely to raise children with high self-esteem.

SPECIFIC BELIEF WITHOUT GLOBAL BELIEF

There are some successful children who develop confidence in their ability in a specific achievement activity *without* first having developed a more general sense of competence as a person. These children often demonstrate a natural talent for a certain activity and quickly experience considerable success in it without first having the opportunity to gain the belief that they are competent people. For example, two studies of gifted adolescent dancers indicated that they had, on average, lower self-esteem than their high school counterparts despite the fact that they were highly confident in their dance abilities. Unfortunately, this specific belief is narrowly based, can be easily shaken when faced with setbacks and failure, and doesn't generalize to other aspects of their lives.

These children feel generally inadequate outside of their achievement activity and tend to be unhappy. Their singular reliance on validation from that one activity causes them to become overly dependent on the activity for their self-esteem—like a drug addict to a drug—and any failure in the activity can be devastating. They will often also believe that as human beings they are of little value without the activity. This narrow view of their competence can keep them in a state of continual fear that they will not be viewed as people worthy of love and respect. Thus, their continued success in their achievement area only provides them with the *appearance* of competence rather than the actual achievement of the deep and enduring trust in their competence that would come from a belief in their general ability to succeed in the world.

Having demonstrated great talent from an early age, Hailey's world had revolved around gymnastics since she was six years old. Her parents had expectations of her becoming an Olympic gymnast, she moved to another city with her mother to train at a prestigious gymnastics academy, she had no friends outside of gymnastics, she believed that the only reason people liked her was because of her gymnastic ability, and all of her efforts had been directed toward making the Olympic team. Hailey had what appeared to be supreme confidence in her gymnastic ability, but she felt totally inept in the rest of her life. She often thought that if she wasn't a gymnast, her life would be over.

When she was sixteen, Hailey qualified for the U.S. Olympic Trials, from which the Olympic team would be selected. Two weeks before the trials, Hailey had what she called "a complete meltdown." For a week she was in a state of panic. She alternated between uncontrollable anger and overwhelming sadness. Seeing that she wasn't getting any better, her parents had her meet with a sport psychologist. It soon became clear that Hailey saw the competition as much more than an opportunity to advance her gymnastics aspirations. Rather, Hailey believed that her entire life was on the line with the meet. Discussions with the sport psychologist revealed that she believed her performance at the trials would determine her self-esteem, her social world, and her future. In the week before the trials, the sport psychologist focused on challenging Hailey's beliefs about the importance of the competition and providing other perspectives that emphasized the meet as only one step in her athletic development. With these healthier beliefs, Hailey calmed down, performed well in the competition, and was named to the U.S. Olympic Gymnastics Team.

SELF-REFLECTION

Successful achievers are able to "look in the mirror" and realistically see their strengths and weaknesses. To become competent, successful, and happy, children must be capable of examining both what they are good at and areas in which they need improvement. Being aware of their strengths gives children confidence and shows them what areas they can count on to help them succeed. But only paying attention to their assets will limit their ability to succeed. Contrary to what many believe, people's strengths do not usually determine what their upper limits of achievement are. Rather, people achieve only what their greatest weaknesses will allow them. Thus, for children to realize their capabilities and gain their fullest sense of competence, they must be willing to focus and work on those areas that are holding them back.

A child's ability to self-reflect depends largely on her sense of competence. A child with confidence in her capabilities has the ability to view her weaknesses positively. She can see her weaknesses as areas that, if worked on, will enhance her ability to succeed. In contrast, a child with a less certain sense of competence views his weaknesses negatively, as threats to his self-esteem, and as problems that will lead him to failure.

If you emphasize improvement more than immediate results and encourage your child to focus on his long-term development in his achievement activity, he will come to see the importance of self-reflection in his progress toward his goals. You should not take it upon yourself to point out what your child's weaknesses might be, but rather help him to be his own reasonable judge. For example, if your child comes home having played a bad soccer game, you can ask him what caused his poor play. You can guide him in this process of self-reflection by helping him recognize what skills (or lack of skills) hurt his ability to play well in the game; for instance, he doesn't dribble well with his left foot. You can then ask him what he can do to overcome this weakness, show confidence that he can improve his skills, and encourage him to get out and practice for the next game.

Your perspective about so-called imperfections affects your child's ability and comfort in self-reflection. Parents who are uncomfortable with self-reflection in their own lives will convey this distress to their children. Parents who cannot recognize or accept their own faults will show anxiety when shortcomings—either their own or those of their child—inevitably arise. This reaction will act as a powerful deterrent to their child to look in the mirror and gain the benefits of self-reflection.

You can act as a positive role model by openly discussing your own shortcomings and demonstrating that it is not only acceptable but necessary to acknowledge inadequacies. The recognition of your imperfections should be accompanied by lessons you have learned from them and how you try to correct them. For example, when your child wants something right away, you could tell her that you sometimes get impatient too, but you have learned that if you just wait a little while, you can often get what you want. Or, when your child is putting off doing her homework, you can tell her that you sometimes procrastinate at work, but you always regret it because then you have to rush to get the project done and it never comes out as good as it could have. Being able to talk about, laugh at, and learn from your own imperfections conveys to your child that having weaknesses is just part of being human.

At the same time, you don't want to use so-called imperfections as excuses for bad behavior. For instance, saying you're not coordinated enough to practice yoga is not sharing your imperfections. It's a rationalization for not wanting to put in the time necessary to become proficient at yoga. But you can tell your child that mastering new skills takes longer for you than it does for most people, so you have to work extra hard to reach your goals. Parents who tell their children that looking in the mirror is a healthy part of being successful and happy will instill in them a constructive outlook toward viewing areas that may be holding them back.

ACCURACY OF SELF-PERCEPTIONS

A child can think she knows what her strengths and weaknesses are, but these perceptions are only useful if they are accurate. Without a reality check, children can develop inaccurate, and often inflated, perceptions of themselves. These distortions can be about their perceived abilities, effort, potential, or goals. Self-reflection can teach children to test the perceptions they hold about themselves so that they can choose a path that is consistent with their actual strengths and weaknesses.

There are a number of reasons why children develop erroneous beliefs about themselves. Children may inadvertently distort reality because they have little experience on which to base their judgments. They form their impressions on what information they have available. For example, a child in a painting class is complimented by her teacher and doesn't hear the teacher also commend other students. Based on this limited information, the child comes to believe that she is more artistically talented than the other students.

Children often base their perceptions about themselves on comparisons with their peers. If they are better than their peers at something, they may come to believe that they are talented despite the fact that their peers may not accurately reflect a high standard of ability.

Children may develop misperceptions about the level of required effort. With little experience, children do not typically know what can be considered significant effort. Most commonly, when children begin to feel discomfort, they believe that they have worked hard enough despite the fact that their efforts may be far from adequate. They may also look to more successful achievers to gauge the effort that is needed to be successful. Unfortunately, effort is not easy to judge: Everyone sees the successes of Michael Jordan, Yo-Yo Ma, and Mikhail Baryshnikov, but few saw the many years of intense effort they put in to reach such high levels of achievement.

Children may develop inaccurate perceptions of themselves as a means of bolstering their self-esteem. By believing that they are more talented and hard working than they actually are, children can, at least temporarily, enhance their overall belief about themselves. Parents, too, may believe that these impressions will build their children's self-esteem. Most parents also want to believe that their children are gifted and special, so they sometimes delude themselves and their children into believing these overestimations.

Overstatements can have some immediate benefits for children by increasing their confidence. Yet there are dangers to these inflated impressions. These perceptions can reduce motivation to work hard and persist because children's inflated views of their abilities may allow them to believe that their talents will lead them to success and that they don't need to work hard to succeed. They may also not be compelled to direct their fullest focus and energy into their achievement efforts.

The long-term effect of these false judgments occurs at two levels. First, a child's progress will be slowed because of the overstated perceptions of ability and effort. With little effort put into their achievement activities, children will show little improvement and their progress will stagnate. Second, and more important, when children who have been misled about their abilities are ultimately forced to face the inaccuracy of those beliefs—the big fish in the small pond syndrome—the experience can be traumatic. Inflated self-perceptions can lead to frustration, anger, and sadness when children are confronted with these realities. Children can come to associate the whole idea of achievement in general with these negative emotions and, because they feel bad most of the time, children will want to avoid achieving anything.

Appropriate understanding of the levels of ability and effort that are required to succeed in an achievement area enables children to accurately assess their current ability and their long-term promise. It also allows them to make informed decisions about their aspirations, effort, and future involvement in the activity. This doesn't mean that a child should drop out of an achievement activity because he is not enormously gifted in it. Not every child can be a star in an activity, but every child can reap great benefits from vigorous participation. The positive experiences gained from committed involvement—regardless of the absolute level of success they attain—provide children with great enjoyment and satisfaction and offer invaluable lessons that they can use in other parts of their lives.

The accuracy of children's self-perceptions also influences the emotions that they attach to their achievement efforts. Children who hold inaccurate beliefs about their capabilities will have expectations that are out of proportion to their true abilities. When they participate in their achievement activities, success is unlikely because of their unrealistic expectations. The accompanying failure will be emotionally devastating to them because they will perform far below what they thought themselves capable of, however out of reach that may be in reality.

Children who have a realistic understanding of their abilities will have a healthy balance of emotions relating to their achievement participation. Because they have an accurate impression of their capabilities, these children will experience success most of the time and will feel joy and excitement with their efforts. At the same time, the inevitable setbacks and failures that they experience will not be overwhelming. Though these children will naturally feel some disappointment and frustration, unsuccessful experiences will not elicit unreasonable pain and sadness. Because the preponderance of emotions associated with achievement is positive, children will learn from their successes and their failures, and use both to their benefit in future achievement activities.

Because your child has little experience on which to base her perceptions, you can act as an important guide in assisting her in reality testing her perceptions. You can initiate a dialogue in which you ask your child about how she perceives herself, compare her beliefs with what you believe to be true, and, if inaccurate, guide your child toward more realistic perceptions. Questions you should ask: How well did you perform today? How good do you think you are? How much effort do you put in? How much fun do you have? What are your goals? You can also listen to your child's offhand remarks—"I'm going to be the next Sarah Chang"—and observe her talent and efforts to see if they are consistent with her goals.

Your child's reflection on her abilities, effort, promise, and aspirations actually begin with your own reflection on your child's capabilities. You will have difficulty helping your child to reality test if your own perceptions are distorted. Many parents find it difficult to admit that their child is not the brightest and most gifted. The first time she kicks a soccer ball, she is the next Mia Hamm. The first time he throws a football, he is the next Joe Montana. You need to reality test your own beliefs about your child. If you lack the expertise to objectively assess your child's abilities, efforts, and goals, you should seek out teachers, instructors, and coaches to help you make realistic judgments about your child's capabilities.

RULES FOR ACHIEVEMENT AND HAPPINESS

1. Let your attitude determine your achievement. Don't let your achievement determine your attitude.
2. Our emotions get in the way of doing for ourselves what we would like to do for others.

3. Don't be afraid to be a kid—have fun.
4. Don't let self-esteem get mixed up in achievement; achievement is different from life.
5. Don't run away from yourself. Wherever you go, there you are.
6. Faced with obstacles, do not ignore them, overcome them.
7. Confidence is born of proper practice.
8. Learn to forgive yourself.
9. The inability to forget is devastating.
10. Get into the process, not the result.
11. Doubt is the number one cause of poor achievement.
12. Follow your dream and enjoy the trip.

Love, III, D. (1997). *Every shot I take· Lessons learned about golf, life, and a father's love.* New York: Simon & Schuster.

CHAPTER 2

Can't You Just Love Me for Me?
Bartering vs. Giving Love

"Unconditional love" is another catchphrase that emerged from the self-esteem movement. The basic idea behind the emergence of unconditional love seemed quite reasonable. Parents should love their children regardless of what they do. Children shouldn't have to worry whether their actions will cause their parents to love them less. They should be able to count on that love no matter what. Much like many aspects of this shift in societal perspective, this idea became misunderstood, misused, and, ultimately, did more harm than good.

Conditional love was big in the fifties. It was a way to maintain control, foster conformity, and instill certain values and beliefs held by parents and society at large. But something happened in the sixties. Perhaps it was a reaction to the rigidity of the postwar era. It was as if the children of the forties and fifties said, "That's enough. We want to be loved regardless of what we do." Within a short time, America went from "Love if you obey and behave" to "Free love without limits."

Unfortunately, the pendulum swung too far. Looking at unconditional love carefully shows us why this grand experiment failed to benefit America's children. The problem is that unconditional love renders all choices, decisions, and actions meaningless. Rewarding children—love is really the ultimate form of reward—regardless of their behavior robs children of one of their most important lessons—that their actions have consequences. What more powerful inducement to good action is there for your child than the threat of losing your love?

I think we should give up our belief that unconditional love exists. Most things in life have strings attached and love is no different. Our society made a big mistake. Instead of figuring out what kinds of conditional love work and what kinds don't, we cut all of the strings and made love conditional on nothing.

In reality, we constantly use love to reward or punish our children's behavior. When you show disapproval toward your child, you are actually showing him or her that your love can be momentarily withheld, and that your love is in fact conditional. For example, you probably do not act lovingly when your child is disobedient, selfish, whines, or is cruel to her siblings. Are you truly withholding your love in these situations? Probably not. You still love your child. But children are generally not sophisticated enough to tell the difference between "We disapprove of your behavior" and "Because of what you did, we are taking away our love." Your child's perception is that love has been temporarily suspended. To your child, it feels like, "I did something wrong and my parents don't love me anymore."

Advocating unconditional love not only did not solve the achievement problem, but it also created a decline in moral behavior and the safety of children in America today. The strings that held America's youth—and perhaps our entire society—together were severed. By taking away conditional love, parents lost their ability to influence their children. Parents gave their children carte blanche in the misguided belief that this freedom would build their self-esteem, foster maturity and independence, and allow them to become successful and happy people. But what it actually did was take away children's responsibility for anything, including their achievement and ethical behavior. Simply put, parents stopped holding their children to any standards.

At some point many parents saw that the pendulum had swung too far and they realized that unconditional love wasn't working. Many children were lazy, uninterested, and out of control. These children weren't good people and they weren't successful. Clearly, a change needed to be made. So, many parents decided to return to conditional love.

Unfortunately, many parents reinstated the wrong kind of conditional love. Parents maintained their unconditional love for their children regardless of their children's values and general behavior as people. Parents gave their children unfettered freedom, few responsibilities, didn't hold them accountable for their actions, provided no consequences, and continued to love them no matter what they did. Perhaps because of the economic uncertainty of the eighties, parents decided to direct their conditional love to achievement, believing this approach would motivate their children to work hard, become successful, and overcome the difficult economic times. Parents began to make their love conditional on how their children performed in school. If Johnny got an A, his parents heaped love on him. When he received a D, they withdrew their love by expressing disappointment, hurt, and embarrassment. So, children's self-esteem became overly connected to their achievement efforts. This conditional love caused achievement to become threatening to children because success and failure were too intimately linked with whether their parents would love them. At the same time, it continued to be disconnected from who they were as people, so their behavior had no consequences. This dichotomy exists today and lies at the heart of many of the difficulties parents and their children have in navigating today's complex social landscape.

The problem has never been that parents love unconditionally but that they placed the wrong conditions on that love. Parents must reverse their use of unconditional and conditional love. You need to give your child unconditional love for her achievements so that she will be free from the fear that you will not love her if she fails to meet your expectations. This unconditional love will motivate your child to give her best efforts and to achieve the highest level of which she is capable. At the same time, you should make your love conditional on whether your child adopts and acts on positive and life-affirming values. If your child behaves poorly, she knows that you will withdraw your love—at least temporarily. If she behaves well, she knows that you will give your love. In time, your child will learn to internalize this healthy conditional love and it will guide her in acting in ethical ways. This careful and appropriate use of unconditional and conditional love is what will help you raise a successful achiever.

RED FLAGS

RED FLAG #1: CONDITIONAL LOVE

One of the dangers to a child's success and happiness occurs when parents use their love as a weapon to threaten and control their child. Love becomes a weapon when parents make their love conditional on their child's success or failure. Says the novelist John Steinbeck, "The greater tumor a child can have is that he is not loved, and rejection is, the hell he fears." This type of conditional love is called *outcome love*, and it can be communicated openly or subtly to children.

Some parents become so invested in their child's achievements that they actively reward success and punish failure. These parents lavish their children with love when they succeed and withhold love when they fail. They reward success by giving their love freely and expressively in the form of effusive praise and physical contact such as hugs and kisses. They also give outcome love materially by buying sometimes extravagant gifts when their children succeed.

When these parents perceive that their children have failed, they behave in a vastly different manner. They may show their disappointment by punishing their children's failure. The punishment may be in terms of anger, verbal abuse and disdain, or the withholding of love with neglect, emotional distance, absence of physical contact, and withdrawal of support and encouragement. Parents who offer outcome love believe that love is not an entitlement for children, but rather something that must be earned. They implicitly believe in a "transactional" approach in which love is a reward for success and withdrawal of love is a payment for failure. An example comes from a family with whom I worked in the Northwest.

Often, without realizing it, parents may create subtle outcome love that can have an equally destructive impact. When your child is successful, it is natural for him to feel happy and excited, and when your child does poorly to feel sad and disappointed. Because parents experience their children's successes and failures vicariously, you may have emotions similar to those of your child. When you express these emotions empathically, you don't intend these feelings to be expressions of outcome love. But your child may not yet be sophisticated enough to understand that you are simply sharing the experience vicariously. Unfortunately, what your child may see is strong positive emotions from you when he succeeds and strong negative emotions when he fails. This inadvertent communication creates the perception of conditional love, however unintended, and produces many of the same difficulties in children as those resulting from a parent actively expressing outcome love.

David was a thirteen-year-old figure skater who traveled with his mother, Susan, to all his competitions. Since David had begun to compete, four years earlier, Susan had unwittingly developed a pattern of expressing conditional love after every event. When David skated well, Susan would hand him her cellular phone and he would call his father, Carl, a successful and very busy banker, and tell him the good news. They would then go to the mall to buy David something special before returning home. In contrast, when David skated poorly, he would often come off the ice crying with disappointment. Susan would cry empathically with David and be there to comfort him. Then, Susan would call Carl to tell him the bad news rather than have David call his father and tell him about his performance.

This pattern led David to believe that he was hurting his mother and angering his father when he skated poorly. Inexplicably to his parents, David developed a reluctance to compete, often coming up with excuses to avoid an event. When he did skate, he was extremely nervous before competitions and skated very poorly. David soon began talking about quitting the sport even though he loved skating and showed considerable promise.

Columbia University researchers Melissa Kamins and Carol Dweck discovered that children who believed that their self-worth was dependent on how they performed were highly self-critical, showed strong negative emotions, judged their performances severely, and demonstrated less persistence following setbacks. This research shows that outcome love produces children who live in a constant state of fear. They are maniacally driven to succeed in order to receive their parents' love, yet they have a powerful dread of failure and the anticipated loss of love from their parents. These children come to believe that they will be loved by their parents and, by extension, everyone else, only if they are successful. Unfortunately, all children will experience failures and setbacks in their achievement efforts. These times will be extremely difficult for these outcome-dependent children because they will be so sensitive to even the smallest failures that they will be unable to focus on their many successes and to maintain a healthy perspective on the setbacks. They may become depressed and anxious because of the threat to their self-esteem. Persistent outcome love will, in time, overwhelm them and drive them to some form of destructive attempts at relief.

RED FLAG #2: DANGLING-CARROT LOVE

A more painful and destructive form of conditional love is *dangling-carrot love*, in which love is promised by parents and held seemingly within reach, but is never truly attainable. This expression came from my work with a young professional athlete who introduced me to a song by Alanis Morissette in which she sings of the "transparent dangling carrot." Much like the donkey who keeps moving forward in the belief that it will be able to reach the carrot tied at the end of a stick in front of it, children are impelled to keep trying to reach the love that they desperately seek from their parents.

Unfortunately, no matter how hard these children try or whatever high level of success they achieve, nothing is ever good enough to gain the love from their parents that they want so badly. Parents who use dangling-carrot love put their children in a hopeless position. Their children are never rewarded for their efforts, yet they are loath to give up. To do so would be to surrender the hope that their parents really do love them. And that would be much too hurtful to accept. So, these children keep striving, chasing that elusive carrot, however fruitlessly, to be good enough to earn their parents' love.

If you are a parent who communicates dangling-carrot love, you would show it by never being completely satisfied with how your child performs. For example, your son brings home a test in which he earned a score of 93 and you ask him why he missed a particularly easy question. Or your daughter receives a standing ovation for her dance performance, but the first thing you say is that she missed three steps in her choreography. In both examples, your child succeeded by anyone's standards, yet his or her achievements were still not completely worthy of your love. Why do parents use this destructive kind of love? Probably in the mistaken belief that if you give complete and unlimited approval for some achievement, your child will take it as a cue to lessen his or her efforts.

Parents also express dangling-carrot love by severely punishing failure. Complete withdrawal of any communication with a child or strong expressions of anger make love seem so distant as to seem forever unreachable for the child. The most extreme example of dangling-carrot love I have ever seen came from the mother of a young athlete with whom I worked. Prior to my involvement, over the course of a summer of competitions in which the girl had some difficult losses, her mother smashed her daughter's equipment, abandoned her at a competition, told her daughter repeatedly that she didn't love her, and, on two occasions, didn't speak a word to her daughter for a week. Sadly, this story doesn't have a happy ending. After several months, I was fired by the mother for "undermining" her efforts to help her daughter. The girl later informed me that she had quit her sport and hated her mother.

RED FLAG #3: CREATING A HUMAN DOING

An unfortunate aspect of outcome love and dangling-carrot love is that parents convey to their child that she is worthy of love only if she lives up to her parents' expectations and is successful. This conditional love creates a child who is a *human doing* in which how she feels about herself is overly connected with her accomplishments. This relationship between outcome and self-esteem becomes the basis for her own self-love. Having internalized her perceptions of being a human doing from their parents, a child comes to love herself only when she is successful and experiences self-loathing when she fails. Unfortunately, human doings cannot be successful achievers because, though they may attain some degree of success, their accomplishments bring them little happiness.

This connection is so strong that human doings judge themselves not only on how they perform in important activities in their lives, but also on how they do in the most mundane tasks. They are so desperate for validation that they gain affirmation from the most trivial accomplishments (I had a client who judged herself on how well she brushed her teeth). For example, human doings are often "list people," who wake up with a list of tasks and are not satisfied or happy until they have crossed every item off the list.

A child's basing his self-esteem on what he does rather than who he is places him in a desperate and untenable position. Failure is a normal and inevitable part of life, yet, for these children, failure is unacceptable and a source of great pain. So, whenever children who are human doings experience failure, they perceive it as an attack on their self-esteem—they feel worthless and undeserving of love. This condition causes children to feel tremendous anxiety over the fear of not being loved and in a persistent position in which their primary motivation is to avoid failure and protect their self-esteem. These children live in a constant state of discomfort. They feel worthwhile only when they are doing something to validate their self-esteem. This ever-vigilant state that human doings are in causes them to feel as if they *must* be successful to be happy, yet, paradoxically, even when they are successful, they don't feel happy.

RED FLAG #4: UNHEALTHY PARENTAL EXPECTATIONS
Unhealthy expectations are one of the most destructive signs of parents who are using either outcome love or dangling-carrot love. "Many people suffer all their lives from this oppressive feeling of guilt, the sense of not having lived up to their parents' expectations," writes psychoanalyst Alice Miller, the author of *Prisoners of Childhood.*

To provide your child with healthy expectations, you need to understand the difference between goals and expectations. Goals are possibilities. They are objectives toward which children can strive that may or may not be reached. When goals are achieved, children feel great excitement because they were not guaranteed. When goals are not attained, children feel some disappointment, but they usually feel satisfaction in any progress toward the goal.

Expectations are assumptions that something will be achieved. An expectation can make something uncertain seem more tangible, almost as if it has already been reached. This perception causes tremendous disappointment when expectations are not met because you feel as if something you already had was taken away from you, even though you never had it in the first place. Expectations are also all-or-nothing—

they're either reached or they're not—so anything less than complete fulfillment of the expectations is a failure.

Many parents defend their use of expectations by saying, "If we don't expect things of our children, they won't amount to anything." The problem is that parents often set the wrong kind of expectations. You should expect your child to be honest, considerate, responsible, hard working, and appreciative. But those expectations are vastly different from expecting your child to get straight A's, go to Harvard, or become a professional athlete.

Expectations are both essential tools for creating successful achievers and potential weapons that parents use against their children. As Shirley Gould, the author of *Teenagers: The Continuing Challenge*, so aptly puts it, "Our own expectations often interfere with our relationships with our children. Not only do we have expectations of what they ought to do and think and be, but we have expectations of ourselves, of how we ought to feel and behave as parents." Whether parental expectations are beneficial or detrimental to a child's pursuit of achievement and happiness depends on the types of expectations that parents place on their child.

An unfortunate mistake that many parents make is to set expectations over which a child has little or no control. An *ability* expectation is one in which a child is expected to achieve a particular result based on his natural ability—"You'll do well in the chess match because you're so smart." An *outcome* expectation is one in which parents expect their child to produce a certain outcome—"I know you'll win."

There are few things more destructive to children than not fulfilling their parents' expectations. "Too many children live with the feeling that they are not accepted for who they are, that, somehow, they are 'disappointing' their parents or not meeting their expectations, that they don't 'measure up,' " write the Kabat-Zinns. If children fail to meet ability expectations, they're forced to attribute their failure to a lack of ability—they weren't smart enough, strong enough, or skilled enough. This type of attribution is harmful because ability is not within children's control; they may come to believe that they are simply inadequate and incapable of being successful in the future and feel helpless to do anything about it. Children may view future achievement as futile and pointless. Children who attribute their successes and failures to their abilities—which they believe to be fixed—tend to have lower achievement. Statements I have heard from young people include "I'm just too uncoordinated to be good, so why should I even try?"

Not meeting their parents' outcome expectations can be equally detrimental. Our society places great emphasis on competition and winning. Shirley Gould argues that "Parents are afraid that if father and mother do not place sufficient stress on winning, on high grades, on awards, then their children may not strive. The opposite is true. . . . Anxious parents who place emphasis on success often contribute to the very discouragement that prevents their offspring from becoming successful." Moreover, outcome expectations are often based on how a child compares to his peers—"You are a much better football player than your friend Eddie. You should definitely start ahead of him." Yet how a child compares to other children is also not within his control. A child may do his best but still fail to perform up to the level of his peers and fail to meet his parents' outcome expectations. This is particularly unfair because children develop at different rates. A child who is less successful at age ten may surpass his peers at age fourteen.

Ability and outcome expectations become connected with outcome love. Children perceive that their success or failure in meeting their parents' expectations will determine whether they receive their parents' love. This emphasis on ability and outcome expectations puts children in no-win situations. If children meet the expectation, they feel no great joy—just relief that their parents still love them. If children don't satisfy the expectation, their greatest fear—that their parents won't love them—is realized.

The perception that nothing a child ever does is good enough and the pressure they feel in response to these escalating expectations takes a heavy emotional toll. Observe Drs. Dinkmeyer and McKay, "The setting of an increasingly difficult standard makes success impossible and discourages the child; for example . . . the child who gets all B's is now expected to get all A's." Parents who communicate unusually high achievement expectations produce angry children. Children who express this hostility learn to associate achievement with the negative emotions and avoid achievement to avoid the bad feelings. Children who suppress their hostility experience guilt over their anger and fear of the loss of their parents' love. Both kinds of children come to view achievement as a painful experience to be avoided.

A further danger of parents expressing expectations about their children's ability or likely success is that children will eventually internalize their parents' unhealthy expectations. Children will no longer need their parents' expectations to feel this pressure and discomfort. Rather, children will create their own unhealthy expectations. These internalized expectations shift from being about gaining their parents' love to allowing self-love. These internalizations will interfere with a child's ability to achieve and be happy even when his parents are not present and on into adulthood.

A special example of expectations that is particularly destructive is what I call the *heir apparent syndrome,* in which the eldest son (occasionally the eldest daughter) of a highly successful father—the heir apparent to the family throne—crumbles under the weight of that expectation. If you are grooming your son as your heir apparent and he is unable to handle the pressure of attempting to follow in your footsteps, you will discover, if you haven't already, that your child will find a number of ways to avoid that overwhelming responsibility. Some heirs apparent simply underachieve until their parents give up the expectations and pass them on to another sibling who is up to the task. The former heir apparent then settles into a life of underachievement and low expectations. This path usually involves the loss of a close relationship with his parents due to his feelings that he failed and disappointed his parents and his anger at his parents for having placed him in such an untenable position. Others choose careers diametrically opposed to their fathers' work and become successful in their own right, thereby maintaining the love and approval of their parents. As a last desperate resort, an heir apparent may develop a substance abuse problem that requires regular treatment and care into adulthood, thus absolving him forever of the responsibility of his parents' expectations.

A happy ending can occur with the heir apparent syndrome. Tony was the prodigal son of a successful and socially prominent investment banker. Tony's parents expected him, from an early age, to attend an Ivy League school and then take over the family business. By the time Tony got to high school, he was doing everything he could to avoid that future. He was the classic underachiever—little effort, poor grades, drug problems, and minor scrapes with the law.

Instead of going to his father's Ivy League alma mater, Tony chose the large state university near his home. For the next few years, he partied a great deal, received poor grades, and was regularly threatened with academic probation. Whenever Tony got into trouble, his parents used their wealth and position to bail him out and clear up the situation.

At their wits' end for how to help their son, Tony's parents sought the assistance of a psychologist who suggested that they completely reverse their approach. Instead of taking responsibility away from him, the psychologist recommended that he be given full ownership of his life and be held accountable for his actions. Though this course of action worried Tony's parents, they gave it a try. In the next year, Tony still struggled with his grades and had minor scrapes with the law, but he didn't have his parents to fall back on (he had to do community service and work to pay all fines). For the first time, Tony was forced to take responsibility for his life, and slowly his life began to change. Tony found a major that he liked, his grades improved, he had no more trouble with the law, and he gave up cigarettes and drugs. Three years later, having graduated from college, he went to law school and began interning with his father during the summer. The heir apparent who had initially crumbled under the weight of his parents' expectations is now the heir confirmed, driven by the strength of his own motivation to succeed and carry on his father's legacy.

RED FLAG #5: UNHEALTHY PRAISE AND PUNISHMENT

You should be careful how you praise your children when they meet your expectations. The Columbia University researchers Claudia Mueller and Carol Dweck found that children who were praised for their intelligence, as compared to their effort, became overly focused on results. Following a failure, these same children persisted less, showed less enjoyment, attributed their failure to a lack of ability (which they believed they could not change), and performed poorly in future achievement efforts. Says Dweck: "Praising children for intelligence makes them fear difficulty because they begin to equate failure with stupidity."

Too much praise of any sort can also be unhealthy. Research has found that students who were lavished with praise were more cautious in their responses to questions, had less confidence in their answers, were less persistent with difficult assignments, and less willing to share their ideas. The educator Alfie Kohn observes, "The more we say 'I like the way you did that,' the more he comes to rely on our decisions about what's good and bad, instead of forming his own judgments. He is led to measure his worth in terms of what prompts us to dole out more approval."

How you punish your child for not meeting expectations can also have a significant impact on his or her future achievement. Another study from Columbia University, also by Carol Dweck, with Melissa Kamins, found that children who received "person criticism"—feedback related to their competence or value—attributed their failure to their lack of ability, lowered their expectations, showed negative emotions, and performed more poorly in the future. The Kabat-Zinns say that "a great deal of unnecessary pain and grief is caused by this withholding, judging behavior on the part of parents. When has parental disapproval, in the form of shaming, humiliating, or withholding, ever been a positive influence on a child's behavior? It might result in obedience; but at what cost to the child, and to the adult that child becomes?"

Children equate person criticism with punishment for failing to meet their parents' expectations. Children often respond by avoiding criticism, which can become their dominant motivation. Criticism hurts a child's motivation to achieve and maintains his dependence on his parents. Eventually, the burden of being constantly criticized will interfere with a child's achievement and his necessary move to independence as he progresses through childhood and adolescence. As Dr. Wayne Dyer offers, "The more criticism a child receives, the more likely he is to avoid trying the things that engendered the criticism. . . . The more you rely on external criticism, the greater the chance that your child will internalize these very same kinds of assessments and, before long, develop a self-picture that is based upon—you guessed it—being critical of himself."

RED FLAG #6: BEING A BOTTOM-LINE PARENT

If you are a bottom-line parent, you are placing too great an emphasis on the outcome of your child's achievement efforts. Bottom-line parents communicate this focus hoping to motivate their children, but end up undermining their children's achievements because the weight of success and failure becomes too great a burden to carry.

Bottom-line parents treat their children like "little employees." These parents expect their children to "produce" in the form of achievement and success. If the desired results do not occur, then these "bosses" show their displeasure and their children may perceive that their parents will "fire" them. Imagine how that feels to children!

A child of bottom-line parents experiences a painful realization when he sees that his parents don't equate his achievements with who he is. Rather, the child "comes to the emotional insight that all the love he has captured with so much effort and self-denial was not meant for him as he really was, that the admiration for his beauty and achievements was aimed at this beauty and these achievements, and not at the child himself," observes psychoanalyst Alice Miller.

RED FLAG #7: CREATING A UNIDIMENSIONAL CHILD

By focusing intensely on directing your child to a high level of achievement in a single area, you run the risk of creating a unidimensional child. Observes Dr. Linda Hamilton: "In dance, competition and career pressures deprive many adolescents of the opportunity to explore. Serious dancers may also believe that all of the important relationships and skills lie within the dance world. Consequently, it is common for the dancer to identify primarily with the values and standards of the profession." This insight can be applied to any child committed to achievement in the arts, academics, sports, or other areas.

A child's identity is comprised of all of the people, things, and experiences that provide a sense of worth and meaning. Typical components of identity include family, friends, school, sports, and cultural activities. A unidimensional identity is one that is predominantly invested in a single area. Singular devotion to a particular achievement activity at too early an age can limit the number of possible sources of meaning and validation of self-esteem for a child.

If your child develops few sources of validation, she can become overly invested in her special activity and become too dependent on it for how she feels about herself. This places great pressure on your child to succeed and creates an exaggerated threat to her self-esteem when she fails. When unidimensional children succeed, they view themselves as worthwhile, competent, and valued, but failure in perhaps the only activity in which they are invested can result in feelings of anxiety, worthlessness, helplessness, and despair. If some event such as an injury or not making a team occurs, halting their participation in their achievement activity, unidimensional children are vulnerable to an identity crisis—"Who am I and what value do I have?"—because the primary basis for their identity has been removed.

I have worked with many achievers who had reached the highest levels of success. For a number of them, the single-minded pursuit of achievement resulted in lives with surfaces of celebrity and wealth, but also of discontent, failed relationships, and limited interests. For others, these quests led to futures of unrealized dreams and lifelong dissatisfaction.

Oksana Baiul, the 1994 Olympic gold medalist in figure skating, exemplifies the unidimensional child turned adult. With no parents or family to support or guide her, Baiul committed herself to her sport at a young age and had no life outside of figure skating. As Brian Boitano, the 1988 Olympic champion, says of his friend, "Upbringing is so important to how young star athletes deal with pressure, and she didn't have any backup. . . . She needed good examples of how to be a responsible person." After winning in Lillehammer, Norway, and turning professional, Baiul went into an emotional tailspin that culminated in committing herself to an alcohol abuse treatment facility. During her stay, Baiul learned two things that most children learn from their families—self-respect and wisdom. Observes Baiul: "I thought I was a big shot, but I wasn't. I knew how to skate, but there was nothing else I knew. What a gift, to have a chance again to make a life."

The antidote for the development of unidimensional children is for you to ensure that you provide your child with opportunities to gain competence, enjoyment, meaning, and validation in areas outside of his primary achievement activity. This requires that you find the time to create and share experiences that your child can use to contribute to his self-identity. As Dr. Ruth Strang, the author of *Helping Your Gifted Child*, emphasizes, "It's especially meaningful to develop a balanced and responsible whole personality and guard against one-sided development."

Darren, an eighteen-year-old former football player, was headed down a narrow path. From an early age, he dreamed of being an NFL quarterback and devoted his life exclusively to achieving that goal. His father, a former collegiate player, wanted his son to attain the success on which he missed out. All aspects of Darren's life were directed toward facilitating his development as a football player. Through high school, Darren was on track toward his goal, having been recognized as one of the top quarterbacks in the country and recruited by many leading college programs.

Unfortunately, during his senior year, Darren sustained a serious back injury that forced him to give up his dream or risk permanent paralysis. For the first time in his life, Darren did not know who he was or where he was going. If he was no longer a football player, then who was he? This led to a period of clinical depression and thoughts of suicide as Darren struggled with accepting that he was no longer a football player. Only after months of reflection, reevaluation, and redefinition was Darren able to emerge from what he later called his "pit of despair" and dedicate himself to developing a more balanced self-identity that included numerous sources of meaning and validation in his life.

RED FLAG #8: PERFECTIONISM

Perfectionism is perhaps the most destructive aspect of outcome love and dangling-carrot love that can severely damage a child's achievement and happiness. Yet perfectionism is ubiquitous throughout the world of those who strive to achieve. You can cause your child to become a perfectionist by never giving complete approval of anything he achieves. Children come to believe that nothing short of perfection is good enough for their parents, so anything less than perfection is absolutely unacceptable. Because of their need to gain the love of their parents, perfectionists push themselves unmercifully to achieve their goals. They also internalize these impossible standards and punish themselves for falling short of perfection. Laura Vanderkam, a recent Princeton University graduate, writes, "Parents want the best for their kids—but some also want the perfect kid. Somewhere along the way to achieving these perfect children . . . overachieving parents stunt the growth of their children's souls."

Drs. Austin M. Antony and Richard P. Swinson, the authors of *When Perfect Isn't Good Enough*, suggest that perfectionists are typically people who set extremely high standards of achievement and are excessively critical in their self-evaluations. Psychiatrist David Burns further clarifies our understanding of perfectionists by describing them as people "whose standards are high beyond reach or reason . . . who strain compulsively and unremittingly toward impossible goals and who measure their worth entirely in terms of productivity and accomplishment."

Perfectionism is a double-edged sword. Healthy or positive perfectionism is characterized as fostering high goals, achievement, self-actualization, confidence, and success. Healthy perfectionists have high expectations, yet also show the ability to be flexible, adapt, and accept less precision when needed. In seventeen years of consulting with high achievers, I have found very few healthy perfectionists.

Neurotic or unhealthy perfectionism is distinguished by compulsive precision, neatness, and organization. Neurotic perfectionists set unrealistic expectations, demonstrate a rigidity in their thinking, view achievement as opportunities to fail, have little tolerance for mistakes, are never satisfied with the fruits of their efforts, respond poorly to adversity, and show little enjoyment in their achievements. Neurotic perfectionists tend to associate mistakes with negative judgments of themselves and worry that failure will cause others to lose respect for them. They often lack confidence in their capabilities, question the quality of their efforts, and are highly critical of themselves. Neurotic perfectionism has been found to be associated with a variety of psychological problems, including eating disorders, social phobia, procrastination, fear of failure, depression, performance anxiety, and poor stress coping.

Some researchers have concluded that the difference between healthy and neurotic perfectionists hinges on the severity of how perfectionists evaluate themselves rather than the high standards they set for themselves. Healthy perfectionists set high expectations for themselves, but don't berate themselves for minor imperfections. Neurotic perfectionists hold themselves to the same standards, but cut themselves no slack for anything less than total achievement of those standards.

If you are a perfectionist, you hold yourself to the same exacting standards that you hold your child to because you were probably exposed to perfectionism and conditional love as a child. Perfectionistic parents abhor failure, cannot accept their own perceived imperfections, and show great distress when they are unable to live up to their own impossible standards. For example, a parent punishes himself for failing to land a business deal or even something relatively unimportant like playing poorly in a round of golf. Or a parent becomes angry and frustrated when she is faced with obstacles on a work project.

If you are not a perfectionist, yet expect your child to achieve perfection, then you are setting the stage for your child's failure and doing serious harm to your relationship. What you may be doing is expecting your child to repair the flaws you see in yourself. This responsibility is an impossible task for your child to fulfill, and no matter what happens with your child, your imperfections remain.

You can communicate perfectionism in many ways. Parents who raise neurotically perfectionistic children set very high goals and are excessively critical of their children. They also give their children consistent, negative feedback about their achievements and, not surprisingly, their children weigh these evaluations heavily in their own self-judgments. Children see the perfectionistic messages of their parents, internalize them, and their parents' dangling-carrot love and neurotic perfectionism become their own.

Neurotic perfectionists are fundamentally unhappy because they strive toward goals they can never achieve. Imagine what life must be like for perfectionists, living in a constant state of fear of being unworthy of love. Every morning waking up and needing to prove to themselves and to the world that they are deserving of love and respect. Every success is only the briefest respite from the fear of not being loved. Every failure is a direct attack on their self-esteem. Perfectionistic children raised with the dangling carrot are caught in a trap of their parents' creation, with little chance of escape. Imagine the frustration, the anger, the despair, of chasing that unreachable goal!

The story of Sarah Devens, a gifted student-athlete at Dartmouth College, offers a powerful cautionary tale about the dangers of perfectionism. A star three-sport athlete, Devens was loved and admired by all. She seemed to have everything—athletic and academic success, close family and friends—except happiness. As a long-time friend expressed, "Sarah couldn't just go out and enjoy herself. She had to be great. If you're the Devil [her nickname], people expect perfection." Devens wanted to be all things to all people. Her ex-boyfriend said that "she wanted to be the best girlfriend, the best athlete, the best student." She also struggled emotionally. Her friends saw that she was down and depressed, though she always tried to put on a happy face. Observed another friend: "The thing is, she was so good at everything, as a person and an athlete, that she got on this vicious cycle. She wanted to please everybody, and she couldn't stop." In 1995, at the age of twenty-one, Sarah Devens, "arguably the best female athlete in the history of Dartmouth College," shot and killed herself. "She wanted to rest, and this was the only way she knew how," her ex-boyfriend surmised.

Giving Healthy Love

VALUE LOVE

Love should have strings attached. Most things of importance in life are earned, whether values like trust, respect, and responsibility, or substantial things such as education, career, and other achievement successes. Why should love be any different? *Love is your most powerful tool for influencing your child.*

Instead of outcome love, you should use *value love*, in which love is conditional on your child's adopting essential values and acting in socially appropriate and ethical ways. Value love nurtures the development of positive values and moral behavior, fosters healthy growth, and encourages achievement and happiness. You can instill values such as accountability, discipline, hard work, consideration, emotional maturity, and generosity by showing disapproval—withholding love—when your child doesn't demonstrate these values and by giving praise— offering love—when your child demonstrates these values. By using love this way, your child learns the importance of these values and can internalize them as his or her own. "Effective parenting centers around love: love that is not permissive, love that doesn't tolerate disrespect, but also love that is powerful enough to allow kids to make mistakes and permit them to live with the consequences of those mistakes," say Dr. Foster Cline and Jim Fay.

CREATE A HUMAN BEING

Your goal is to raise your child to be a *human being*. Human beings believe that the kind of person that they are—the values they hold, their effort, how they treat people—determines how they value themselves. Human beings gain satisfaction and validation from, among other things, being honest, considerate, and responsible. They also have complete control over what primarily affirms their self-esteem.

Part of being a human being is accepting one's basic humanity, which includes understanding that no one is perfect and that failure is a necessary and acceptable part of life. Failure then loses its power to harm self-esteem. "Help them to be responsible people by loving them for their errors, telling them that it is okay to make mistakes, and letting them know they are loved even if they do get jelly on the carpet, or fail a biology course, or wet the bed, or anything else that they do as human beings," says Dr. Wayne Dyer. As a human being, self-esteem is not threatened because your child is not a perfectionist, he has no fear of failure, and he doesn't fear losing your love.

Being a human being doesn't mean that your child will be satisfied with just being happy with herself and not care about achieving. To the contrary, it liberates your child from the dangers of trying to achieve because success and failure are not so centrally connected to her self-esteem. The removal of this threat to self-esteem will allow your child to pursue achievement from a position in which she wants to seek out achievement opportunities. Your child feels none of the pressure—from you or herself—that may interfere with her becoming successful.

Ironically, success is not really about what children do. In school, the arts, sports, and other achievement pursuits, no one has the market cornered on strategies that foster success. Children do pretty much the same things. Rather, success comes from being—who children are, what they value, their work ethic, and their ability to connect and work with others.

But your child cannot just *be* to become successful. He needs to do something, but it has to go beyond just his achievement efforts. Your child's efforts must come from his being, from who he is. Achieving as a human being is very different from achieving as a human doing: your child's efforts are imbued with who he is and what he values. Children who are human beings find meaning in their achievement efforts and they connect their passions and commitment to their efforts. In a sense, their achievement efforts are filtered through their being. The efforts that result are determined, confident, energized, and focused. Children

who are human beings experience a sense of happiness in their achievement efforts because their efforts come out of and affirm who they are.
This connection between who children are and what they do is what
separates children who are successful achievers from those children who
merely succeed or don't succeed at all.

HEALTHY PARENTAL EXPECTATIONS

You should be tough on your child! But being tough does not mean
being negative, critical, or punitive. Expectations should never motivate
by demeaning, threatening, or scaring your child. Though these expectations can be motivating at first, they will only hurt your child in
the long run. For example, telling your child (using a harsh and un-
forgiving tone), "Any grade other than an A is unacceptable. If you
don't excel in school, your mother and I will be very disappointed in
you. Perhaps we overestimated your capabilities," will only cause fear,
anger, and hurt, and will ultimately cause your child to be unsuccessful
and unhappy.

Being tough means holding your child to high standards that reflect
your values and beliefs about yourself, family, education, career, and
society, to name a few areas. Your challenge is to set expectations that
will help your child achieve his goals, internalize essential values, and
develop beliefs and attitudes that will foster his growth as a successful
achiever. Expectations should be positive and motivating. For example,
you can say to your child (with a positive and confident tone), "Good
grades are important for you to get into a good college, which we know
is important to you. We know that by working hard, you can achieve
your goals. We are behind you all the way." This communicates your
expectations in a context that focuses on your child, emphasizes his
goals, and models determination and positive emotions.

As your child grows, your role in setting expectations should diminish and your child's involvement should increase. Instead of telling your
child what you expect of her, you should ask her what she expects of

herself. Questions like "Why do you want to do this?," "What do you hope to get out of this?," and "What would make this a really great experience for you?" will help your child clarify why she wants to participate in an achievement activity and what goals and expectations she might have for herself. You can still have input in your child's expectations by reality testing her expectations, offering her different perspectives that might help her clarify her expectations, and then showing your support for her participation in the achievement activity based on her expectations.

You need to be sensitive to your own expectations and what expectations you are communicating to your child. The first step in ensuring that you convey healthy expectations involves gaining insight into your own ambitions for your child's achievement efforts. "Too often parents harbor an idealized mental image of what their child should be and how he should perform. But it is important to recognize that none of these standards, values, and goals we set for the child can be achieved until he himself feels adequate and self-satisfied," say Drs. Dinkmeyer and McKay. You should compare your own expectations with those of your child and identify similarities, differences, and points of contention. If your child's expectations are at odds with your own expectations, either you should come to a consensus with your child so that the conflict is resolved or you should respect your child's expectations and allow those expectations to guide his achievement efforts. For example, your child may want to play Little League baseball mostly to be with his friends and may not be concerned with how much or how well he plays. You, in turn, may feel that if he is going to devote so much time to playing—and you are going to commit time and money to his participation—then he should take it more seriously. If you allow him to play while each of you hold such divergent expectations about his participation, conflict will arise between you and your child, and his Little League playing experience will not turn out to be positive.

The Kabat-Zinns suggest that you ask yourself the following questions: "Are our expectations realistic and age-appropriate? Do they contribute to a child's growth? Are we expecting too much or too little? Are we setting our child up to experience unnecessary stress and failure? Do our expectations enhance our child's self-esteem, or do they constrict, limit, or belittle the child? Do they contribute to a child's wellbeing, to his or her feeling loved and cared for and accepted? Do they encourage important human values such as honesty, respect for others, and being responsible for one's actions?"

With these questions in mind, you should ensure that you only set expectations over which your child has control. *Effort* expectations emphasize how much determination, hard work, and persistence you expect your child to put into her achievement activities—"We expect you to always try your hardest and do your best." If your child meets your reasonable effort expectations, she will learn the essential relationship between effort and outcome. If your child doesn't meet your effort expectations, she learns the downside of this relationship, but the lesson is still learned. Your child may be disappointed, but she also knows what she must do to meet those expectations next time—work harder. Thus, meeting the expectations in the future are within your child's control. This realization provides your child with ownership of her achievements and it empowers her to meet those expectations. For example, a reasonable expectation for your child in school might be that she will work hard in all of her subjects, which translates into paying attention and participating in class, making homework a priority over social activities, checking her homework for mistakes and completeness, and making sure assignments are finished well in advance of their due date. This not only states clearly the general expectation you have of your child, but you also remove any ambiguity of how that expectation can be met. Your child will also receive three types of feedback about the expectation. You will give her feedback about whether you believe she is fulfilling the practical aspects of the expectation. Your child will also obtain feedback from the grades she receives from her efforts. Finally, your child will be able to decide whether she met the expectation.

Value expectations are those that you place on your child to behave in a way that is consistent with the values that you want to teach your child, such as honesty, fairness, responsibility, hard work, persistence, and consideration of others. Expectations that reflect particular family values may include fulfilling household responsibilities, completing homework assignments, and helping those less fortunate. Because meeting value expectations are within your child's control, he has further opportunities to make a natural connection between effort and outcome and he can internalize these life-enriching values, making them his own. For example, you can tell your child that you expect every member of the family to show love and respect for one another. This expectation includes having him look out for the safety and well-being of his younger sister, which involves his keeping an eye on her when they are playing in the backyard, helping her with her homework, and sharing his toys with her. This value expectation communicates clearly what the value is—love and respect for family members—and what your child can do to meet the expectation.

Even the healthiest expectations have little value if parents don't have the ability to enforce them. You need to clearly state your expectations and establish and communicate the consequences of your child's meeting or not meeting those expectations. You should explain why you are setting the expectations and the consequences so your child can see the benefit of acting in accordance with those expectations. This explanation process helps ensure clear communication and understanding, and encourages open dialogue between you and your child.

A typical dialogue about expectations and consequences goes as follows.

You: "Being honest is something we expect of you and ourselves. This means that we always tell the truth even when something bad happens. Do you know why it is important to be honest?"

Your child: "Because then we can believe what we say to each other."

You: "Very good. And we all need to be able to trust each other. You know that nothing you do would be bad enough to lie about. And we will always love you. Why do you think lying is bad?"

Your child: "Lying makes things worse and I would get into even more trouble."

You: "That's right. We both need to keep in mind that no one's perfect and even you may not be honest on occasion. If you aren't honest, what do you think a fair consequence should be?"

Your child: "You could tell me not to do that again."

You: "You might not take me seriously if I only said something. What if you couldn't do something you really liked for a few days?"

Your child: "How about not being able to play with my friends for three days?"

You: "That sounds fair to me. Would that be fair to you?"

Consequences must be meaningful to your child. She needs to see the personal value of meeting the expectations. External benefits can include parental approval or receiving some predetermined reward (for example, receiving her allowance). Internal value can mean the intrinsic satisfaction of doing the right thing.

Consequences must also be reasonable to your child—they should be commensurate with the expectation. This fairness allows your child to justify her punishment when she doesn't meet the expectations and encourages her to internalize the expectations because the consequence is not so severe that she is being "forced" to comply. For example, a child's finishing her homework might merit her favorite dessert, but doesn't justify a shopping trip to the mall. Similarly, failure to help with the dinner dishes could warrant no phone use for the rest of the evening, but doesn't deserve a weeklong grounding. If you explain the rationale behind the expectation, create a fair consequence—ideally with your child's input—and emphasize that she has the power to choose whether to meet or violate the expectation, then she is more likely to see the value in the expectation and accept it as her own.

Parents who enforce excessive or arbitrary consequences risk anger, resentment, and resistance in their child. If you set an expectation and establish a consequence that is harsh and excessive, your child may meet the expectation for a while out of fear of punishment, but she will, at some point, rebel against it; she will not internalize and accept the expectation as her own and she will cease her efforts at meeting the expectation as soon as she is out of your reach.

At the same time, consequences that are insufficient for the transgression are equally ineffective. In other words, *the punishment should fit the crime.* Observes John Rosemond: "The fact is, the outrageous offense requires an equally outrageous response. Today's parents are often reluctant to employ outrageous consequences—and by this I definitely do not mean hurtful, cruel, or mean—because professional psychobabblers have intimidated them into believing that outrageous discipline is psychologically harmful. Big Consequences cause children great discomfort and inconvenience, which is precisely the idea. But are they psychologically harmful? Not unless you think that improved behavior is bad."

You need to then *firmly and consistently* adhere to the expectations and consequences that you establish. Yet, parents don't always do this. It takes time and energy for parents to consistently hold their children to the standards that they have established. When a working parent comes home tired at the end of the day, the last thing he wants to deal with is the stress of providing consequences for his child's misbehavior. It's easier to let his child off and tell her that if she does it again, then she will really get it. Children can also be persuasive in talking their parents out of consequences. Promises of better behavior in the future and demonstrations of love can seduce parents into letting their children off the hook. Yet, if children are successful, they will come to believe that the threatened consequences will not be administered next time. Every time a child is let off without a consequence for failing to meet an expectation, the value of the expectation is lost. Your child must learn that you mean business!

Finally, setting expectations alone is not sufficient to foster achievement and happiness in your child. He must also have the skills to meet those expectations. When your child lacks the tools to successfully meet the expectations, you ensure failure and limit his ability to learn from these experiences. Many children develop problems because they have expectations placed on them without the necessary skills—often psychological and emotional—to effectively meet them. Much like a teacher would never give an exam to students without first teaching them the relevant lessons, you should be sure that your child possesses the practical or psychological information and skills to meet the expectations that you set for him. For example, you can't expect your child to give his best effort in school if he doesn't have the materials and support (for example, books, supplies, your attention and help) that will allow his best effort to be realized. Or you can't expect your child to be responsible if you don't explain to him what it means to take responsibility (for example, helping with the dishes, cleaning his room).

Meeting expectations should be a choice that your child can make about her behavior and achievement. Your child can choose to meet realistic expectations and reap the internal and external rewards of successful achieving, or she can choose not to meet the expectations and accept the consequences of parental disapproval, low achievement, and dissatisfaction. Considering *expectations as choices* places more of the onus for meeting the expectations on your child rather than her feeling forced to accept the expectations. Thus, the responsibility for meeting the expectations is her own, and this sense of ownership motivates your child to meet the expectations. Expectations as choices also give your child control over how she responds to the expectations, further fostering the essential perception that her actions matter.

The final goal of creating healthy expectations is to help your child learn to set his own expectations. At an early age, your child will not have the experience and perspective to develop expectations on his own. You are in a position to guide him in creating expectations that are consistent with his wants and needs. You can ask your child the following questions: What achievement activities are important to you? What do you most like about these activities? What are your goals in these activities? What are you willing to do to achieve those goals?

As your child matures and gains the necessary experience and perspective, you need to then give her the freedom to establish her own expectations. You can still help your child by offering different viewpoints and testing her expectations against her goals, capabilities, and level of development to ensure that her expectations are reasonable and attainable.

HEALTHY PRAISE AND PUNISHMENT

Children learn about the relationship between their actions and their outcomes by seeing the consequences of their actions. Two ways that you can offer consequences—and assist your child in making this connection—is to provide your child with healthy praise and punishment in response to his or her actions.

Researchers Mueller and Dweck found that children who were praised for their effort showed more interest in learning, demonstrated greater persistence and more enjoyment, attributed their failure to lack of effort (which they believed they could change), and performed well in subsequent achievement activities. Rewarding effort also encouraged them to work harder and to seek new challenges. Adds the Clark University researcher Wendy Grolnick: "Parental encouragement of learning strategies helps children build a sense of personal responsibility for—and control over—their academic careers." Based on these findings, you should direct your praise to areas over which your child has control—effort, attitude, commitment, discipline, and focus. You should look at aspects of your child's achievements and specifically praise those areas that enabled him to be successful and which he can do something about (for example, "You worked so hard preparing for this test," "You were so focused during the entire chess match," and "You gave it everything you had today").

You should also consider not giving praise every time your child is successful. Alfie Kohn recommends three alternatives to praising children. First, say nothing. Your child doesn't need to be stroked every time he does a good deed. He can experience his own self-satisfaction. Second, report what you see. A brief, nonjudgmental statement (for example, "You spent a lot of time on that project") shows your child that you are interested in his efforts and noticed his accomplishment. Third, ask questions. You can find out what your child thought and felt about his achievement (for example, "What did you enjoy most about your performance?" and "How do you feel about what you just did?"). Allow your child to decide for himself how he feels about his accomplishments, enable your child to reward himself for his own good actions, and encourage him to internalize what he observed about his own achievement efforts.

How you punish your child for not meeting expectations can also have a significant impact on future achievement. The use of the word "punish" is perhaps a bit harsh in this context. Punishment suggests a negative and punitive orientation in which children did something wrong and they must pay the price for their transgression. A more appropriate term is "feedback," in which you convey to your child why she behaved or performed poorly.

Kamins and Dweck found that children who received "process criticism"—feedback associated with their effort or the strategies they used—had a positive reaction, attributed their failure to controllable factors such as poor effort or ineffective strategies, maintained their expectations, showed little emotion, persisted longer, and performed better in later achievement efforts. Much like praise, "punishment" should focus on contributors to achievement over which children have control. You can point out areas that influenced your child's poor performances that he can change in his future achievement efforts: "It seems like there were times when you could have been studying, but chose to play with your friends instead," or "It looked to us like you weren't paying attention during the game."

The emotional content of your feedback is also critical to how it influences your child. If your tone when you administer the punishment is angry and hurtful, your child will focus on the underlying emotions rather than the meaningful content of the message, so the message will be lost. Your child may also connect the negative emotions with the withdrawal of your love, which may convey outcome love and hurt her self-esteem. When you respond emotionally, your child may also question whether you are putting her needs first and acting in her best interests.

You can maximize the value of your punishment by communicating it in a calm and loving tone and focusing on how your child can do better in the future rather than on what he did wrong. With this supportive air, your child will clearly hear your message, feel the caring beyond the message, and recognize that the punishment, though he may not like it, is for his own good.

This "process" approach to punishment has several benefits. It requires your child to assume ownership and responsibility for her poor performances—"I didn't do well because I didn't do the things I needed to do to be successful." It has fewer negative connotations associated with it and keeps your child at an emotional distance from her perceived failure. Your child also doesn't need to be concerned about your being angry or upset by her performance. Instead, she will view the feedback as positive and constructive, because she can use it to improve in her future achievement efforts.

STRIVE FOR EXCELLENCE

Excellence is the antidote to neurotic perfectionism. Whereas perfection is unattainable and, consequently, a fruitless pursuit, excellence is an achievable and worthwhile goal toward which you should encourage your child to strive. I define excellence as *being successful most of the time.*

This redefinition of acceptable standards of achievement takes the best that healthy perfectionism has to offer and removes the harmful aspects of neurotic perfectionism. Excellence still demands that your child set high expectations. It still encourages him to give his best effort and to do the very best job he can. However, excellence lightens the burden of having to avoid mistakes and failure, relieves the unrelenting pressure of receiving overly critical evaluations, removes the fear of failure because your child won't be afraid of losing your love, and allows your child to enjoy his achievement efforts.

This simple understanding of excellence has several essential benefits. Excellence is an aim that any child can reach. They have the control to achieve excellence. With hard work alone, your child can achieve some level of excellence. Excellence also allows for mistakes and failure. Your child doesn't have to be perfect. It's not only okay to fail, but also encouraged. Some failure is important when your child strives for excellence because failure offers valuable lessons that will help her to strive for excellence. For example, your child can be satisfied with a score of 94 on a test. She can make a mistake in a chess match or a soccer game and still be happy with her performance. Your child can even lose periodically and find some gratification in having given her best effort and performed well despite not winning.

Perfection is a huge burden on a child's shoulders. Author Shirley Gould offers: "If you don't expect your offspring to be perfect, you encourage them to accept themselves as they are, freeing them to function in productive ways." Striving for excellence lifts the burden of perfection from your child. Excellence takes the pressure off him to achieve the unachievable. Your child can say with confidence, "Yeah, I can do that. I can strive for excellence."

PARENTAL DOS AND DON'TS

DO FOR YOURSELF

1. Take vicarious pleasure in your child's achievement efforts.
2. Try to enjoy yourself during your child's achievement activities. Your unhappiness can cause your child to feel guilty.
3. Look relaxed, calm, positive, and energized when watching your child in his or her achievement activity. Your attitude influences how your child feels and performs.
4. Have a life of your own outside of your child's achievement activity.

DO WITH OTHER PARENTS

1. Make friends with other parents at achievement events. Socializing can make the event more fun for you.
2. Volunteer as much as you can. Many achievement activities depend on the time and energy of involved parents.
3. Police your own ranks: Work with other parents to ensure that all parents behave appropriately at achievement events.

DO WITH TEACHERS (INSTRUCTORS, COACHES)

1. Leave the teaching to the teachers.
2. Give them any support they need to help them do their jobs better.
3. Communicate with them about your child. You can learn about your child from one another.
4. Inform them of relevant issues at home that might affect your child in his or her achievement efforts.
5. Inquire about the progress of your child at the appropriate time. You have a right to know.
6. Make teachers your allies.

DO FOR YOUR CHILD

1. Provide guidance for your child, but do not force or pressure.
2. Assist your child in setting realistic achievement goals.
3. Emphasize fun, skill development, and other benefits of achieving, such as motivation, confidence, focus, responsibility, and ability to handle pressure.
4. Show interest in your child's achievement activity: Provide resources, attend performances, ask questions.
5. Provide regular encouragement.
6. Provide a healthy perspective to help your child understand success and failure.
7. Emphasize and reward effort rather than results.
8. Intervene if your child's behavior is unacceptable at achievement events.
9. Understand that your child may need a break from the achievement activity occasionally.
10. Give your child some space when needed. Part of achieving involves your child's figuring things out for him- or herself.
11. Keep a sense of humor. If you are having fun and laughing, so will your child.
12. Be a healthy role model for your child by being positive and relaxed and by having balance in your life.
13. Give your child value love: Show your love regardless of the outcome.

DON'T FOR YOURSELF

1. Don't base your self-esteem on your child's achievements.
2. Don't care too much about how your child performs.
3. Don't lose perspective about the importance of your child's achievements.

DON'T WITH OTHER PARENTS

1. Don't make enemies of other parents.
2. Don't talk about other parents, talk to them—it is more constructive.

DON'T WITH TEACHERS (INSTRUCTORS, COACHES)

1. Don't interfere with their teaching.
2. Don't work at cross purposes with them. Make sure you agree philosophically and practically on why your child is involved in the achievement activity and what he or she may get out of it.

DON'T FOR YOUR CHILD

1. Don't expect your child to get anything more from the achievement activity than a good time, mastery, love of an activity, and transferable life skills.
2. Don't ask your child to talk with you immediately after a performance.
3. Don't show negative emotions while attending an achievement event.
4. Don't make your child feel guilty for the time, energy, and money you are spending and the sacrifices you are making for the achievement activity.
5. Don't think of your child's achievement activity as an investment for which you expect a return (except for #1).
6. Don't live out your own dreams through your child's achievement activity (get your own dreams).
7. Don't compare your child's progress with that of other children.
8. Don't badger, harass, use sarcasm, threaten, or use fear to motivate your child. It only demeans your child and causes ill feelings toward you.
9. Don't expect anything from your child except his or her best effort and good behavior.

10. Don't ever do anything that will cause your child to think less of him- or herself or of you.

Taylor, J. "What kids really need: How to (positively) push your child to achievement and happiness." Invited speaker, Town School, San Francisco, CA, February 27, 2001

CHAPTER 3

Who Is the Real Me?
False Self vs. True Self

All children, as they grow, experience the discovery of their identities, the development of their personalities, the growth of who they are and what they will become. This developmental process is similar to the building of a house. The brick and mortar of a child's self include his genetic predispositions and the influences of different levels of society—his parents and family, his peers and social world, his schools and communities, and the larger culture of society as communicated through television, radio, books, magazines, and the Internet.

Ideally, as a child develops, all of the materials that are used should be of the highest quality and should complement one another. The construction process proceeds smoothly and on schedule, and what results is a completed person, who, like a well-constructed house, is strong, stable, and resilient to the elements. If problems arise, however, owing to substandard materials or poor construction, the house may either not be completed or, on completion, may be shaky, unstable, and offer little protection from sudden storms. Poor construction of a child's self is caused by a parent who pushes inappropriately, too hard, or not enough. This faulty construction creates a child who is vulnerable to life's elements and results in an adult who cannot withstand the inevitable inclement weather of the adult world.

The construction of a child's self needs to begin with a solid foundation that facilitates the creation of her *true self*, which is comprised of materials from her parents' use of value love and the teaching of values, beliefs, and attitudes that foster the growth of successful achievers. "The capacity to be true, 'to thine own self,'" says Dr. Daniel Goleman, "allows acting in accord with one's deepest feelings and values no matter what the social consequences." The true self believes in a child's goodness and value. The true self loves the child it inhabits and is truly happy. The true self has confidence in being loved and in being competent, thus it acts as the basis for self-esteem. It has no conditional self-love; the true self accepts a child's imperfections and failures. The true self liberates a child to pursue her goals and accept successes and failures with equal equanimity. Research has found that children who perceive their parents' support positively exhibit the most positive emotions, highest self-worth, greatest hopefulness, and most knowledge of their true selves.

Unfortunately, construction of the true self can be halted and the creation of a *false self* can begin any time during a child's development. As your child becomes involved in an achievement activity, there is the danger that you can lose perspective, become overly invested, and shift from value love to outcome love. All of a sudden, without realizing it, you might be changing the construction plans of your child and using different materials to complete the house that is your child's identity. This radical change will cause your child to begin to internalize certain destructive beliefs and attitudes—such as valuing results over effort, a demand for perfection and nothing less, and a dangerous dependence of self-esteem on narrowly defined success or failure—that conflict with his true self. The child is now at a point where he can no longer be his true self and still function in the world in which he finds himself. Ultimately, your child will be driven to construct an alternative self, a false self. This false self will enable him to meet both his own needs and the demands of the real world that you have created for him.

Unfortunately, though this false self will allow your child to survive in this hostile world, he will find no happiness or peace in it.

The false self sees a child as a bad person who is unacceptably imperfect and will constantly fail to live up to the internalized expectations of his parents and society. In order to receive love—from society, from his parents, and from himself—the child who is controlled by his false self must meet the impossibly high standards that have become his own. Because these standards are unreachable, the false self causes a child to view himself as a failure who is not deserving of love. The false self not only doesn't think that the self is worthy of love, but that it is incapable of love because it receives only outcome love from his parents and society. Because it has not experienced true love, the false self can't show, give, or receive love for itself.

The false self is also greedy. There are momentary periods of satisfaction when a child meets the demands of the false self, but the false self always needs more, more, more. Effort and excellence are never good enough. Only perfection is sufficient to provide even the briefest glimpses of self-validation. The false self no longer needs parents to dangle the carrot of love; it has offered its own unreachable carrot to the child.

Alice Miller, the author of *The Drama of the Gifted Child*, describes how many children lose their true selves at an early age because they are faced with a choice that really isn't a choice: They can remain true to themselves and forsake their parents' love or they can accept the unhealthy false self and ensure their parents' love. These children repress their true selves with their positive perspectives and healthy needs and allow their false selves with their faulty judgments and dangerous prohibitions to gain dominance.

The messages that society as a whole communicates to your child can conflict with her true self and further strengthen the false self. Whether the importance of wealth and power, being handsome or beautiful, or the necessity of being thin, your child is often unable to avoid internalizing powerful negative messages. If these internalizations are consistent with your messages, your child can be overwhelmed with the construction of this unhealthy false self. The need to gain love from you *and* to be accepted by society causes the true self to be pushed far into the background of your child's psyche and allows the false self to come to the fore and assert control.

It is nearly impossible for your child to combat the unhealthy messages—image is everything, it's all about consumption, a sound bite is enough—that society communicates through television, magazines, and the Internet. Your child lacks the experience, perspective, and maturity to resist the allure. The real danger occurs when you are seduced by society's messages and become a part of the problem by reinforcing societal messages. If you don't protect your child from these messages, you are building a house without a roof. Your child is left vulnerable to society's elements and is unable to shield him- or herself from the destructive path of our culture's tornadoes and hurricanes.

Maryann is a twenty-one-year-old world-class swimmer. Until she was ten years old, Maryann was a happy kid. She had loving parents and enjoyed hanging out with her friends, studying, and playing different sports. When she was ten, her father, Sam, introduced her to swimming. In a short time, Maryann showed promise and she became committed to pursuing her goals in swimming. Sam also became very involved in her swimming.

By the age of thirteen, Maryann's development as a swimmer accelerated and her growth as a person halted. Sam no longer saw or seemed to care about Maryann the person, only Maryann the swimmer. During the previous three years, the happy child that Maryann had been seemed to disappear. The only friends she had were from swimming. All of her time was devoted to swimming or to school.

During this time, Maryann also internalized her father's beliefs and attitudes about competition and achievement. Winning was everything. Failure was unacceptable. Nothing was ever good enough. She had to be right and in control. As Maryann entered adolescence, society's messages asserted themselves even more. Already a big girl because of genetics, Maryann's body began to develop further with the onset of puberty. At the same time, she was being bombarded by messages that thin was beautiful and fast, and big was ugly and slow. Sam (and her coach) encouraged the internalization of these messages, telling her that she had to be thinner if she wanted to reach her goals. Maryann was being assailed from all sides by messages about three things that meant everything to her—being thin, being fast, and being loved.

Sam and her coach—who, though well-respected in the swimming world, was known as a taskmaster and as decidedly unsympathetic to the general health of his swimmers—encouraged Maryann to lose weight and she did. They then told her that she had lost too much weight and it was hurting her swimming. Maryann was in an impossible situation created by society, her father, and her coach. Maryann felt trapped—no matter what she did, she couldn't seem to please the two most important people in her life. She was unhappy and depressed, and felt helpless and out of control. Then she found a solution: She became a bulimic. Finally, she felt in control of something.

Maryann exemplifies the dangers of a child's having a true and false self that are in conflict. Her authentic self couldn't satisfy the demands that her father, her coach, and society placed on her. She needed to create a new self that would be able to function in a world that demanded she control her weight; the only way she could do so was to learn how to throw up her food on demand, even though, to her true self, this would have been an abhorrent thing to do. This unhealthy resolution of the conflict gave Maryann a false sense of control and provided some temporary relief from her pain.

Children are faced with the need to absorb unhealthy pressures that come from every level of society, from the culture communicated through the media to the educational, artistic, and athletic systems in which they participate. Peers can be victims and carriers of this virus as well. Children are often helpless to resist and become victims of their false selves. When this happens, adds Dr. Pipher, "young [people] have lost their true selves. In their eagerness to please, they have developed an addiction that destroys their central core. They have sold their souls."

RED FLAGS

The false self is difficult to spot early in your child's life. The false self develops slowly, yet it is unrelenting and, in time, will engulf your child. How can you tell if your child is creating a false self? And how can you find out if you are part of the problem? Here are some symptoms to look out for.

RED FLAG #1: SELF-HATE

How much does your child love herself? If your child is beginning to be dominated by a false self, the first sign will be that she will not seem to like herself: "I hate the way I look." "I'm stupid." "I can't do anything right." If this sounds like your child, you need to understand that she doesn't hate herself so much as she has begun to hate the failures of her false self. If this describes your child, she lives in a constant state of fear that she will never measure up and earn self-love or your love. Even worse, she feels totally helpless to do anything about it.

If your child has created a false self, then she will have a greater conflict than the one just between her true and false selves. She will also have a conflict with you, because the need to create that false self was caused by you in the first place. Because your child's false self and her self-hatred came from you, then your child, at some level, is really expressing hatred for you. Your child's feelings toward you collide with great force. Her greatest need is your love. Her greatest fear is that you don't love her. Allowing herself to believe that you are to blame for her pain would negate her profound need for your love, so your child makes the only possible choice: She chooses to hate herself.

RED FLAG #2: SELF-PUNISHMENT

To reconcile this conflict, your child may convince herself that she deserves her self-hatred for failing to live up to her internalized standards. Your child then might turn that hatred toward herself by criticizing herself, being angry at feeling unhappy about herself, withholding pleasurable experiences, pushing herself unreasonably, adhering to perspectives and beliefs that make her unhappy and unproductive, and being closed to other, more balanced views.

The emergence of this self-hatred from the false self is expressed with increasingly harsh self-judgments, beginning with your child's making critical statements about grades, sports performance, appearance, or social prowess. These self-criticisms may increase in frequency and intensity. Strong and seemingly unreasonable expressions of negative emotions such as frustration, anger, and sadness are also evidence that the false self is surfacing. You might also be seeing that your child is no longer enjoying the things she used to, or that she's generally unhappy, or that her grades are slipping.

You might notice that your child is putting less energy into her friendships. Constant fighting, intense expressions of anger toward a sibling or a peer, and social withdrawal may be signs of the emergence of the false self. Though sibling and peer conflict are normal parts of growing up, prolonged and frequent squabbling among your children is a sign that something serious may be going on. You will need to talk with teachers, instructors, coaches, and parents of friends who can provide you with information about how your child is feeling and behaving.

These signs are usually expressions of either depression or anger. As Dr. Pipher says, "If that pain is blamed on themselves, on their own failures, it manifests itself as depression. If that pain is blamed on others—on parents, peers or the culture—it shows up as anger. This anger is often mislabeled as rebellion or even delinquency. In fact, anger often masks a severe rejection of the self and an enormous sense of loss."

Punishing himself protects your child by removing the conflict that it is actually you who is causing him pain. Punishing himself excessively also preempts the punishment that your child expects to receive from you for failing to live up to expectations. If your child punishes himself severely enough, then perhaps you will see that he has already suffered enough and will not cause him more pain (and may even show him love). By justifying his pain in this way, your child actually feels better than if he had to acknowledge that his pain is unfair and wrong. This resolution of your child's conflict also gives him a false sense of control over his pain, which allows him to believe that he can lessen the pain because he is inflicting it on himself rather than its being administered by you.

All attempts at self-punishment serve three essential purposes: Your child experiences temporary relief from his pain; you are forced to show love, caring, and support for your child; and finally, your child can exact revenge on you by inflicting pain on those who are the true source of his pain.

RED FLAG #3: SELF-DESTRUCTION

To this point, if your child has created a false self, she may simply be unhappy and troubled. If the emergence of the false self is not halted and the self-punishment continues, the ways in which your child punishes herself will become more severe. As the false self gains strength—and the pain your child feels from her continued failure to satisfy the false self grows—the self-punishment will show itself in more self-destructive ways.

Substance abuse is one way a child may anesthetize his pain. In a study of young substance abusers, researcher Lynn Woodhouse discovered that most had experienced emotional pain for many years from repressed fear, anger, self-hate, depression, and guilt. Depending on the type of substance used, drugs can either numb children to their pain or temporarily replace the pain with feelings of pleasure.

Eating disorders, particularly among girls, are also attempts to take away their pain. Having apparent control over their eating and how much they weigh acts to moderate their pain by giving them small victories, which "nourish" their false selves. A girl might not realize, however, that as she feeds her false self, she starves her true self!

These are serious issues and need to be addressed as soon as you see them arise. Children who find themselves under the control of false selves may begin to feel deeply alienated and despair of ever finding their true selves and happiness again. The idea of suicide arises as a way to end the conflict between the false self and the suffering true self that can find no way out. Dr. Darold Treffert noticed an increase in adolescent suicides with the young people who were wrapped up in the pursuit of success. He tells of a straight-A student who received a single B on her report card who said, "Mom and Dad have never said anything to me about having to get good grades. In fact, we rarely talk about it. But I know they do not want, nor could they tolerate, a failure. And if I fail in what I do, I fail in what I am."

DEVELOPING YOUR CHILD'S TRUE SELF

KNOW THE TRUE SELF

Helping your child resist the false self begins with your child's knowing and identifying with her true self. Your child can't become her true self if she doesn't know who her true self is. This understanding and connection with your child's true self allows her to clearly separate her values and beliefs from those of society and her potential false self. A well-defined true self can provide your child with the awareness necessary to recognize the unhealthy, though seductive, pressures of society and the strength and resilience to oppose them.

Your child's true self develops in two ways. You need to expose your child to essential life-affirming values such as honesty, integrity, genuineness, emotional expression, and compassion. If you can expose your child at an early age to values, beliefs, and attitudes that counter society's messages and are consistent with her true self, you lay the foundation from which your child's true self can emerge.

You must then help your child understand what her true self is. This realization entails assisting your child in recognizing what makes her unique—her strengths and her weaknesses—what she values about herself and the world, what is most important to her in her life, and what she can offer others. You need to help your child distinguish between what society communicates and what she chooses to believe on her own. This process includes encouraging your child to acknowledge all of her perspectives, beliefs, and feelings, especially if they differ from those of society. It also means helping your child develop the sensitivity to be able to critically judge society's messages and understand that those messages are frequently at cross-purposes with her real values. And all this needs to be done without creating a cynical or alienated child. For example, finding teenage magazines stupid doesn't mean that our society is stupid. You need to balance the negative aspects of our society by emphasizing the good things our society has to offer—democracy, justice, equality, freedom, opportunities, and so on.

This understanding of your child's true self obviously doesn't occur overnight. Rather, it is a process the evolves over years as she matures. You need to maintain an ongoing dialogue, live a life consistent with your values, and encourage your child to cultivate her true self. These continuing experiences will give your child the perspectives and resources that will enable her to create her own value system and allow her true self to emerge, gain strength, and maintain its dominance. Consistent emphasis on the true self keeps its presence in the forefront of your child's mind and allows her to more deliberately weigh and select or discard the messages that she gets from the culture that envelops her. Teaching your child to see the difference between our culture's positive messages—serious conversation, good literature, the arts—and pop culture—mass media, which aggrandizes sexuality and violence—and showing her how to examine the underlying values in the messages she receives on a daily basis is an essential responsibility of parenting. Helping your child to develop a conscious awareness and the ability to separate the healthy from the unhealthy messages is fundamental to the development of a person strong enough to withstand this daily assault. The emergence of your child's true self—and the actions that you need to take to foster that emergence—needs to be ever present in your psyche throughout her formative years and you need to play an active and nurturing role in this process.

WAGE WAR AGAINST THE FALSE SELF

From an early age, your child wages a war against the development and dominance of his false self. As unfortunate as it is to say, society at large is an enemy in this war. The messages that society conveys in magazines and on television, film, and the Internet can be destructive to the growth and preeminence of a child's true self.

Your child cannot win this war alone. He simply does not have the perspective, experience, or resources to marshal an effective defense against society's armies. Your child has only one hope—that you are willing to fight with him against the forces of the unhealthy false self. Whether your child can win this war outright, given the omnipresence and potency of society's forces, is questionable. However, you can at least keep society at bay by allying yourself with your child from the beginning and teaching him the perspectives, beliefs, and skills that will help him make healthy decisions about which messages he chooses to accept and reject.

You can facilitate these changes by not falling victim to the unhealthy societal messages yourself. This challenge is great because you may already possess something of a false self that influences your beliefs and behavior, which you may then unwittingly pass on to your child. In committing to ally yourself with your child in this battle against the false self, you need to examine your own beliefs and, if they are guided by a false self, consciously decide to not infect your child with those messages, and choose to communicate healthier messages to your child that will foster his true self.

In support of the development of your child's true self, you must convey messages that contradict society's destructive directives. You can act as a role model for your child by showing that in your own life, you are not seduced by the sirens' call of these messages. You can also defend against unhealthy messages by openly discussing their allure and dangers, and by offering your child a healthier alternative perspective to internalize. For example, a common message in our society is that success is defined in terms of accumulated wealth and material possessions. You can counter this view by showing your child how you define success. This message can be especially powerful if you and your spouse have careers that model your personal values about success. You can also introduce your child to alternative definitions of success, such as helping others or expressing one's creativity, and letting your child express her feelings about what success means to her. Giving examples of people you and your child know and admire can illustrate this healthier definition. You can show your child the destructiveness of society's messages, why these messages are so prevalent, and how they interfere with true success and happiness.

Another way to alter our culture's messages is to reframe them in a way that better reflects your fundamental values. For example, rather than the goal of success being accumulating wealth for its own sake, you can connect this traditional kind of success with what wealth can provide, such as freedom, opportunity, travel, education, sharing, and the ability to donate to charity.

For the swimmer Maryann, whom I described earlier, there was a happy turn of events. In the proceeding months, it became clear to Maryann's father that something was wrong. Maryann's swimming times became slower, she became increasingly moody, and she began to withdraw from her friends and teammates. Finally, one of Maryann's close swimming friends had the courage to tell Sam that his daughter was bulimic. Though angry at first at this apparent betrayal, Maryann also felt relief at no longer having to keep her "dirty little secret." Expecting her father to be furious with her, Maryann was surprised and touched by how loving, supportive, and concerned Sam was. For the first time in her life, Maryann talked openly with her father about what she had been going through and he responded. A light finally switched on in Sam's head and he saw what he had been doing. He found a sport psychologist with training in eating disorders to work with Maryann and they made the mutual decision to have her change swimming programs so she could work with a coach who had a reputation for sensitivity to young women's health concerns. Sam also changed. This threat to his daughter's health was a wake-up call that caused him to reexamine his motivations and behavior with Maryann over the last decade. Though Sam could not undo the damage he had done, he was committed to not causing any more harm to his daughter and to doing everything he could to turn the tide on Maryann's health and happiness. Sam realized that he was pushing his daughter for his own reasons rather than because it was best for her. He saw that he had lost sight of Maryann as a person and had only seen her as a swimmer who competed to achieve *his* goals. Sam decided that he would put Maryann's needs first from then on. If she wanted to continue swimming, it would be her choice, and she would do it her way. He would support her in whatever she decided. Sam's new priority was that he would do everything he could to ensure that Maryann was as healthy and happy as she could be.

FALSE SELF OR TRUE SELF: YOUR CHOICE

1. Negativity breeds negativity.
2. Disparagement breeds distrust.
3. Continual criticism breeds defensiveness.
4. Lectures breed resistance.

5. Sermons breed passivity.

6. Low expectations breed poor performance.

7. Lack of faith breeds insecurity.

8. Anger breeds fear.

1. Optimism breeds enthusiasm.

2. Positive expectations breed achievement.

3. Love breeds trust.

4. Affirmation breeds motivation.

5. Success breeds self-confidence.

6. Active involvement breeds active learning.

7. Faith breeds security.

Greene, L. J. (1995). *The life-smart kid: Teaching your child to use good judgment in every situation.* Rocklin, CA: Prima.

PART II

OWNERSHIP

Successful achievers must have "ownership" of the activities in which they participate. Ownership means children perceive that their participation in an achievement activity is truly their own—their motivation, their determination, their efforts, their successes and failures, and their rewards. Successful achievers care deeply for the chosen activity. Children who have ownership of an activity have a great passion for it and join in for no other reason than the value they place on it for themselves. As a result of their ownership, successful achievers take responsibility for all aspects of their achievement efforts because they are *internally* motivated and believe they have control over their efforts and their outcomes.

If you have to tear your child away from building a model airplane or practicing her free-throw shooting or reading a good book, then you know what ownership looks like. But if your child needs to be forced into everything she does and never develops a self-sustaining drive to really get into it, then you need to understand why your child lacks ownership. Are you doing something that is keeping your child from gaining ownership, such as being too involved in her achievement activities or taking on responsibilities that should be hers? Has your child simply not found something that excites her?

There are two levels of ownership related to successful achievers: philosophical and practical. Philosophical ownership relates to a child's basic feelings about her involvement in the activity and why she participates. Practical ownership is the expression of the philosophical ownership in her achievement activities and her life.

Perhaps the thing that most separates children who have philosophical ownership from other children is in the kind of satisfaction and enjoyment that each experiences. If your child doesn't have philosophical ownership, he probably gains most of his validation solely from the *outcome* of his achievement efforts. He likely relies heavily on the outside benefits derived from his participation, such as social status, trophies, and attention from parents or friends. Your child may lack an internal motivation to achieve and is dependent on external factors to justify his efforts in the achievement activity.

In contrast, if your child has philosophical ownership, then you will see that he gains most of his gratification from the *process* of achieving. Your child probably enjoys "the grind," the seemingly endless, and often tedious, repetition required to become successful in any activity. He loves the process of the activity as much as or more than the performance itself and the accolades that may result. Though the external rewards are nice, your child will simply love to achieve for its own sake.

Philosophical ownership is best developed in the early stages of participation in an activity. You can facilitate this process in several ways. As a role model, you can show your child what philosophical ownership looks like. If you live your life with philosophical ownership of the activities in which you participate—if you express passion and joy for your own achievement efforts—such as your career and your hobbies, it is almost impossible for your child to not adopt a similar perspective. You can show your child your own philosophical ownership in your career, for example, by demonstrating commitment to your work, allowing your child to see your focus, effort, and intensity when working, and sharing with your child your work experiences that communicate your enjoyment of it.

More directly, you can encourage your child to develop philosophical ownership by placing greater emphasis on the importance of effort and enjoyment of the process and downplaying the importance of the outcomes. You can nourish philosophical ownership when you assist your child in setting goals related to the activity. If goals focus on teaching your child the relationship between effort and outcome and on the joy and satisfaction gained from the process, he will come to believe that the process is most important. For example, if you tell your son that his goal should be to win the upcoming chess tournament, the message is that winning is all important. In contrast, if you suggest that the goal should be to work hard in practice in the weeks leading up to the chess tournament, to give his best effort in the matches, and to have fun playing, the message is that preparation, effort, and fun are most essential. Paradoxically, the child who doesn't focus on winning is often the most successful.

You can also encourage ownership following your child's achievement efforts. After your child receives a good grade in a class, instead of telling her, "You are the best student in the class. You are so smart," you might say, "You worked hard to earn that grade. It must feel good to see your efforts rewarded." Comparing your child to others puts her in a world outside of her control. But placing the emphasis on your child's hard work and pleasure in those efforts reinforces the value of ownership.

Your child will have difficulty developing philosophical ownership if you do not encourage it. If you either stress results too much or take ownership of your child's activities for yourself, he is helpless to do anything about it. Philosophical ownership is a gift that you give your child rather than something that your child can gain readily on his own.

Children who have practical ownership are the first to arrive and the last to leave. They put in time and effort beyond the threshold of what is simply "expected" of them, often working on their own outside of classes, practice, and lessons. Children who have practical ownership often stand out because they are inquisitive about the activity and take particular care of their equipment, whether it's a musical instrument or sports gear.

Children with practical ownership of their activity work hard and maintain their focus for long periods of time. They are typically organized in their efforts and are careful to check their work to ensure quality and minimize mistakes. They, for example, are good at structuring their study time and diligently review their homework so that they don't have any careless errors. These young achievers don't need to be asked whether they did their work. Rather, they regularly ask for additional opportunities to learn about their activity. Children who have practical ownership are also voracious consumers of their activity, often expressing a fascination for its most esoteric aspects and reveling in its minutiae—for instance, the young guitarist who reads about guitar greats such as Les Paul and Jimi Hendrix, collects guitar memorabilia, and enjoys polishing his guitar.

You can show your child what goes into practical ownership: giving his best effort, putting extra time into his practices and lessons, and being organized. Through role modeling and discussion, you can place the focus on these functional aspects of ownership, encourage your child in these steps, point out the satisfaction and pleasure that is gained from this active participation in the activity, and reward him for his practical ownership.

Of course, kids are kids and there will be times when even a child with practical ownership will be distracted, bored, or interested in doing other things. In these situations, if your child needs to finish homework, for example, you can give her a little nudge of encouragement and offer a small reward on completion. If her responsibilities aren't pressing, it can be healthy to give her permission to take a break from her work and go have some fun.

A few years ago, I attended a staff meeting at Burke Mountain Academy, an accredited private school for ski racers in Vermont of which I am an alum and a trustee. During the meeting, the teachers and coaches reviewed each student-athlete's progress to that point of the school year.

They described the strengths of and areas in need of improvement for each student-athlete, and discussed what each young person needed to work on in the near future. In talking about one boy, a coach said, "He takes pride in everything he does." At the time of the meeting, this simple statement struck me as being an interesting insight, but I needed to explore its full meaning further. I talked to the coach about what he meant and thought further about what this statement suggested. After lengthy consideration, I concluded that *taking pride in everything you do* was the greatest compliment a young person could receive and the ultimate goal of having ownership of an achievement activity.

What does this statement mean? When your child takes pride in everything she does, she is expressing her self-respect and she is thoroughly engaged in every aspect of her life. She values her achievement efforts enough to attempt to imbue all of her efforts with the greatest quality she can. Doing the very best she can in everything she does is a fundamental value that directs her life. If your child has this pride, she understands that life itself is an opportunity. She takes the challenge of the opportunity seriously and appreciates and respects the gift by giving her best effort in all of her pursuits. Your child recognizes that one of the true joys of life is experiencing the process of achieving. If your child is living this way, then she accepts the rewards of success and makes no excuses for failure because she understands that, ultimately, *there are no excuses*, only her efforts and her outcomes.

Taking pride in everything is both a goal toward which children strive and the result of their considerable efforts. It can be considered the ultimate objective of *Positive Pushing*. Every recommendation in this book is aimed at creating the kind of ownership in your child that results in your child's developing pride in what he does. If your child takes pride in everything he does, he is going to be an achiever because he will always do his best. Most important, your child will also be happy because he knows how to derive satisfaction and joy from his efforts. By both of these realizations, your child will be a successful achiever.

CHAPTER 4

Whose Life Is This, Anyway?
Parent Needs vs. Child Needs

In an ideal world, becoming a parent is the most unselfish thing a person can do. By having a child, a person is making a commitment to putting the needs of his child ahead of his own. Yet, the world we live in is not ideal. Parents often struggle in a tug-of-war between their own needs and those of their children. This conflict usually results in a battle over ownership of the child's life.

At the heart of this conflict between parents' needs and a child's needs are parents who are unable to gain sufficient meaning, validation, and satisfaction from their own work, relationships, or other activities. It's not uncommon to find needy parents in an unhappy marriage or unfulfilling jobs in which they're not able to meet their own needs. If you are like this, then you might find that you are compelled to turn to the most available source of support—your child—to have your needs met. As the Kabat-Zinns have observed, "A subtle entraining may take place between parent and child—wholly beneath the conscious awareness and intention of the parent—in which the child learns to tune in to the emotional needs of the parent, often without anything being said. Rather than the parent being empathic and compassionate, the child takes on that role and is expected to empathize with the parent's feelings, troubles, and stresses. . . . The child's own feelings, needs, desires get buried."

You might simply be living an unsatisfying life and have no other outlet for your needs other than your child. In other instances, parents may have more severe psychological and emotional difficulties, such as depression or anxiety, and their children become essential tools for their own survival (I encourage parents with these problems to get into psychotherapy to help them address these problems and to better understand their impact on their children).

I have noticed in my work with families that many children who struggle with issues involving achievement and happiness often have one parent who has no life of his or her own (that is, no real sources of validation from his or her marriage, career, or friendships) and who cares too much about the child's life while the other parent is totally focused on his or her own life and does not care enough about the child. If you are the needy parent who is not getting any of your needs met, you might, without even realizing it, be turning to your child for psychological and emotional sustenance. On the other hand, your spouse, who is so absorbed in his work, may be so preoccupied that he has not enough concern for the needs of your child. If this is your family, then your child is caught between two undesirable extremes of parental needs: being overwhelmed or being neglected. Your child's needs are relegated to a secondary status and your child feels unfulfilled and overburdened.

Are you putting your own needs ahead of those of your child? Are you using your child's life to find meaning and satisfaction in your own? *Are you stealing your child's life?*

Parents who put their own needs first ensure that their child won't gain ownership of his or her achievements or life. Says Alice Miller: "Children who fulfill their parents' conscious or unconscious wishes are 'good,' but if they ever refuse to do so or express wishes of their own that go against those of their parents, they are called egoistic or inconsiderate. It usually does not occur to the parents that they might need and use the child to fulfill their own egoistic wishes."

At the age of twenty-four, Deborah left college to marry and have children. Her husband, Jason, was a salesman who worked long hours, traveled extensively, was rarely home, and felt constant financial pressure to support his family. Deborah was lonely, unfulfilled, and depressed. Neglected by her husband, she stole the lives of her two daughters, Emily (sixteen) and Tanya (eleven), in very different ways.

Deborah became Emily's "best friend." They did everything together and Deborah shared her innermost thoughts with Emily, including her loneliness, her sadness, and her feelings about her relationship with her husband. Emily realized that her mother depended on her and Emily did everything she could to make her mother happy. She got straight A's in school, regularly chose to spend time with her mother over her friends on weekends, and decided to apply to colleges near their home. Though she sometimes felt angry and resentful, Emily would punish herself for these feelings because of all of the sacrifices her mother made for her. Deborah never noticed that Emily didn't seem to have many friends or that she had become increasingly sullen. Jason was happy that Emily filled his wife's time when he was not home. It took Emily years to fully realize how unhappy she was.

Tanya, the younger daughter, showed promise as a singer at an early age. Though she enjoyed it, there were other things she liked to do better. But her mother had decided that Tanya was going to become a famous singer. To that end, Deborah threw herself into her daughter's singing, learning everything she could about voice, hiring the best voice coaches she could find, and attending every lesson and recital. At the same time, Jason was so busy in his own life that he showed little interest in Tanya's singing. He was glad that Deborah was so busy with their younger daughter. Tanya began to think that her father didn't love her. After a while, Tanya started to lose interest in singing, but every time she brought it up, Deborah cried. Once, when Tanya skipped a voice lesson, her father sat down with her and expressed his disapproval. At the time, Tanya thought how nice it was that he showed interest. She also found herself becoming angry at her mother for not allowing her to stop singing. Tanya learned that by skipping lessons and singing poorly in recitals she felt less anger toward her mother (though Deborah was more angry at her) and she got more attention from her father. This tug-of-war spiraled downward into a vicious cycle of mutual anger and resentment until no one's needs were being met.

Your child can be surprisingly astute at knowing when you are not acting in her best interests. At some nonconscious level, your child can sense when you might be placing your own needs ahead of her own and that your actions are motivated by what is best for you rather than what is best for her. If your child comes to believe this, she will lose trust in you. Your child's self-esteem may also weaken if she concludes that she may not be worthy enough for you to place her needs ahead of your own. This diminishment of your child's self-esteem will produce anger and resentment toward you for making her feel so bad. These beliefs and emotions can lead your child down a road toward adulthood filled with dissatisfaction, distrust, and unhappiness.

YOUR NEEDS VS. YOUR CHILD'S NEEDS

The needs that drive you are no different from the needs that we all feel and want to have satisfied: to be loved, to be valued, to be competent, to be in control, to receive gratification, to have meaning in our lives. These needs are normal and healthy parts of being a human being. The problem arises when your efforts to meet those needs for yourself are compensation for not having had them met as a child or if you are now unable to have your needs met through healthy interactions with others. What ought to be healthy needs become compulsions that demand satisfaction at any cost in order for you to maintain your psychological and emotional equilibrium.

Your child too has fundamental needs that are essential for her development into a successful and happy adult: to feel loved, to feel safe, to feel competent, to grow, to explore, to become independent. Unfortunately, your child has limited ability to meet these needs for herself early in her life. Rather, you must give her the freedom to meet her own needs. If you don't give your child that freedom, she may be forced to meet her own needs in any way she can. If this happens, your child may seek out unhealthy outlets to meet her frustrated and unfulfilled needs and look for alternative—and sometimes destructive—ways to take her life back.

RED FLAGS

Perhaps the single greatest barrier to the development of an achieving and happy child occurs when you steal your child's life in order to meet your own needs. There are a variety of red flags that you should look for in yourself and your spouse to judge whether either of you is putting your own needs ahead of those of your child, whether you are stealing your child's life.

RED FLAG #1: FIXING YOUR IMPERFECT SELF

A necessary, though uncomfortable, thing that you must face is acknowledging your own imperfections. This realization of your imperfect self can be painful because you may be forced to look at weaknesses you internalized from your own parents. To avoid having to face your imperfect self, you may project your imperfections onto your child. This bestowal relieves you of having to accept and take responsibility for these so-called flaws in yourself and enables you to "fix" your own imperfect self in your children.

Joanne felt unappreciated and unloved by her husband and felt great anger at him for not meeting her needs. As he was a school principal and she had not worked in years, Joanne felt stupid and inadequate around him. She projected these feelings onto her daughter, Jessie, with the use of outcome love and by driving her daughter unmercifully in all of her achievement activities in an attempt to ensure that Jessie would never feel stupid or inadequate in her own life. Sadly, in attempting to fix her own imperfect self through her daughter, Joanne replicated rather than repaired her imperfect self in Jessie.

At its worst, you may project your own inadequacies onto your child, hating that part of your child that is so like yourself, and then desperately try to correct those flaws. If you are doing this, you are punishing your child for your own imperfections. Irrational expectations and demands, spontaneous expressions of frustration and anger in response to failure, prolonged depression, a sense of failure and loss, and an inability to let go of your child's perceived failures are red flags of attempts to repair your imperfect self by "fixing" your child.

RED FLAG #2: MERGING WITH YOUR CHILD

Arthur devoted his life to developing the pianistic talent of his young daughter, Gwen. Although Arthur had an older son, Gwen's music career was becoming the central focus of the family's activities. On several occasions, Arthur changed the date and location of family vacations so as not to conflict with Gwen's planned recitals. Jealousy began to develop between Gwen and her older brother, who felt neglected and unloved. Arthur constantly hounded Gwen to practice and, before every recital, humiliated her by reminding her to go to the bathroom. Every time her father did this, Gwen would let out a huge sigh of frustration and become angry at him. Not surprisingly, her anger would often interfere with her performance.

Gwen's increasing anger at her father began to undermine their relationship. What began as love and support for an enjoyed activity became an oppressive force driving Gwen away from something she loved. Their relationship deteriorated as Arthur, indignant that Gwen didn't appreciate all of the sacrifices he was making, expressed her anger by pushing harder and becoming more forcefully involved. Because they were no longer able to communicate effectively, Gwen got back at her father by resisting all of his efforts. Their relationship became a tug-of-war for control over Gwen's music and life.

Gwen began to take control by putting little effort into lessons, feigning a hand injury, and sabotaging her recitals by not warming up and then playing poorly. A vicious cycle of pressure, resistance, and mutual anger developed between Gwen and Arthur. Though at one time Gwen couldn't wait to sit down at the piano to practice and perform, now she showed little interest or enjoyment in playing. This destructive scenario culminated in Gwen's announcing one day that she was quitting the piano forever.

In your zealousness to see your child achieve, you are in danger of becoming so involved in your child's achievement activity that you may not distinguish between your own needs for achievement and those of your child. University of Washington researcher Frank Smoll calls this the "reverse dependency trap" in which parents overidentify with their child's experience and define their own self-worth based on the success of their child in the achievement activity. "Be cautious when you take an interest in your child's activities and accomplishments that your own self-esteem is not at stake. Just as the child's worth does not depend on his or her own accomplishments, the adult's worth does not rest on the achievements of the children. . . . Your own self-esteem need not rise or fall with your teen's success and failure," writes Shirley Gould.

The activity may actually become more important to you than to your child, which, in turn, diminishes its importance to him. This excessive interest on your part, rather than promoting your child's participation, undermines his interest by taking away his ownership of the achievement activity. Your child may develop the perception that the activity is no longer his because you seem to be doing more in the activity than he is. In essence, you *merge with your child* in his achievement efforts.

If you merge with your child, you will assume roles that are outside of your purview as a parent, such as doing all scheduling without your child's input, talking too much about your child's achievement interests, attending all practices and performances, and instructing or coaching your child. An early sign that you might be merging with your child is that you take responsibility away from him, such as constantly asking him whether he has fulfilled his practice requirements, maintained his equipment properly, and is adequately prepared for an imminent performance.

A profound warning that you may have merged with your child would be if you notice that your child's achievement activity has begun to dominate family life. Are you planning your vacations around your child's performance schedule, or sacrificing your own needs and activities to serve your achieving child? Are you favoring your higher-achieving child to such an extent that your other children feel that their sibling is the favorite and that they are being neglected?

The impact of your merging with your achieving child is especially hurtful because it harms not only the achieving child, but also your other children. Excessive love, attention, energy, and resources that are given to the achieving child may leave your other children lacking in these areas. Your other children may feel unloved, inadequate, and abandoned. Your persistent favoritism will likely cause conflict and lasting harm in your family. Additionally, many of the red flags that we have already looked at—low self-esteem, low achievement, and emotional immaturity—will not only show up in the your high-achieving child, but also in your other, increasingly neglected, children.

And finally, the clearest and scariest sign that you might be merging with your child is if you discover yourself discussing your child's performances in terms of how "we" did: "We played great today," "We just weren't on today," and "We just need to work harder." I have never seen parents actually performing with their children on the field, on the stage, or in the classroom. Are you using "we"? If the answer is yes, this should send up a red flag for you.

RED FLAG #3: PLACING YOUR HAPPINESS ON YOUR
CHILD'S SHOULDERS

One of the great joys of being a parent is sharing in your child's achievements. Your excitement for your child's successes and your disappointment for your child's failures are a normal and healthy part of parenting. But *sharing* your child's achievements doesn't mean *living through* your child's achievements. Lawrence J. Greene, the author of *The Life-smart Kid*, writes, "The parent who tries to live vicariously through a child's accomplishments imposes a heavy emotional burden on the child. He's asking her to assume responsibility for *his* contentment. . . . The child who agrees to conform to this script cannot help but feel unfulfilled, frustrated, resentful, and angry. . . . She's clearly in a double bind. . . . She'll respond to this emotionally wrenching dilemma by becoming withdrawn and depressed or by acting out her rage in some counterproductive way."

Sharing in your child's achievements and living vicariously through him is a subtle but powerful distinction. Sharing your child's experiences places the focus on him. The emphasis is on what the experience means to him, the emotions he is feeling, the lessons he learns, and the benefits he gains from the experience. When your child succeeds, you are thrilled for him. When your child fails, you feel his sadness. With sharing, it is *all about your child*. When you are living vicariously through your child, the focus is on you: your emotions, what the experience means to you, what you gain from it. When your child succeeds, you feel that you have succeeded. When your child fails, you feel that you have failed. With living vicariously through your child, it is *all about you*.

It's tough being a kid these days. Your child has so many responsibilities, including school, family, social life, sports, arts, and religious activities. You may overschedule your child's life and he may have little time to just be a kid. These challenges alone are sufficient to burden your child. Yet you may also thrust the additional responsibility on him of making you happy. If you do not gain sufficient meaning and satisfaction from your own life and look to your child as the primary source of ego-gratification, your self-esteem becomes dependent on the success of your child. And he knows it!

Imagine the burden. Every time your child performs, your happiness and well-being are squarely on his shoulders. If he succeeds, you will be happy, but only until the next performance. If he fails, you will remain unhappy until he can provide you with a successful performance.

The first red flag that might signal that you are placing your happiness on your child's shoulders relates to the strength of your emotions compared to your child's. Do you feel stronger emotions than your child does regarding her achievement activities? Are you more nervous before a performance than your child is, more excited when she succeeds, and more disappointed when she does not perform up to expectations?

The second danger sign is how long these emotions last. Do your emotions remain with you for an extended period? Are you depressed for days after your child's poor performance? Do these emotions dominate your life and are you unable to put them behind you? Do they interfere with your daily functioning, rather than your being able to let go of them and get on with your life?

The third indicator of trouble is if you are more focused on how *you* feel and less aware of how *your child* feels about his performance. After an achievement activity, do you dominate the conversation about it? Do you evaluate his performance and tell him what it meant to you? Are you so absorbed in your own feelings that you don't notice or inquire about your child's impressions or feelings about the performance?

The fourth red flag is if you're more concerned with results—standings, rankings, grades, and test scores—than the developmental benefits of the achievement activity. What is the first thing you ask your child after a performance—"How did you do?" If the outcomes of your

child's performances take precedence over the process of her performances, for example, how much fun she had or what she learned from
the experience, then you may be placing your happiness on your child's
shoulders.

Several years ago I was contacted by a dance instructor about working with a young ballet dancer, Danielle. The instructor had sensed
that my primary emphasis should be on the mother, Karen, rather than
on Danielle, because Danielle's problems seemed to stem from her
mother. I soon saw that Karen was placing her own need for happiness
on the shoulders of her daughter. I learned that Karen had felt tremendous guilt about her older son, who was having a number of serious
problems. Her husband had magnified these feelings of guilt by placing
the blame for his son's difficulties on Karen. Karen was struggling with
the perception that she was a terrible mother who had screwed up her
son. Her only possible redemption was to raise Danielle right, proving
to herself, her husband, and the world that she was a good mother.

Karen poured every ounce of her energy into ensuring that Danielle
would be successful. Unfortunately, her efforts were having the opposite
effect. Her daughter began to show anger, resentment, and resistance
to her mother's efforts. Their relationship deteriorated, and Danielle's
dancing suffered as well. Karen's greatest fear—that she was the terrible
mother that she thought others believed her to be—was being realized.

RED FLAG #4: LOSING PERSPECTIVE

Many achievement activities are very seductive. Fame and fortune resulting from success in school, sports, and the performing arts appear
to be waiting for your child if only he or she has the talent and determination to reach that level. This dream can cause you to lose perspective on achievement's intrinsic value.

Your child has a limited perspective because of his or her lack of
experience. Your child views the world narrowly and only into the
immediate future. Your child can be easily enticed by the slogan, image,

or appearance of the pot of gold at the end of the rainbow of achievement. Your child rarely is able to see what it takes to get there or the unlikelihood of such a dream. One study shows, for example, that 70 percent of inner-city boys expect to play professional sports when, in reality, the chances are that 1 in 10,000 will reach that level.

If you also buy into this unrealistic perspective and direct your energy based on this illusion, you are setting your child up for failure and you up for disappointment. If you are seduced by the same naive perspective and encourage this view in your child, you are inflicting potentially long-term and irreparable harm on your child's development. You and your child may only see the upside of achievement. You may not be aware of its price: the sacrifices, limitations, loneliness, and emotional, social, and physical tolls. If you could see the downside of achievement, you might reconsider the value of setting such a singular and unrealistic goal for your child.

The odds of achieving greatness are also infinitesimally small. How many Pavarottis, Navratilovas, or Hawkings emerge in any generation? What is the likelihood that your investment will be returned with fame and fortune? Extremely unlikely. Without both you and your child understanding the downside of achievement, you would be investing in fool's gold. If you think the way out of the ghetto for your child is to become the next Michael Jordan, the chances are 999,999 times out of 1,000,000 that you are choosing a dead end for your child.

Nowhere is this loss of perspective better illustrated than in the age scandal at the 2001 Little League World Series. A pitcher for a Bronx, New York, team threw a no-hitter, a perfect game, and led his team to a third-place finish in the tournament—and became a national hero in the process. An investigation later revealed that he was fourteen years old, not twelve—thus ineligible—and that his father had altered his birth certificate so he could play. Though the reason for the deception is still unclear, there had been speculation that the boy's father wanted to jumpstart his son's career toward the major leagues. Ironically, only twenty-one players in the fifty-three-year history of the Little League World Series have gone on to play in the major leagues.

RED FLAG #5: OVERMATCHING YOUR CHILD

In your zealousness to encourage your child's development, you are in danger of pushing your child to higher and higher levels of achievement, even when your child may not be prepared for the increased demands. For example, parents of a chess player may enter him in increasingly competitive tournaments or parents of a percussionist may have her try out for a more advanced orchestra. Dr. T. Berry Brazelton, the author of *What Every Baby Knows*, observes that "parents today seem to be anxiously concerned with early learning. With a [child] who has a slow start, parents' anxiety to prove she's OK may lead them to push her to do things before she's ready. . . . An environment full of pressure is likely to become a strained, joyless one. . . . Eventually they have trouble coping with the demands of our complicated society." By placing your child in achievement settings in which he is overmatched, you may be inadvertently inhibiting, rather than facilitating, his interest, achievement, and enjoyment in the activity.

The essential question: Why would you put your child in situations in which he or she is overmatched? One reason may be that you might overestimate your child's capabilities. You may not have a realistic understanding of your child's capabilities in an achievement activity. You may use peer comparisons in your judgments. You may think, "My Stephanie is a better math student than the girl next door, so she's ready to take an advanced class." Your own ego and achievement needs can cause you to overmatch your child. Because of your emotional investment in your child, you may have difficulty admitting that she is anything but the brightest and most talented. Seeing your own imperfect self in your child can drive you to ensure that those imperfections are exorcized from her as soon as possible by pushing her to achieve at higher and higher levels.

Wanting to "fast-forward" development is another common reason for overmatching your child. In our society where achievement and competition are so highly revered and rewarded, you may feel pressure to give your child any advantage by putting him or her on the fast track to success. This urgency shows itself in the need to get your child involved in unnecessary private lessons, gifted programs, special tutoring, and other extracurricular activities. You may also feel the need to "keep up with the Joneses." You may feel that you aren't doing as much as other parents, and your child will suffer from this "neglect." Unfortunately, you may not realize that development can't be rushed; the necessary time and effort have to be put in and your child has to be allowed to develop at his or her own pace.

Dr. Benjamin Bloom, the author of *Developing Talent in Young People*, believes that pushing children too quickly up the development ladder will actually slow their progress. He describes the initial romance stage of development as emphasizing play, fun, and exploration. During this stage children learn fundamental skills and develop a love for the achievement activity. Dr. Bloom found that rushing children through their development interfered with the emergence of these areas and left them with inadequate motivation and skills to be successful later in their development in the achievement activity.

Your child himself can also be responsible for becoming overmatched. Your child can be motivated to move ahead prematurely due to perceived pressure from you, a desire to keep up with his peers, or to live up to role models portrayed in the media. Your child can't know that this desire will actually interfere with his development. You should provide appropriate perspective and guidance that encourage him to develop at his own pace.

The noted University of Chicago psychologist Mihalyi Csikszentmihalyi developed a simple and elegant theory of motivation and achievement that shows the danger of overmatching your child. If your child's ability surpasses the demands of the situation, she will probably get bored and lose interest. This is common among bright students who are not adequately challenged in school. But if the demands of the situation far exceed your child's ability, she will feel frustrated in her efforts and will probably fail badly. If you allow your child to be in a situation where she is greatly overmatched, there is a very real danger that she will lose interest and motivation in her achievement activity because it will have become downright unpleasant.

How you react when your child inevitably does poorly because he is in over his head may affect whether he is hurt by the experience. Instead of understanding that your child's difficulties are rightfully caused by being overmatched, you risk blaming him for his "failures." If you don't understand that your child is in over his head, you might even develop, however unintentionally, the perception that your child is slow or incapable, and then subtly convey this belief to your child. Consistent exposure to circumstances in which your child feels that his ability is surpassed by the situation's demands will eventually make him feel incompetent. If these experiences are frequent, this sense of incompetence may result in lowered self-esteem and he may begin to believe that he is incompetent in everything.

Recently, I attended a tennis tournament that had attracted a number of fairly high-level players. It had been organized to ensure that every player would play at least three matches over two days. When I arrived at the tennis facility, I saw a father warming up his daughter on the court. It quickly became clear that this young player had not been playing long and was not very skilled. In her first match against the fourth seed, she lost 6-0, 6-0 and won only a handful of points. She came off the court in tears and, though her father was supportive and encouraging, it was obvious that he was disappointed too. Her other two matches followed a similar pattern: She didn't win a single game and won only a few points. After each match she was upset and, while the other girls talked or played cards with one another, she was off to the side with her father, looking very sad. Interestingly, the girls she lost to found no joy in beating her. The player I was working with came off the court after their match almost in tears, feeling awful that she had beaten the girl so thoroughly. Not surprisingly, I didn't see the girl at tournaments the remainder of the summer.

RED FLAG #6: BATTLE OF WILLS

Perhaps the most glaring red flag arises when you and your child get into a battle of wills for control of your child's life. Some conflict is a natural and expected part of the parent-child relationship. But if you and your child are constantly in disagreement, arguing, and feeling anger more than love toward each other, you can become locked in a tug-of-war in which there can be no clear victor and both of you will be victims.

Early in this struggle for power, you may think you have the upper hand because you are the parent and you can assert your needs more forcefully than can your child. But this apparent control may be an illusion that you cling to when the reality is that if you even enter into a battle of wills, you automatically lose, and your child and your relationship with him will also be casualties of the war.

The battle of wills can begin at a young age when, for example, you try to force your child to eat something, to obey you, or to behave in public. Your child can retaliate by going against your directive, by throwing a temper tantrum and embarrassing you in public, for instance. At this point, sides have been taken and the war is in danger of escalating.

The battle of wills usually carries on because you enable your child to take control first. You relinquish power if you don't stand your ground, give in to your child's behavior, and allow him to act as he pleases. When this happens, you immediately lose the war because your child learns what he needs to do to get his way. You also cede control if you react like a child yourself by, for example, having a temper tantrum of your own. Your child also wins if you try to bribe him to get him to behave. In all instances, your child learns that he owns you!

A second battle of wills can occur in adolescence as your child begins the transition from childhood to adulthood. Some conflict is a natural part of the separation process that your child must go through to become an independent adult. Your child will test his limits, experiment with this new thing called adulthood, and flex his new-found "muscles." Much as with the earlier battle of wills, you must remain resolute in maintaining reasonable boundaries, but with an emphasis on what is age-appropriate.

Unfortunately, if you are more concerned about meeting your own needs rather than those of your child—such as your need for love, support, and validation—you may be reluctant to let your child go. Your child's only possible response will be resistance and this conflict may then shift from the normal and healthy quarrels that occur between child and parents into a pitched battle of wills over control of your child's life. At this point, the battle lines are drawn and the battlefield can extend across all aspects of your child's life, including family, school, friends, dress, boundaries, and activities.

This struggle for power will continue as long as you refuse to accept your child's burgeoning independence. And this battle of wills can only end badly for both you and your child. Your child will eventually win because, at some point as he enters adulthood, he can wrest control of his life from you and, if he chooses to, walk out of your life. Then your child loses, because he has lost the love and support of his parents. You lose completely because you will have lost the battle for control of your child's life and you may have lost your child, perhaps forever.

PUTTING YOUR CHILD'S NEEDS FIRST

Putting your child's needs first is your foremost responsibility. Just as your child can sense when you are putting your own needs ahead of his, he is also aware when you make his needs a priority. Your child can "smell" your intentions. If your intentions are self-serving, your child will likely respond with resistance. If your intentions are directed toward helping your child, he will usually be cooperative. Your child may not always like what you do, but if you consistently convey that what you are doing is for the right reasons—because it is best for him in the long run—he is more likely to accept and respond to it.

RECOGNIZE YOUR OWN NEEDS

A significant challenge for you is to recognize your own needs in your child's achievement activities. What makes this process difficult is that people are often driven by needs of which they have little awareness, much less control. These needs may be grounded in experiences and perceptions that arose when they were children and have been reinforced for many years. Your ability to acknowledge your needs and understand how those needs may be hurting your child is one of the most important things you can do to help your child become a successful achiever.

The first step in this recognition process is to be able to "look in the mirror" and examine your wonderful but imperfect self. Admittedly, this can be a difficult process, yet it can determine whether your child ever finds success and happiness. With the help of a psychotherapist, your spouse, a friend, or by some other means, you can examine parts of yourself that you don't like and which you may be projecting onto your child. A way to help identify your imperfect self is to recognize those moments when you have emotional reactions to a situation you are in that seem extreme or inappropriate—anger, disappointment, or hurt. You might notice this occurs with special intensity when your child does poorly in an achievement activity.

Ask yourself: What is the source of those emotions? What part of you is reacting to this situation in which your child is involved? You may find that the root causes are painful emotions that you felt as a child—inadequacy, uncertainty, fear—that were responses to your own parents' reactions to your achievement efforts.

With these insights, you should then understand what reactions might be more beneficial to your child. When you are next faced with a situation that provokes a similar reaction, you must recognize it, maintain a healthy perspective, and modify your response in a way that is in your child's best interests—not yours. Though this change process won't be easy—it will take time and considerable effort—your efforts should be girded by knowing that your courage and resolve in putting your child's needs ahead of your own will help your child become successful and happy.

GAIN AND MAINTAIN PERSPECTIVE

You should not involve your child in an achievement activity unless you have a healthy perspective on your child's participation. Without this outlook you are setting your child up for failure and ensuring your own disappointment in her efforts. You need to ask yourself questions such as the following: Why do I want my child to participate in this activity? What will she get out of the experience? What are my expectations for her involvement? What obstacles might interfere with her experience in the activity? What are the potential downsides to her participation? What are the possible upsides?

Perhaps the simplest and healthiest perspective you can have is summed up as follows: The primary purpose of my child's participation in this achievement activity is to gain its life lessons and psychological, emotional, social (and possibly physical) benefits including, but not limited to, fun, love and mastery of an activity, motivation, commitment, confidence, focus, emotional maturity, ability to handle competition and pressure, responsibility, discipline, cooperation, leadership, teamwork, and time management, which will benefit my child later in life. Anything else—for example, great success, fame, and fortune—is just icing on the cake.

Another part of gaining and maintaining a healthy perspective involves reality testing your perceptions. Even with the best of intentions, avoiding the allure of an achievement activity is difficult, particularly if it is one that has a high profile (for example, professional sports, acting) or for which your child has shown some early talent. When your child begins a new activity, if you fantasize about her becoming its next great performer because you are absolutely sure she is gifted, you need a reality check. First, you should immediately return to the healthy perspective I provided above (you should write it down and place it on your refrigerator until your child leaves for college).

Then, as your child makes a greater commitment to an achievement activity, you should test her capabilities. Unless you have experience in the activity (if you were a participant, teacher, instructor, or coach in the activity), you are not in a position to make accurate judgments about your child's abilities or promise in the activity. You are more likely to distort your impressions. To keep this from happening, you should seek out feedback from experts who can reasonably evaluate your child's skills.

Just because your child might not be the next great one in her achievement activity doesn't mean that she shouldn't pursue it vigorously. If she has a great love for the activity and is determined, she will reach some level of success and, returning to the perspective I described above, your child will learn valuable life lessons that will serve her well in the future. As I told one parent of a young athlete with limited athletic ability, "Your son may not become that successful in his sport, but he will become successful at *something*."

Also, remember that predicting future success is an uncertain endeavor. Think of all the "phenoms" and "can't miss kids" who didn't turn out to be phenomenal and did, in fact, miss. And recall the ones who just "didn't have what it takes," yet somehow they became superstars anyway. An assessment of your child's capabilities should not be used to determine how much support and encouragement you give her. And it should never be used to set limits on your child's dreams and goals. As someone once said, "If you don't aim for the stars, you will never even reach the top of the mountain." Rather, you should understand your child's ability so you can keep your perspective grounded in reality and focus on what you can do to offer your child appropriate support.

With a healthy perspective and reasonable reality testing, you are in a position to support and encourage your child in a way that will meet his needs rather than yours. Regardless of your child's ability or future promise in the achievement activity, you will be doing what you need to do to ensure that he achieves the higher level of which he is capable and gains the greatest benefits from his participation that will serve him well in his future endeavors.

UNDERSTAND YOUR CHILD'S NEEDS

Most essential to putting your child's needs ahead of your own is understanding what your child's needs are. Perhaps the best way to judge what a child's needs are is to observe her. A child's actions speak the loudest for what she enjoys most, what she likes about an achievement activity, and what her goals are in the activity. Simply watching a child engage in the activity can tell you a lot about your child's needs.

You can also ask teachers, instructors, and coaches about your child's needs. Because they see your child most often in the achievement activity (this assumes there already is a specific activity, but you may only be in the process of finding out), they are often best suited to know how your child feels about it. This feedback is valuable because your child may behave differently with you—to please you—than she would with others, where she may behave more spontaneously. In these settings children will often demonstrate their true feelings about their involvement in an achievement activity. You may see a side of your child of which you were not aware, but need to be. Finally, you can ask your child about her needs to hear directly from her what she would like to do. Writes Alice Miller: "Many parents, even with the best intentions, cannot always understand their child, since they, too, have been stamped by their experience with their own parents. . . . It is indeed a great deal when parents can respect their children's feelings even when they cannot understand them."

AVOID THE BATTLE OF WILLS

What your child won't realize but you must understand is that the only way she can gain independence and take true control of her life is to give you control early on. If you can establish your control at the first battle, before the war truly begins, you create an environment of love, security, and boundaries in which your child can feel safe to explore her world and her capabilities, and slowly and reasonably gain power over her life.

To avoid this battle of wills, you must communicate to your young child the unmistakable message that you are in charge until he is mature enough to take command of his own life. Start to defuse the battle of wills by being the adult. If you can act like an adult—which means being mature, in control, calm, forceful, and positive—you win the first battle by not lowering yourself to your child's level in terms of your emotions or your behavior. You also neutralize the struggle for power by being the parent and doing what is best for your child. Assuming the role of the parent means establishing clear expectations and definitive consequences, and then holding your child to those expectations and enforcing the consequences firmly, lovingly, and consistently.

Later, in your child's adolescent years, a second battle of wills may emerge when your child's need to assert her separateness becomes an important part of her development. This battle is one that your child should and must win—and you must allow her to—if she is to become a mature and independent adult. To keep the normal conflicts that arise between you and your child from escalating into a battle of wills, you need to find a balance between maintaining enough control to ensure your child's safety, and progressively and age-appropriately ceding control to your child in her decision-making, boundaries, and freedom.

Early on in this process of letting go, you want to give your child small "victories" so she feels that she has taken control of parts of her life, such as what she wears and what music she listens to, while, at the same time, you maintain control of "big" issues, such as effort in school, curfew, and the types of social activities in which she is allowed to participate. Later in the separation process, you need to trust that you have done a good job of raising a mature child who will make thoughtful and responsible choices in her life. Ultimately, everything discussed in this book is aimed at helping you maintain the balance of control and freedom with your child, avoid the potentially destructive battle of wills, and do what is in your child's best interests.

CHALLENGE YOUR CHILD

Achievement is a process of small steps rather than big leaps. As a coach I work with put it, "Success is a marathon, not a sprint." A common mistake parents make is to push their children to take bigger steps than they are prepared for. Contrary to parents' intentions, trying to take big steps actually slows their children's progress.

You should do everything you can to ensure that your child stays interested and motivated in the achievement activity and that he maintains steady progress toward his goals. Csikszentmihalyi suggests that this can be best accomplished if the demands of the achievement situation slightly exceed a child's ability. This relationship challenges and motivates children by enabling them to see that if they push themselves a bit beyond what they believe themselves capable of and persevere in the face of those achievement demands, they will be successful.

You can play an essential role in this process by ensuring that two things occur. First, you need to have an understanding of your child's level of development in the achievement activity. At what level is he currently performing? What kind of progress has he been making?

What is a reasonable next step for your child? What types of demands can be expected for the next step in his progress?

Second, you need to assess your child's skills at his current level of development. What skills does your child currently have? What tools will your child need in order to continue his development? How can these skills be best obtained and learned? Knowing what skills he has will help you determine what more your child will need to learn to be successful at the next level of achievement.

For you to ascertain this information, you must become an informed consumer, seeking out the best information to meet your child's needs and maximize his or her achievement experiences. Resources such as teachers, instructors, coaches, and more experienced parents can help you educate yourself sufficiently so that you create Csikszentmihalyi's ideal achievement scenario for your child.

THE SIBLING FACTOR

If you have more than one child, you will see that your children's temperaments, interests, motivations, and capabilities can differ greatly. Having one child in a family who demonstrates greater interest, motivation, and ability than her siblings is common. If you lose perspective with your high-achieving child, your whole family will suffer, particularly the siblings, because they are the ones who are often left out. Putting the higher-achieving child's needs ahead of those of siblings, who may still be finding their own special areas of achievement, sends a destructive message to all of your children—love and attention have to be earned by achievement. This message further conveys that if one of your children is less talented than another, then he is not as worthy of love and his needs are less important.

To prevent this from happening, you need to be aware of the time, attention, resources, and affection you give your children and you must be especially sensitive to the needs of the less accomplished siblings. Because the high-achieving child will usually demand more attention and require more time, you need to be particularly vigilant in the distribution of your energy. Your other children are no less deserving of your love and attention and, though perhaps not yet as successful, their dreams and goals are no less important. They must be supported and encouraged for them to also gain the life lessons and benefits of whatever activities they choose and to whatever level of achievement for which they strive.

Perhaps most important in your treatment of the high-achieving child's siblings is to help them find something for which they have passion, support their participation, and give them the time and attention necessary for them to feel loved and valued. In keeping with my views of conditional love, your goal in achieving a sibling balance is to ensure that each child feels appreciated and respected for who they are, regardless of their accomplishments.

At a practical level, this balanced approach toward your children involves giving equal time and energy to all your children in play, helping with homework, and showing interest in all of their achievement efforts. It also means being balanced with your children in assigning responsibilities, establishing discipline, and meting out consequences without favoritism. As a general rule, you should treat all of your children equally and without concern for their talents and accomplishments.

GET A LIFE

This chapter concludes with a piece of advice that is reiterated in some form throughout this book: *GET A LIFE!* This seemingly harsh directive is a form of tough love from me to you. It means that to be a parent of an achieving and happy child, you must have a life of your own that meets your own needs and provides you with the meaning, satisfaction, and validation that will enable you to be happy and productive. If you have a life of your own that offers something beyond the real but insufficient rewards of being a good parent, then you won't have to find a life within your child. You will not need to merge with your child nor will you need to place your happiness on his or her shoulders. Having your own life will allow your child to have his or her own life. It is one of the most important gifts you can give your child.

CONTROL* VS. NURTURE YOUR CHILD

CONTROL

1. *Emotional Blackmail:* "Do what I want or I'll get very angry and go all to pieces."
2. *The Guilt Trip:* "How could you do this to me after all I've done for you?"

3. *The Bribe:* "Do what I want and I'll make it worth your time."

4. *By Might and by Power:* "Shut up and do what I tell you."

5. *The Humiliation:* "Do what I want or I'll embarrass you at home and abroad."

NURTURE

1. *Emotional Exchange:* "Let's figure out what works best for both of us, so we are both happy."
2. *The Commitment Trip:* "I wonder why you are no longer committed and what you can do to get recommitted."

3. *The Encouragement:* "Try this and see how you feel. You might actually like it."

4. *By Love and by Fairness:* "I think you should do this because I love you and I think you will enjoy it. The choice is yours."

5. *The Affirmation:* "Do this and I'll bet you will feel great about it."

---

*Dobson, J. C (1987). *Parenting isn't for cowards: Dealing confidently with the frustrations of child-rearing.* Waco, TX: World Books.

CHAPTER 5

Who's in Charge Here?
Forced vs. Guided Participation

The journey of raising your child to become a successful achiever begins with her participation in achievement activities. This participation stimulates interest, exploration, and motivation to achieve. It should initiate the process of instilling the values that are necessary for becoming a successful achiever. Participation in an activity should teach your child about the fun and satisfaction of engaging in and committing to an activity. Experimenting with a number of activities will help your child find those in which she loves to participate and which may lead to continued involvement as a vocation or avocation. Participation in an achievement activity that she chooses freely provides the opportunity for your child to eventually experience ownership.

You are faced with maintaining a delicate balance from the very first experience that your child has with an achievement activity. This equilibrium involves providing the impetus for your child to participate in new activities long enough for her to decide whether she wants to continue, yet not pushing so much that it acts to stifle your child's interest and motivation, and interfere with her development of ownership. This distinction is between forced vs. guided participation.

FORCED PARTICIPATION

"So, the paradox is that *parents who try to ensure their children's success, often raise unsuccessful kids.* But the loving and *concerned* parents who allow for failure wind up with kids who tend to choose success," Foster Cline and Jim Fay have written. Forcing your child to participate in an achievement activity can produce a wide range of difficulties. A child's most common reaction to being forced to participate in something is anger, resentment, and resistance toward his or her parents. This response will increase as the child gets older and begins to assert his independence. Some negative feelings toward parents are a natural aspect of adolescence, but when the negative feelings become fixated on one area, are unusually strong, and they persist, the negative emotions can become destructive and lasting.

If you force your child to participate, he may express his anger by showing little desire or effort in practice. Your child may sabotage his participation by breaking his equipment, behaving poorly in the activity, or directing his anger at the teacher or coach. In sports, your child may play well, but exhibit tantrums, poor behavior, and unsportsmanlike conduct. He may sabotage his own performances, intentionally performing at a low level. If you have demonstrated a high level of commitment to your child's activity, his actions are calculated to embarrass and anger you, thereby exacting revenge for his forced participation.

Forcing your child to participate in an activity in which she has little intrinsic interest hurts her ability to achieve in any endeavor by producing negative thoughts, emotions, and behavior that she associates with achievement. Your child may come to associate achievement with bad feelings. This forced participation also removes any possibility of your child's gaining ownership of the achievement activity because she is doing it for you. The anger and resentment interfere with the possibility of future enjoyment and success in the activity. Dr. Ron Taffel has noted that "the more you try to mold your child in ways that run counter to her temperament, the more she will rebel when she hits her school years. You still won't get what you want, and your relationship will suffer."

Why would you force your child to participate in an activity? The reasons are many, some well-intentioned, others ill-conceived, and all hurtful to a child. You may see an achievement activity as a way for your child to become successful. Forcing your child to pursue a particular course of study in school or participate in a certain sport, for example, may in your mind ensure that your child will achieve a level of success. Unfortunately, you may not consider—or perhaps not care—that the path you force your child to follow may not be the path your child wishes to take.

Forced participation occurred with the son of a couple I knew who were passionate about skiing. The father, Tim, was an absolute skiing fanatic, and he and his wife, Sara, made skiing a central part of their lives. After watching Bill Johnson win the 1984 Olympic downhill gold medal, Tim decided that his son, Trevor, was going to be a skiing champion. They started Trevor skiing before he could walk, and he became a remarkable skier by the time he was seven years old. His parents began to enter him in races when he was eight, and Trevor immediately showed promise.

Tim coached Trevor throughout his development as a skier and provided him with every opportunity to succeed, including summers away at training camps in Europe. Trevor couldn't say he ever really loved ski racing, but it was something he had grown up doing and it was important to his father. But by the time Trevor was thirteen, Tim wouldn't let him try out for other sports and Trevor was devoting so much time to skiing that he began to lose touch with his friends at home. Trevor was becoming angry, but every time he tried to talk to his father about it, Tim would tell him that he would never be good at those other sports anyway and he had good friends in the ski world.

Trevor's anger at being forced to race increased, and having no effective outlet for releasing it, he began to resist his father's efforts in his ski racing.

Trevor stopped taking care of his equipment and showed little effort in his training. His father became angry at Trevor's "laziness." Their relationship deteriorated quickly. Finally, Trevor decided that enough was enough and told his father that he hated skiing and would never put on a pair of skis again. And he hasn't.

GUIDED PARTICIPATION

"The greatest power parents have is the power to guide their children," Dr. John Gray has written. Raising a successful achiever involves *guiding* your child along the path of achievement and happiness, not *forcing* her down a path of your choosing. Guided participation gives your child the support she needs to overcome the many challenges of achievement. It also gives her the freedom she needs to choose her own route to achievement and happiness.

Guided participation provides your child with the initial impetus to achieve, but more important, it allows her to gain ownership of, motivation in, and desire for the achievement activity. You need to strike a balance between giving your child the first push toward achievement in terms of direction, opportunities, and resources, and then stepping back and enabling her to find her own personal connection with the activity. Your involvement must shift from *direction and guidance* to *encouragement and freedom*, and your involvement must decrease as time goes by. "I never tell [Tiger] to do something; I will give him information and let him make a choice," reflects Earl Woods. As your involvement decreases, the opportunity and space for your child to develop ownership will increase.

RED FLAGS

RED FLAG #1: TAKING AWAY THE FUN

You can ensure that your child doesn't gain ownership of an achievement activity by *taking away the fun*. Nothing is more damaging to a child's motivation, desire, and excitement than when an achievement activity becomes a joyless, tedious, and stressful task. Lack of fun is one common reason why children lose their motivation to achieve.

Because achievement is a long-term process in which its greatest rewards are not always immediate, your child needs to have fun to maintain her interest and motivation. Take away the fun and your child will find few reasons to continue to participate. Achieving will become work for your child, a burden that she feels obligated by you to bear. Your child's participation will become drudgery that is not only not looked forward to, but is viewed with dread.

This perspective of achieving as work typically develops from parents' attitudes toward the activity. If you push your child too much and his participation becomes a burden, he will lose sight of the intrinsic benefits of achieving and begin to participate for extrinsic reasons. He will begin to participate for you rather than for himself.

Pressure from you to participate may keep your child involved in the activity for a while, but the immediate and long-term consequences will be significant. In the short term, your child may be unmotivated and will only achieve enough to appease you. In the future, at the first opportunity in which you no longer have control over her participation, your child is going to quit and find activities that are more fun and intrinsically rewarding.

RED FLAG #2: LOSS OF MOTIVATION

The most obvious red flag of forced participation is a loss of motivation. This decline may show itself as little sustained effort in the activity. Your child may be easily distracted by other activities. She may give up easily in the face of minor obstacles. The quality of your child's efforts may deteriorate substantially or she may simply no longer want to participate in the activity.

When parents first ask me to work with their child, the most common questions they ask are "Why isn't he motivated?" and "Can you motivate him?" What parents don't realize is that they are asking the wrong questions. The issue is not "Why isn't this child motivated?," as if the child lacks the requisite desire and abilities to achieve. Rather, the question is "What is *keeping* this child from being motivated?" in the belief that the motivation is inherent, but something—or someone—is holding it back.

I go under the assumption that, whether a student, athlete, or performing artist, whether gifted or simply passionate about what he does, your child wishes to achieve and to find joy in what he does. Yet your child may move in the opposite direction from which he would want to naturally strive. A loss of motivation is often a sign that your child is being forced to participate, ownership is being taken away, or he isn't gaining satisfaction from his involvement.

FIND THE FUN AGAIN

Fun cannot be taught or given to your child. He needs to simply see that participation in the achievement activity is enjoyable and rewarding in its own right. You cannot *make the activity fun*. All you can do is clear the obstacles that cause an activity to lose its enjoyment value so that he can once again *find the fun*.

If your child appears to be going through the motions with little joy or pleasure, then you can assume that she no longer sees her participation as a positive experience. You need to explore why she is no longer having fun, especially if it is an activity that she had previously enjoyed. Is your child performing poorly, having conflicts with the instructor or her peers, or having other difficulties in her participation that would take away the enjoyment? You must look in the mirror and consider how you might be affecting your child's experience. Are you overly invested and overinvolved? Are you pushing your child too hard or inappropriately? How might you be stifling her enjoyment? Earl Woods says, "But through all the teaching, training, and coaching, my operative theme was teaching Tiger *the game of golf was fun* [italics added]."

If the activity is no longer fun because it has become tedious or because your child feels he is missing out on other activities in which he is interested, you may be able to reestablish the fun by changing his participation, perhaps by allowing him to take fewer lessons each week so the activity is no longer such drudgery and he can get involved in other activities. This reorganization may cause you to feel that your child will no longer continue to progress in the activity. However, it is better for him to develop more slowly than for him to quit and cease to develop at all.

If your child is having some difficulties in the activity itself—for example, she doesn't like her instructor or she doesn't get along with her teammates—you can use this opportunity to teach your child about communication and resolving conflict with others. You can also speak to the instructor about the problems and enlist his or her help in resolving them. If these difficulties cannot be resolved and your child still enjoys the activity itself, you can consider finding another program in which she can participate (if the activity provides for this option).

As your child's most powerful role model, how you approach an activity will often determine how she looks at it. If you are serious and intense, your child will come to believe that she better take it seriously too. You will communicate to her that the activity is work and that her participation is serious business that isn't about fun. If you are happy, positive, enthusiastic, laugh, and have a good time with your involvement in the achievement activity, then the message you are conveying is that your child should also look at the activity this way and the goal is to have fun.

A final point about achievement and fun: In reality, the process of achievement is not always fun. It can sometimes be repetitious, monotonous, tiring, and painful. An important lesson you can teach your child is that genuine fun comes from different aspects of his achievement efforts. Sometimes, the actual process of engaging in the activity is fun. Other times, your child will find satisfaction in the improvement that he makes because of his hard work. Still other times, your child will find great pleasure in achieving the goals he has set for himself. And, yes, it is fun to succeed. If you can teach your child this lesson, then when the learning process becomes difficult and it is not fun for a while, he will keep working hard because he will be looking for fun in the other areas.

REGAINING MOTIVATION

Once your child loses her motivation, can it be regained? Possibly, but it can be difficult because your child may have already made a strong connection between the achievement activity and her negative feelings and correctly labeled it as a bad experience. Like fun, motivation is not something that you can give to your child—at least you can't give healthy, internal motivation. Rather, your child must find motivation within herself. Whether your child can recapture her motivation will depend on the cause of its loss and what you can do to remove the obstacles that are suppressing it.

To resurrect your child's motivation, you must first understand why your child lost it. You can ask your child directly why he is no longer motivated, but if he believes that you are overly invested in the achievement activity and that you will be disappointed or become angry if he is truthful, then he will probably not be honest with you. You can try an indirect route by asking more generally how things are going. You can ask what he likes and dislikes about the achievement activity, how he feels about his teacher (instructor, coach) and his peers, and if there have been any problems lately. You should also speak to others who may shed light on your child's loss of motivation. Teachers (instructors, coaches) and others who have observed him in the achievement activity may be able to give you firsthand information. You can also speak to parents of your child's peers who may also have useful insights.

You must also look at your involvement in your child's achievement efforts and consider whether you have contributed to the loss of motivation. Useful questions to ask yourself include these: How invested are you in your child's participation in the achievement activity? How would you feel if she left the activity? Whose needs are most being met by her continuing to participate? What is most important is for you to understand the reasons for the loss of motivation and act in a way that is in your child's best interest.

If you are able to learn the cause of your child's loss of motivation, you may be in a position to resolve the problem, enabling his motivation to reemerge. Children lose their motivation for many reasons. Sometimes, their concerns are reasonable—an abusive teacher, lack of fun, not enough time to do other things, too much pressure from you. You must decide whether your child's loss of motivation is legitimate, and if so, he should be allowed to end his participation in the achievement activity. In this instance, you should help him to understand the difficulties he had and the lessons he learned from the experience, and how he can prevent them from occurring in the future. With these insights, your child can leave the activity after having gained some benefits from his participation. You should also make it clear that a part of his being allowed to discontinue his involvement is that he must commit to another activity—doing nothing is not an option.

At other times, your child's reasons may be less compelling—she has experienced some disappointment, she is not getting along with her peers, she just doesn't feel like doing it anymore. You must decide whether your child should be pushed to stay with the activity in the hope that her motivation will return. This decision should always be collaborative with your child to help her maintain ownership of the activity. You can help your child better understand her loss of motivation and, perhaps, help her regain it. Some relevant questions: What would you miss about the activity? What wouldn't you miss? What are the benefits of continuing with the activity? How can your current difficulties be resolved? If they were resolved, would you want to continue? What would you do in place of this activity? Would you be willing to stay with the activity for a little longer to see if you could get back your desire?

Your child's loss of motivation may not be related to the achievement activity itself. There may be something going on in another part of his life. Perhaps he had a fight with a friend who also participates in the activity. Maybe your child is having some other peer difficulties such as trying to avoid a bully. You should recognize that there are many things in his life that can distract him to the detriment of his participation in his achievement activity.

Ultimately, the decision of whether your child continues is yours. You should base your decision on several essential concerns. What harm could come to your child if she is pushed to stay involved in the activity? What lessons can she learn from continuing to participate? Is the damage done to your child's feelings about the activity irreparable? What is the likelihood that your child would regain her motivation? Is your child willing to stick with the activity a little longer? I cannot provide you with clearly defined guidelines in your decision. Only by carefully examining all aspects of the situation, obtaining all relevant information, asking the right questions, taking a good look at your child's reaction to the activity, knowing your child's temperament, including your child in the decision-making process, and, most important, trusting your intuition will you come to the best decision.

If you decide that your child should remain in the achievement activity, how you "push" your child to buy into your decision will be crucial to how he responds. Ideally, you want the decision to be mutual.

The best approach is to explain to your child the reasons behind your decision and the benefits of staying involved, and that if he continues for a while he is likely to look back on this decision and see that it gave him a real opportunity to triumph over adversity. That, of course, is the best possible outcome from sticking with something when the going gets tough. You also want to encourage him to make this decision on his own, using your discussions and what he thinks will be best for him in the long run. To give your child as much control as possible, I recommend that you tell him that this decision is not irreversible and that you and he can revisit and reevaluate it some time in the near future, perhaps in one month. If your child finds his motivation again, he will know that it was a good decision. If your child continues to be unmotivated, he will know for sure that the activity wasn't for him and he can look for a new activity in which to participate. Being calm, upbeat, supportive, and encouraging in this discussion can help put the decision into a more positive light.

PROCESS OF GUIDED PARTICIPATION

EXPOSURE TO ACHIEVEMENT ACTIVITIES

The process of guided participation begins with exposing your child to a wide variety of activities in the hope that one will pique her interest and become an activity in which she can derive great satisfaction and enjoyment, and, possibly, become an avenue of achievement in the future. Parents usually first introduce their children to activities that are of interest to themselves. Rare is the child who becomes a classical musician if her parents have never taken her to a concert or who develops a love of a sport in which her parents did not participate.

You should not, however, limit your child's exposure to achievement activities in which you have knowledge and experience. For you to assume that what is good for you will also be good for your child is presumptuous and potentially restrictive, much as a lawyer might decide that his son must also be a lawyer and forces him on the path to law school. "Parents naturally feel more experienced in the ways of life and thus more competent to plan for the future. They may overlook their teens' inner strivings or assume always that as parents they know best," observes Shirley Gould. One of your great challenges is not to impose your own interests and needs on your child, but rather to *help your child to identify his or her own.*

This first step in guided participation is about being attuned to the interests of your child and letting her guide you as you guide her. This guided participation will encourage your child to experience many activities and find those to which she is attracted and best suited based on talent, temperament, challenge, and interest. Your child has a great capacity to communicate her likes and dislikes to you. You need to hear these messages and respond in your child's best interests rather than your own. Providing opportunities for diverse experiences and then allowing your child to choose her path is a powerful demonstration of your respect for your child's true self and her desire for self-determination.

TIME MANAGEMENT

While exposure to many achievement activities is desirable, I recommend exposing your child to one or two at a time rather than multiple activities concurrently. A ubiquitous—and unfortunate—phenomenon that has emerged in the last ten years is the overscheduling of a child's life. Today's child is often taking ballet classes, playing soccer, and acting in her school play, in addition to being tutored at home and having her normal school responsibilities. These overly ambitious lives do more harm than good to the entire family. The child is overloaded with work, feels stressed by the time constraints, and has little time for free play, creativity, and just being a kid. This overplanned life interferes rather than fosters her achievement and happiness. With so much to do, she has limited time to devote to or focus on any one or two activities to find out whether she actually enjoys them enough to want to explore them further.

Parents are similarly overloaded trying to organize the schedules of one or more children, experience even greater stress trying to juggle all of these demands and to "keep up with the Joneses," and have little free time to spend with their families and even less time for themselves and their spouses. They also put themselves under such stress trying to live up to society's image of "good parents" that they lose sight of what really makes parents good.

One family I know has three kids. The mother was a world-class performing artist and the father was an elite athlete. They both have successful careers. Both parents are high achievers who want their children to adopt similar values. Here is the breakdown of their children's activities. Eldest child: tennis and piano. Middle child: basketball, soccer, baseball, and guitar. Youngest child: cross-country running, baseball, and tennis. All of the children go to two sleep-away summer camps. The mother points out that the sports are played in different seasons and that they don't expect their children to become concert performers, but rather to learn basic musical skills, which are no longer taught in school. She also notes that it is most difficult for her and her husband because they have to manage both family and careers—"This is what makes parents crazy," she says.

Though I can't give you definitive guidelines for how much of your child's life should be scheduled and how much should be unstructured, I can offer a few reasonable suggestions. Your child shouldn't be involved in more than two achievement activities at one time. He should participate in only one achievement activity each day. Scheduling shouldn't interfere with your child's getting a good night's sleep or eating three healthy meals—fast-food dinners in the car going from one achievement activity to another should be a red flag for you. Your family should be able to sit down and eat dinner together more times than not each week. Your child should be able to finish his homework well before bedtime and get to bed at a reasonable hour. Your child should have time at least several days a week to play outside during the day and inside in the evenings. At least several times a week your family should have "hang-out" time, during which you do something—or nothing—together. Your family should share an activity at least twice a month, such as going for a day hike, visiting a museum, or attending a dance concert. You should have time to read a newspaper or a book, watch something you enjoy on television, or share a relaxed, non-child-related conversation with your spouse most evenings each week. You should have time to have dinner with friends away from your child once or twice a month. At least half of each month's weekends should be open and unplanned. These are very general guidelines. The motivation of your child, your values, and the demands of the achievement activities will all cause these guidelines to need to be modified at times. For example, many sports competitions occur every weekend and mastery of a musical instrument takes many hours of practice each week. Ultimately, you are the best judge of how much is too much. I believe that you know when enough is enough, but you may be reluctant to assert yourself because you are afraid you will be viewed as a "bad parent"—in reality, other parents will be jealous of you.

A father of two young children who is a friend of mine recommends that parents choose one activity that the entire family can enjoy. He and his wife chose skiing because he was a nationally ranked ski racer as a youth and she also enjoys the sport. He feels that an activity in which parents are actively involved and which they can share with their children is best for the entire family. On weekends during the winter, they head to the local ski area. While the children are being coached in the mornings, their parents enjoy themselves skiing. During the afternoons, the family skis together. At races, the parents both enjoy watching their kids race and can also go skiing themselves. They find this approach vastly better than having their kids in an activity in which they play a more passive role—driving their children to an event, watching them perform, and then driving home. The father used the example of a three-day chess tournament to which he had taken one of his children. They drove five hours to the tournament; his son played three matches over three days, with the remainder of the trip devoted to sitting around waiting for the matches or going to the mall after matches. Though he enjoyed watching his son compete and his son liked the competition, it was not, overall, a very rewarding or time-efficient experience for either of them. As he noted, "Though the tournament itself was great, we were both pretty bored most of the trip."

Finally, I am often asked by parents for my opinion of video games and television. Though I am perhaps being unrealistic given how popular video games and television are among children, I believe that they offer little benefit to your child. What purpose do video games and television serve in your child's life? They entertain your child. Video games and television keep him out of your hair for a while. They relieve you of having to entertain him. They keep him distracted and quiet. So far, everything I have said is in your best interests, but nothing I have said is in the best interests of your child.

What real value do video games and television have in your child's life? I would say little. Though educational video games and television shows do exist and, if used judiciously, can be beneficial to your child in limited quantity, in all likelihood, the video games your child plays and the television shows he watches have little redeeming value. They do little to foster healthy moral, intellectual, or emotional growth in your child. Video games and television also encourage your child to live a sedentary life at a time when childhood obesity has become a national epidemic. Not only do video games and television offer little benefit, they can also be harmful by aggrandizing gratuitous violence and sex, and making heroic decidedly unheroic characters and behavior. Considering all the important lessons and skills your child will need to develop to become a successful achiever and all the great joys the world has to offer, video games and television are a poor use of the precious hours of your child's life.

INITIAL IMPETUS

Ideally, every achievement activity that you expose your child to should be one in which he is motivated to participate. When your child already has the motivation to take part in an activity, my best advice is "Get out of the way!" All you need to do is provide the necessary resources and support, and your child will take care of the rest. However, not all achievement activities are immediately motivating. Offering your child opportunities to experience different achievement activities sometimes means having him participate in activities in which he may not want to engage or have an instantaneous affinity for—piano lessons and dance classes come to mind. Yet not exposing your child to these types of achievement activities may deprive him of finding an activity that could become his lifelong passion. You should base your decision of what achievement experiences to which you want him exposed on your values and interests, and on what you believe might offer your child new and enriching experiences.

The challenge then is how to get your child to try an achievement activity that she doesn't want to do. Parents often ask me, "Should I bribe my child to commit to an achievement activity?" This is a tricky question with a great deal of conflicting answers from parents, parenting experts, and researchers.

Some parents and many parenting experts swear that "bribery" is a necessary tool that parents use to motivate their children. Considerable research, however, recommends against using external rewards to bribe children to participate, indicating that it actually undermines motivation. However, this same research suggests that there are some conditions in which external rewards can increase motivation. An important distinction needs to be made between inherently interesting activities and those that are dull or boring. Research argues strongly against providing external rewards to children for activities that are interesting and that they already enjoy. The evidence is very clear that this tactic actually reduces their intrinsic motivation.

However, using external rewards to bribe your child to continue her participation in an achievement activity that she does not yet find inherently motivating can be effective—to a point. Although there are no firm rules, I can make some recommendations on how to use external rewards to your child's benefit. The goal of using external rewards is not to force your child to participate in an achievement activity that is clearly not naturally enjoyable and motivating. External rewards are also not aimed at providing lasting motivation to your child. Rather, they are to offer your child some initial impetus to try an achievement activity so that she can give it a fair chance and see whether it might become intrinsically motivating. If, in a short time, your child finds the activity inherently enjoyable, then you can provide the reward you agreed on because a deal is a deal. If, on the other hand, after a reasonable time, your child doesn't find the activity intrinsically motivating, then you should follow through on your agreement and together look for another achievement activity that she might enjoy.

The key question is what kind of external reward should you offer? The reward has to be enticing enough to motivate your child to accept the offer, but not so large as to distract her from finding intrinsic value in the activity itself. There are no set rules here and you should use your own judgment about what is fair and reasonable. You should start by asking your child what she thinks would be a good reward. Say to your child: "I can see that you aren't too psyched about doing this, but we think you would enjoy it and we would like you to try it. What do you think would be a good reward for your trying it for one month?" You can solicit her ideas and then make the decision based on what you think is best. Rewards should be something that your child wants and something that you want her to have. And, hopefully, the reward will have some kind of redeeming value—which rules out junk food, violent video games, and gratuitously expensive clothing. You should also explain the purpose of the reward and emphasize your hope that she will come to enjoy the activity on its own merits. The reward might even be an introduction to another achievement opportunity—a gift certificate for new skates, tickets to a music concert, or to go indoor rock climbing.

An important aspect of external rewards is what the reward communicates to your child. External rewards won't work if they convey incompetence, anger, lack of faith, control, or coercion (for example, "The only way I can get you to do anything is to bribe you"). External rewards are most effective when they indicate to your child that she is valued, competent, and that you believe in her (for example, "We love you and want to reward you for your openness and efforts"). If external rewards are combined with love, praise, encouragement, and physical affection, you are sending your child the right message and providing her with a little push so she can find out if she really likes an achievement activity.

PROVIDE RESOURCES

The next step in guided participation is providing the resources to ensure that your child's initial achievement experiences are positive. This process involves creating a physical and psychological environment that allows your child to explore the activity fully and enables her to decide on its merits whether she wishes to continue with the activity. These resources can include materials such as computers, musical instruments, sports gear, or instruction and other learning experiences that will foster mastery, a fun and motivating atmosphere that encourages participation, and a "toolbox" of skills to facilitate success.

A note of caution here: The amount of resources that you provide should increase progressively based on the amount of investment your child is making in the achievement activity. A danger is that when your child shows an interest in an activity, you go out and spend a lot of money on the necessary equipment and then your child soon loses interest. You can't help but be angry and communicate your feelings to your child. He might feel guilty and stay in the activity even though he really doesn't want to be in it anymore or he may become afraid to express interest in anything in the future. For example, if your child shows an interest in playing the guitar, you shouldn't go out and buy him a Fender Stratocaster. Rather, you could purchase some guitar CDs, some guitar picks, and arrange for a series of lessons with a rented guitar. Later on, if your son expresses a continued interest, you can consider buying him a guitar or helping him earn the money so he can buy one for himself.

The most important of these resources is the toolbox in which your child can place essential tools that he develops. These tools are life skills—emotional mastery, decision-making, communication, social skills—that will serve him not only in the current activity, but also in future endeavors that he chooses to pursue. A significant part of growing up for your child is adding tools to his toolbox that will foster his development as a successful achiever. This entire book is devoted to showing you how to help your child fill his toolbox with the most important tools.

When your child begins a new achievement activity, you should consider what resources she will need to maximize her experience. Making a list of the materials that are required, instructional opportunities that are available, and tools that your child will need will help you deliberately identify and select those resources that will allow your child to explore and appreciate fully the achievement experience.

COMMITMENT

The importance of commitment is a lesson that your child must learn to gain ownership of an achievement activity and to become a successful achiever. When your child initially chooses an achievement activity in which to participate, you have an opportunity to teach your child the significance of commitment as a value and as a practical tool.

Two of the most essential qualities associated with commitment are hard work and persistence. The reality is that there are few fields that require special gifts. Perhaps they're required for becoming a professional athlete, a concert musician, or a quantum physicist. For most endeavors, though, if a child simply works hard and persists at the activity, she will achieve a reasonable level of competence and success.

Dr. K. Anders Ericsson, a researcher at Florida State University, offers some specifics. He has found that inborn ability is not necessary to predict whether a child will be successful in fields such as sports, dance, chess, physics, medicine, and music. His findings indicate that two factors best predict how successful someone will become: how long they have been committed to the activity and how much they practiced. Dr. Ericsson coined a simple rule-of-thumb for becoming an expert in a field—"ten years and 10,000 hours"—meaning that it takes 10 years and 10,000 hours of practice to become successful (that's 1,000 hours a year or 20 hours a week).

In the early stages of an achievement activity, your child will probably feel considerable frustration and discouragement as he learns its necessary rudiments. In the beginning, the costs and discomfort may outweigh the benefits and enjoyment that your child experiences. This rough beginning may cause your child to give up because he finds the activity neither fun nor rewarding. You must, at this point, positively push your child to stick with the activity until the initial unpleasantness declines and the enjoyment takes precedence or it becomes clear that your child will never enjoy the activity.

If you allow your child to end his participation after only the initial discomfort, your child will not learn the value of hard work and persistence that is so essential to commitment and successful achieving. Allowing your child to back out of his involvement also teaches him that he can get out of anything that he doesn't like or that becomes difficult. It also leaves you having committed your time and money to the activity without your child's appreciating or taking advantage of your commitment.

. Most of us remember our parents' forcing us as children to do something we really did not like doing. One of two things happened: Either it became so unpleasant that we stopped doing it as soon as we could—and perhaps, as adults, we are sorry we stopped. Or we finally broke through the discomfort, found enjoyment and reward in it, and begrudgingly thanked our parents for keeping us committed to it.

During a recent trip, I was waiting at the gate for my flight when a mother walked up with her three young daughters in tow, all carrying violin cases. During the hour wait for the flight, she had the girls practice their instruments, each at her own level of ability. I was intrigued by this process and asked her why she chose the violin for all three girls and how she was able to get them to commit to such a rigorous activity at such young ages (the girls ranged in age from six to ten years old). She said that their grandmother had introduced the violin to the eldest daughter and, to make life easier on herself and her husband, she had encouraged the two younger girls to pursue the violin. They, in turn, responded to the encouragement and said they wanted to play. The mother said that she had limited aspirations for their playing—hoping they would play in their church's orchestra—but she was adamant that all of her daughters stay committed to the violin as long as they lived in her house. She indicated that she wanted to teach her daughters the meaning of commitment for later in life. I asked the girls if they liked playing. Each made a face and said, "Not always." In response to my question and their reply, their mother pointed out that her daughters also played sports that they enjoyed. She and her husband had a rule for their children, "One thing we want you to do and one thing you want to do."

When your child makes a commitment, he must be held to it— except in the most extreme circumstances (for example, if continued participation would do him harm)—just as he would expect you to adhere to your commitment. Imagine how your child would feel if, part of the way through a series of music lessons that he was enjoying immensely, you decided to pull him out. He would feel disappointed and let down. You should feel the same way and should not allow your child to break his commitment either.

Commitment is not a single irreversible decision, but rather a series of increasingly more dedicated steps that leads to greater involvement in an achievement activity. You should ask your child to make an age-appropriate time commitment to an activity in which she shows interest. You should establish reasonable time frames, perhaps based on a relevant period of time for the activity, such as a school year, a lesson package, a sports season, or simply a time period that you feel is adequate for your child to be able to experience the benefits of the activity. Your child should be required to stay committed to the activity for the agreed-upon time period. At the conclusion of the time commitment, you and your child can then reevaluate her participation and decide whether to continue or to explore another activity. This agreement should be connected with some consequence, such as the removal of some other desired activity or experience, if your child decides to break the commitment. By having a consequence, your child will learn that her commitments have consequences.

You can facilitate your child's commitment by showing her that commitment applies to both you and her. You can model commitment by showing your child that when she makes a commitment to an activity, you also make a commitment. You should make clear to your child the commitment in terms of time, energy, and money you are making and that you expect a similar commitment from her. You commit to paying for the activity, providing the necessary equipment or supplies, arranging for instruction and performance opportunities, providing logistical support such as getting her to and from the activity, and giving emotional support in the form of interest and encouragement. In turn, your child's commitment includes giving her best effort, being attentive to her teachers, devoting the requisite time to the activity, being considerate of peers, and being appropriately appreciative of her opportunity.

GOAL SETTING

Your child can learn more about his commitment by having you assist him in setting goals for his participation. Goal setting acts as a guide for your child in his understanding of what he wants to accomplish in his achievement efforts and what he needs to do to attain the goals that he sets for himself. Goal setting is a valuable life tool that your child can learn and place in his toolbox to assist him throughout his life.

Goal setting is an important part of teaching your child essential values related to commitment and ownership. It shows your child that she needs to plan for the future and work toward whatever she wishes to accomplish. Goal setting helps your child understand the relationship between her actions and positive and negative outcomes. Your child will learn that when she puts effort toward her goals, she will usually achieve them, and when she doesn't, she probably won't realize them. Your child will learn that the results she produces come from the actions she takes toward achieving her goals, a key aspect of ownership. Your child will also gain appreciation of the satisfaction that comes from setting a goal, working hard in its pursuit, and reaching the goal.

Though a seemingly innocuous process, helping your child set goals is complicated by a number of factors. Particularly at a young age or in an activity in which your child has little knowledge or experience, she may lack the perspective to set her own goals, so she must rely on you for establishing objectives. In a guiding rather than a directive role, you must be careful not to impose your own needs and goals on your child. For example, if your daughter takes up the flute, don't start thinking of her one day being in the philharmonic. Also, if you have little knowledge of or experience in an activity, you are not in a position to know what goals are reasonable for your child. Goal setting is a process that begins simply and increases in detail and complexity as your child's involvement in an activity increases. In addition, from its inception goal setting should be discussed with your child (as is age-appropriate), goals should be decided on mutually, and goals should be explicitly stated.

When your child begins his participation, you should assist him in establishing three goals. The foremost goal is to *have fun*. Enjoying the experience is the most motivating thing for a child early in an achievement activity. If your child enjoys the activity, you will have little concern for motivating him to continue to participate.

The second goal is *commitment*. If your child chooses to participate in an activity—and you make a commitment to his involvement—your child must have a goal of staying committed for the specified duration of the activity. This goal teaches the values of patience and persistence.

The third goal is to give his *best effort*. As I emphasize throughout this book, one of the most important lessons your child can learn is the value of effort because that is something he can control (whereas talent, for example, is not). When your child is in the beginning stages of an achievement activity, avoid any goal setting based on results. Outcome goals place too great an emphasis on results at too early an age and may cause your child to become preoccupied with results. Goals that emphasize effort will show your child its importance and encourage him to develop a healthy work ethic.

You can begin an age-appropriate dialogue with your child about these goals. This conversation should start with an explanation of goals so you can be sure your child understands the concept of goals (for example, "Goals are things you want and that you decide to work to get"). You can then give your child the rationale for these three goals (for example, "You can control whether you reach these goals"). Finally, you can provide practical examples of how your child can achieve the goals (for example, "You can enjoy being with your friends, doing your best, and never giving up").

These three goals act as the foundation for all future participation in an achievement activity because they ensure a sense of ownership of the activity. These goals are likely to be achieved because they are fully within your child's control. They also provide life skills that will maximize your child's success and enjoyment, which will benefit her in her future achievement efforts.

As your child becomes more involved in an achievement activity, goals can become more specific and more performance relevant. The next stage of goal setting should emphasize skill acquisition and maximizing performance (for example, knowing all the major and minor chords or mastering the basic tennis strokes). Only when your child becomes committed to long-term involvement in an activity and chooses to pursue it to the fullest of his abilities should outcome goals be part of his goal setting.

You should recognize your own limitations in assisting your child in setting long-term goals. Unless you have in-depth knowledge of the activity, you can do more harm than good by trying to set goals for your child. The wise course at this point is to seek out experts, such as teachers, coaches, or instructors, who can provide experienced guidance about your child's goals.

Goals should be *realistic, yet attainable.* Goals should be able to be reached, but only with significant effort. Goals that are achieved too easily will have little positive impact on your child because success will be achieved with little or no commitment or effort, reaching the goal will offer little enjoyment in the process, and he will feel no sense of ownership of the outcome. Goals that are too difficult to attain will have a negative effect on your child because, even with significant commitment and effort, he will experience frustration, he won't enjoy the experience, and he won't reach his goals.

The focus should be on the *degree of attainment* rather than absolute attainment. An inevitable part of goal setting is that your child won't reach all of his goals because it's not possible to accurately judge how realistic all goals are. If you and your child are concerned only with whether he reaches a goal, your child may see himself as a failure if he is unable to do so. This response will invariably reduce rather than bolster his motivation. You should emphasize how much of the goal your child achieved rather than whether or not the goal is fully realized. Though your child won't attain all of his goals, he will almost always improve toward a goal. With this perspective, if your child does not reach a goal, but still improves 50 percent over the previous level, he is more likely to view himself as having been successful and his enjoyment, commitment, and effort will be rewarded. For example: Your child's goal is to raise his grade in English from a C to a B, but he receives a final grade of B−. Even though he didn't reach his goal of a B, he did improve from a C to a B−, which should still be rewarding to him. Or your child's goal is to raise her state tennis ranking from thirty-fifth to fifteenth in the coming year. At the end of the year, she is ranked twenty-first. Though short of her goal, she did progress fourteen places in the ranking and that achievement should be a source of pride and confidence.

Your child should receive *consistent feedback* about his goals. This input serves several purposes. It keeps your child focused on his goals, so he maintains his commitment and effort in his pursuit of his goals. Feedback shows progress toward your child's goals, rewarding his commitment and efforts. It also emphasizes the relationship between effort and achievement by connecting his goals with improvement. Feedback can come from you, instructors, from your child himself, or directly from successful experiences.

ONGOING ENCOURAGEMENT

Throughout the achievement process, ongoing encouragement is a valuable gift you can give your child. When most people think of encouragement, what comes to mind are platitudinous comments such as "Nice job" or "Way to go." Real encouragement, though, is much more substantial and purposeful. Being conscious of what you're communicating to your child can have a significant impact on his or her perspectives, attitudes, and reactions to participation in achievement activities.

Meaningful encouragement serves many roles. It acts to focus attention on important values associated with your child's participation in an achievement activity. For example, simple comments like "Great effort," "You really stuck with it when things got tough," and "It must feel great to do your best" clearly communicate the value of effort and perseverance, which are necessary for your child to become a successful achiever.

Substantial encouragement also reinforces why your child is participating. Support that emphasizes fun ("You looked like you were having a great time"), mastery ("You are improving so much"), cooperation ("It's great to work as a team, isn't it?"), and competition ("It is so exciting to compete and do your best") all further facilitate the internalization of ownership in your child's achievement activity.

Proper encouragement keeps the focus on your child's understanding that the achievement is truly his, rather than external validation from you. When your child does something well, you are actually not helping when you say things like "We are so proud of you," "We love you so much," or "You deserve a reward," as nice as they might seem. However well-intentioned, expressions of love or providing material rewards for success mistakenly link your child's achievement with external sources of validation, such as your love and material inducements. Instead, you want to connect your child's accomplishments with the internal benefits of participation, such as fun, mastery, achieving goals, and social interaction. "You really stuck with your game plan even when you were behind. That took guts!," is a good example.

FREEDOM

Freedom is one of the greatest gifts you can give your child. At the appropriate time, you must step back from your child's achievements, both literally and figuratively—just as you will do as she makes the transition to adulthood—and allow her to find her own path. This means letting your child experience both success and failure, joy and pain, and giving her the opportunity to come to terms with these experiences and use them to grow. Only by offering this freedom can you ensure that your child gains ownership of her participation and builds a personal relationship with achievement activity. You want your child to build on her own passion for the activity, joy in its experience, and self-generated rewards of participation and accomplishment.

This does not mean letting your child go completely. A strong connection between you and your child is essential as he expands his boundaries, because it provides a safety line as he explores his inner and outer worlds and a secure haven to which he can return. Also, your child's participation in an achievement activity is a wonderful opportunity for you and your child to share his experiences and growth. Giving your child this freedom actually strengthens your connection. By letting your child go, he is unburdened and free to return of his own accord.

YOUR CHILD'S CHOICE

Almost every child I see wants to be successful. Many want to attain lofty goals. Some expend considerable effort in pursuit of their dreams. Yet, relatively few children fully realize their aspirations. Simply put, most parents and children do not truly understand the level of commitment that is required to become a successful achiever. They may consider achieving their dreams and goals a part-time endeavor, as something they can pursue when they have the time, energy, or inclination. This approach, unfortunately, will not be sufficient.

Successful achieving is not something that is done once in a while or with one or two things in life. Being a successful achiever is not something that your child falls into by chance or luck. She will not develop this quality apart from you and her upbringing. You must nurture this attribute in your child in a variety of ways and then your child, as she matures, must make *successful achieving a lifestyle choice.*

Your child can express the lifestyle choice of successful achieving by dedicating her life to one achievement activity and directing all of her time, effort, and energy into excellence in one activity. This singular devotion can result in your child's reaching the top of her field—she could become a corporate executive, a professional athlete or musician, or build one of the finest art collections in the world. Alternatively, your child can choose to balance her pursuit of excellence among several areas in which she may not be the best, but still achieve substantial success in a number of activities—she could own a neighborhood bookstore, be president of the local chapter of the PTA, and be a great mother to her two children.

At the end of the guided participation process lies this choice for your child: Should I make successful achieving a part of my life? If you have followed the guided participation process, then successful achieving will not really be in question. Rather, your child is likely to have already internalized successful achieving as a way of life because he will have learned its benefits and instilled its values. Your child will possess the ownership and desire to want to commit his life to successful achieving to reap its many benefits.

Suggestions for Raising Successful Achievers

1. Avoid pressuring your child about winning or losing.
2. Do not force your child to practice.
3. Emphasize enjoyment.
4. Provide encouragement and hopeful optimism when needed.
5. Encourage other interests.
6. Encourage self-reliance and acceptance of responsibility for decisions.
7. Do not interfere with your child's teacher, instructor, or coach.
8. Help your child to develop and maintain a healthy perspective.
9. Encourage your child to play for himself or herself—not for you or anyone else.
10. Allow your child to set his or her own standards of excellence.
11. Separate achievement failure from personal failure.

Rotella, R. J., & Bunker, L. K. (1987). *Parenting your superstar How to help your child get the most out of sports.* Champaign, IL: Leisure Press.

CHAPTER 6

Why Won't You Let Me Grow Up?
Contingent vs. Independent Children

The culmination of which path you have chosen in Chapters 4 and 5 will result in your child's either becoming contingent on you or independent of you. The degree to which your child is able to define, understand, and act on his or her own needs, and is given the freedom by you to seek out and participate in achievement activities that are personally meaningful, will determine which path your child takes.

Certainly, in early development, your child is highly dependent on you. As an infant, she relies on you for nourishment, cleaning, and mobility. As your child grows, she becomes more self-reliant in these basic areas of living, but still depends on you for love, protection, guidance, and support. As your child reaches adolescence and moves toward adulthood, she becomes less reliant on you and gains greater independence in all aspects of her life. This process of separation prepares your child for the demands of adulthood.

This evolution into independence is often a tug-of-war between children who naturally want to separate from their parents and parents who often want to maintain their children's dependence. This battle is particularly evident in a family in which parents encourage their child to achieve success, but have done so by fostering his reliance on them. For example: The father of a young golfer has gone to every one of his son's tournaments, packed his bags, found out tee times, located the practice green and the driving range, caddied for him, kept score, and regularly given him technical and tactical feedback. In other words, he has trained his son to be completely dependent on him at tournaments. When the time came for his son to go to tournaments alone or with a group of golfers, the son was totally unprepared, lacking the necessary practical, tactical, technical, psychological, and emotional tools to succeed on his own.

Contingent children are unable to become successful achievers because, though they may attain some level of success, their dependence on others precludes them from being fully functioning and happy adults. In contrast, independent children have the ownership and capabilities that enable them to become successful and happy adults.

CONTINGENT CHILDREN

Contingent children are dependent on others for how they feel about themselves. They need others to validate their self-esteem and can become despondent if they don't receive the affirmation they need to feel good about themselves. If you are a parent of a contingent child you may be, in a way, holding your child's self-esteem hostage for your own purposes. Some parents do indeed want to foster dependence in their child. These parents act on their own needs for power and use control and coercion to ensure that they remain the dominant forces in their child's life. To encourage dependence, these parents offer only outcome love to their child, withholding love until their child is starving for it and is willing to do anything to gain love from them.

Contingent children aren't good decision makers. Parents of contingent children raise them with unilateral decision-making. If you are creating a contingent child, you will hold the belief that you always know what is best for him and will make decisions without soliciting his involvement. As a result, your child will never learn the process of effective decision-making and gain no confidence in his ability to make decisions. Because of his dependence on you, he would have a great deal of difficulty trusting his own choices and would rather have others make decisions for him. Turning decision-making over to others—notably you—absolves your child of responsibility should he make a poor decision. Unfortunately, contingent children also give up the power to change their decisions.

Contingent children are those who depend on others to provide them with incentive to achieve. Contingent children never gain ownership of their participation in an achievement activity because they don't participate for themselves, and the benefits they gain from their involvement are largely external. Extrinsic rewards such as love, money, gifts, trophies, parental approval, and recognition come from outside of children. If you are a parent who offers extrinsic rewards—either emotional or material—your child will never learn to gain intrinsic satisfaction and enjoyment from the achievement activity itself. Your child will constantly look outward for reasons to engage in the activity. Extrinsic rewards lead to children who are motivated only when the rewards are present and produce sufficient effort only to obtain the rewards.

Contingent children are also dependent on others for their happiness. If your child has no ownership of her achievement activities, she has no ownership of herself; has little responsibility for her own thoughts, emotions, and actions; and turns to others for happiness as well. Your child will find little happiness in the process of achieving or within herself and will rely solely on extrinsic rewards for validation. Contingent children equate the good feelings they get when they are rewarded externally with happiness. But that happiness is shallow and fleeting.

Contingent behavior often results from loving parents who don't understand the subtleties of appropriate rewards. If you give to your child without reasonable limits and often reward your child regardless of his actions, your child will never learn the fundamental relationship between his actions and outcomes. Your child will always experience "good outcomes"—thanks to you—regardless of what he has actually done.

In the earliest stages of child rearing, the use of extrinsic rewards offers the seductive benefit of the quick fix: "If you do your homework, you can have some cookies." But sometimes contingent children will not do their homework, yet still receive the promised cookies. When the cause-and-effect relationship becomes muddled, children lose any sense of reward for initiating and persisting at a task.

Parents often reward the wrong thing. Because you might value success highly, you might find yourself rewarding your child's outcomes, such as school grades, artistic accomplishments, or athletic victories, rather than their efforts. If you do, you are sending a strong message to your child that results are what are important to you. Then your child will begin to focus on her results instead of her efforts. You need to be aware of the dangers of using rewards to control rather than to validate your child. If you are using rewards as a means to assert your power over your child, you are encouraging your child's dependence on you.

If you have been rewarding your child's outcomes and not her efforts, you may begin to see that your child is losing her motivation and even her level of achievement. You may even have unwittingly reacted to your child's apparent lessening of motivation in the same way that worked initially—by increasing your rewards in a haphazard way, for homework half done, for instance. This will further undermine your child's motivation and feed into her dependence on you. If you have used extrinsic rewards consistently with your child, the rewards can act like an addictive drug that your child becomes "hooked" on. As your contingent child becomes accustomed to a certain level of external reinforcement, she will demand more and better rewards in order to maintain her level of achievement. You may have begun the reward process with the best of intentions to provide some initial impetus for your child to achieve, but you soon become a "dealer" of extrinsic rewards. If this dependence continues, your child can, in a sense, come to own you! If you have become accustomed to gratification from your child's achievement, which has been sustained by showering rewards on her, you may be loath to give that up. If you find it difficult to imagine stopping those external rewards, you might realize that you have addicted your child and are afraid of the consequences of removing the "drug."

INDEPENDENT CHILDREN

Independent children are different from contingent children in several essential ways. If your child is independent, you have provided him with the belief that he is competent and capable of taking care of himself. As the parent of an independent child, you have offered your child the guidance to find activities that are meaningful and satisfying. Finally, you have given your child the freedom to experience life fully and learn its many important lessons. From these opportunities, independent children learn what thoughts, emotions, behavior, and activities are self-rewarding and they actively seek out experiences that affirm their beliefs about themselves. Independent children learn to validate their self-esteem and to find happiness within themselves.

Independent children are able to consider various options, clarify choices, and make their own decisions. If your child is independent, you have trained her from an early age to be an effective decision maker. You have taught your child about the decision-making process and then shared age-appropriate decision-making with her throughout her childhood. By adolescence, your independent child is already an experienced decision maker who can make generally good choices and trust her own judgment.

If you have raised an independent child, he is intrinsically motivated because you have allowed him to find his own reasons to achieve within himself. You have provided your child with the opportunity and guidance to explore achievement activities of his own choosing. You have allowed your child to find out for himself why he enjoys a particular activity and decide whether he wishes to continue it.

There are a variety of intrinsic reasons for achieving. Your child wants to participate because it is fun, she enjoys the process of the activity, it is satisfying to see her efforts bear fruit, or because she wants to achieve some specific goals she has set for herself. More tangible intrinsic reasons your child might find to motivate herself to achieve may include the sense of mastery she can gain from learning something new, the social opportunities that arise when achievers work together, or simply reaching a personal goal of accomplishment. At the heart of intrinsic motivation lies a great passion for the activity and great joy in its participation. This foundation provides your child with the intrinsic motivation that will drive her to achieve.

As a parent who wants to raise an independent child, you will sense that some external rewards are a natural part of encouraging a child's achievement participation. However, unlike parents of contingent children, you will want to be clear about the true purpose of rewards, what behaviors should be rewarded, what kinds of rewards are effective, and how long rewards should be offered.

You will want to assume a collaborative rather than a controlling role in raising your child, one that fosters healthy separation and independence. For example, you will want to discuss issues and solicit ideas from your child, and to encourage your child to make her own decisions by offering her age-appropriate choices. If you find that the situation calls for you to make a unilateral decision, you will want to explain your reasoning and offer the promise of future options to your child. You will want to make every attempt to create a win-win situation with your child, even if, sometimes, she only wins a little, or can't really win until a later date.

When you are able to remain within the boundaries of a more supportive role, you and your child will be able to maintain a healthier relationship throughout his childhood and into adulthood than you could have with a contingent child. Because you have given your child the guidance and then the freedom to choose his own way, you won't experience the tug-of-war that often develops between parents and children and you both avoid the anger and resentment that is characteristic of contingent children. There is less conflict, fewer battles, less emotional bloodshed, and no casualties. Your independent child doesn't need to "react" to you out of frustration, anger, or hurt, but rather can "respond" to the love, support, and encouragement that you give him.

PARENT AND CHILD RESPONSIBILITIES

At the heart of whether you will be raising a contingent or independent child is that you understand the essential responsibilities that you and your child need to accept. Taylor's (that's me!) Law of Family Responsibilities states that if family members fulfill their own responsibilities and do not assume others', then children develop into independent people and successful achievers, and everyone is happy. However, problems arise when parents take on the responsibilities of their children and their children are not allowed to assume their own responsibilities. This usurping of responsibilities results in parents taking ownership of their children's lives.

YOUR RESPONSIBILITIES

Your responsibilities revolve primarily around providing your child with the opportunity, means, and support to pursue her goals in an achievement activity. The psychological means include providing love, guidance, and encouragement for her efforts. The practical means include ensuring that your child has the materials needed, proper instruction, and transportation, among other logistical concerns.

YOUR CHILD'S RESPONSIBILITIES
Your child's responsibilities relate to doing what is necessary to maximize the opportunities that you give him. Philosophical ownership responsibilities include being motivated, giving his best effort, being responsible and disciplined, staying committed, and giving an achievement opportunity a realistic try. Practical ownership responsibilities include completing all tasks and exercises, getting the most out of instruction, being cooperative, and expressing appreciation and gratitude for others' efforts.

RED FLAGS

It is overwhelmingly important for you to recognize the possibility that you could be raising a dependent child, so that you can begin to change your behavior and learn how to nurture an independent child. I have been able to generalize about five types of contingent children: the Pleaser, the Disappointer, the Reactor, the Frustrator, and the Rejecter. All of the them are created in similar ways. A parent has used outcome love, inappropriate expectations, inappropriate rewards and punishments, and the other unhealthy strategies I have already described. Children develop a particular contingent style depending on their temperament and that of their parents. Their difficulties will reflect your beliefs, your emotions, and the behavior you have modeled.

Contingent children do not escape their upbringings unscathed. Dependence carries a significant price that children will pay throughout their childhood and, most painfully, into their adult lives. If you fall into the trap of creating a contingent child, everyone loses. You lose because your relationship with your child can be severely damaged and your child will not attain the success and happiness toward which you pushed her. Your child loses because she has lost her love and trust in you and she may never develop into an independent, successful, and happy adult. Read these red flags carefully, and if you recognize yourself or your child, consider changing the way you are raising your child.

RED FLAG #1: PLEASERS

The Pleaser's drug of choice is parental love and attention. Pleasers may often be perceived as model children who are exceptionally giving and supportive of others. Pleasers are more concerned about the needs of others than they are about their own needs. Pleasers, for instance, will rearrange their schedules to accommodate someone else's needs at the expense of their own.

Parents create Pleasers by subjecting them to outcome love, perfectionism, and control. If you are raising a Pleaser, you have established clear and unbending rules about what behavior is appropriate and what is not, and offer or withdraw your love as a means of maintaining dominance and instilling dependence in your child. Pleasers learn very early in their lives what they need to do to gain your love and make sure they play by your rules.

Pleasers become overachievers to ensure that they receive the extrinsic rewards they need to maintain even a minimal level of self-worth. Pleasers typically perform extremely well, appearing to be almost ideal children: They get straight A's in school, are successful in the athletic arena, or show great accomplishment in the arts. But Pleasers are rarely ever pleased with themselves. Although their perfectionistic drive provides them with some of the love and attention they crave, it also becomes an unbearable weight that they carry. Always finding fault in their own efforts, they're unable to gain satisfaction and happiness for themselves.

Pleasers have no ownership of their achievements, often feeling that they are just lucky when they succeed. They also believe their successes are transitory and fleeting. These beliefs leave them in a constant state of fear that propels them to higher levels of achievement that might give them the elusive fulfillment and peace for which they desperately search. This compulsion to earn your attention and love can put extreme pressure on children, which can lead them to make unhealthy choices. Observes Dr. James C. Dobson, the author of *Parenting Isn't for Cowards*: "Both anorexia and bulimia are thought to . . . represent a desire for *control*. The typical anorectic patient is a female in her late adolescence or early adulthood. She is usually a compliant individual who was always 'a good little girl.' She conformed to her parents' expectations, although resenting them quietly at times. She withheld her anger and frustration at being powerless throughout her developmental years. Then one day, her need for control was manifested in a serious eating disorder. There, at least, was one area where she could be the boss."

At some point, Pleasers may realize that they are giving too much and getting too little—*they are being cheated*. They begin, often aggressively, to seek out their own needs. Their awareness of this inequity will produce anger and a backlash against you. Pleasers will suddenly sabotage all that they had created while trying to please others, undermining the very achievement and success that you had wanted so much. This attempt to regain control and assert their needs can lead children to attempts at escape, including alcohol and drug abuse, criminal behavior, and, in extreme cases, suicide.

Parents of Pleasers are left wondering, "What happened to my perfect child?"

RED FLAG #2: DISAPPOINTERS .

The second type of contingent children are called Disappointers because they never live up to your expectations. Instead of responding positively to your pressure to achieve, Disappointers deflect the pressure by not giving you what you most want—high achievement.

Disappointers are nonachievers. They are usually bright and demonstrate promise in a number of areas—for example, they often score high on IQ and achievement tests—yet they rarely accomplish anything. Their meager attempts at achievement are permeated with acts of self-sabotage that derive from a fundamental conflict with you. They are dependent on you for love and self-worth, so Disappointers express the desire to achieve and succeed in order to receive that love. At the same time, Disappointers are afraid to give their best effort because if they do try their hardest and they fail, they will have no excuse and they are guaranteed to lose your love.

Disappointers express this conflict in ways that enable them to avoid responsibility for their failures. This expression may be in the form of subtle passive-aggressive behavior, such as neglect of themselves, lack of effort in or avoidance of the achievement activity, or significant problem behavior such as drug use or criminal misconduct. This conduct offers the benefit of providing excuses for their failures (for example, "I would have succeeded if I had tried" or "I've got all these problems") and relieves the pressure to achieve by directing parental attention away from their failures and onto the more salient dysfunctional behaviors.

RED FLAG #3: REACTORS

The third type of contingent children are Reactors. In contrast to Pleasers, who do everything their parents want them to do, and Disappointers, whose parents seem to have little influence on their behavior, Reactors do the exact opposite of whatever their parents want them to do. Parents often interpret this behavior as independence, but in actuality, Reactors are highly dependent on their parents in a paradoxical way.

Reactors feel controlled by their parents and feel powerless to directly assert themselves against their parents' constraints. This sense of helplessness causes anger and resentment, and motivates them to find ways to establish control over their lives. If you are a parent of a Reactor, you unwittingly guide your child's behavior by providing direction and purpose for him. Reactors wait to see what you want them to do and then they choose the course that is in direct opposition to it. Reactors perceive themselves as having separated from you and believe that they are making choices on their own, but in fact they have little ability to consider options and make decisions without your guidance. This reactive behavior usually emerges in the form of nonconformist dress, poor grades, "unacceptable" peer relations, and, possibly, alcohol and drug use.

Reactors, as well as other children who are pushed too hard, hold a powerful and deep-seated resentment toward their parents. Resentful children often sabotage the achievement activity that they once may have loved. They stop trying, disrespect their instructors, behave poorly, and perform well below their capabilities. As a client who was one of her sport's top young athletes said to me, "I think the reason I haven't achieved my—or my father's—goals is that, as I grew more independent, I began to really resent [my sport]. I used to love playing. Now I hate it so much because it has brought me nothing but misery. How could I ever be successful at something that I resent so strongly?"

Reactors sometimes start out as Pleasers or Disappointers, but become Reactors when they can no longer internalize their anger. Because of their long history of dependence, Reactors do not have a clear understanding of what independence is. Reactors confuse doing the opposite of what you want with doing what they themselves truly want, which is the essence of real independence. Their apparent independence is a facade that they hide behind.

Reactors confuse their need to defy you with their own true needs, so they often end up hurting themselves. Responding (oppositionally) to your needs takes precedence over satisfying their own needs. They seem to be saying to themselves, "I would rather get back at my parents than do what is best for me."

RED FLAG #4: FRUSTRATORS

The fourth type of contingent children are Frustrators because frustration is what parents often feel toward them. Frustrators are not "bad kids," and they rarely get into trouble. They do fairly well in school and in other achievement settings, yet they are often viewed as underachievers who don't perform up to their ability.

Frustrators seem to have love-hate relationships with their parents. They generally get along with their parents, but often show anger and resistance toward them because they are frustrated too and they take out their frustration on their parents. Frustrators express their negative emotions in subtle ways, often in the form of less than full commitment and lower motivation in their pursuits. A Frustrator might get a B+ rather than putting in a little extra effort to get an A in a class, or be named as an alternate to perform in a musical recital, or lose a tightly contested sports competition. If your child is a Frustrator, you can't really get angry with him because he is doing, by most accounts, just fine. But you become frustrated in trying to understand why your child doesn't take the extra step necessary to excel. It sometimes seems as if your Frustrator child is subtly torturing you by getting close to high achievement, but not quite attaining it.

Frustrators possess a little of each of the qualities of the Pleasers, Disappointers, and Reactors. Frustrators are the most conflicted of all contingent children because they cannot commit to one course of action. They are caught in an internal tug-of-war of conflicting desires, needs, and motivations. Like Pleasers, Frustrators have a strong need for love and affection from their parents, so they often engage in pleasing behavior. Similar to Disappointers, they never truly excel in their achievement activities. Though Frustrators feel overly controlled by their parents, they don't have the assertiveness to take the extreme steps that Reactors do.

If your child is a Frustrator, in an attempt to get her to take that extra step to become truly successful, you may have hired tutors and coaches. You may have had your child participate in special programs and camps aimed at bringing out her talent. You may have tried to motivate your child with bribes, threats, discipline, and love. But that is missing the point. You would be looking at the overt behavior—your child's lack of motivation—and trying to change it. Instead, you need to consider the "why" of your child's behavior and the underlying dynamics behind it.

RED FLAG #5: REJECTERS

The final type of contingent children are Rejecters. If you are the parent of a Rejecter, your child is rejecting your values and imperatives, choosing a course of his own in spite of your objections. Though similar to Reactors in that they do not follow parents' directives, Rejecters do not simply *react* by choosing the opposite, but rather thoroughly reject whatever their parents have to offer.

Rejecters may be viewed as the most healthy and adaptive of the five kinds of contingent children because they really have separated from their parents and become autonomous and self-directed people. Your Rejecter child, however, pays a price for his disengagement. In order to establish separation, he has often had to take extreme steps to ensure his independence. To make this separation, he may have needed to discard even the potentially positive contributions you have made. Rejecter children use extreme measures, including moving out of the family home, attending college as far away as possible, sometimes even completely breaking off contact with their parents. Rejecters may also find it necessary to spurn most or all of their parents' values and lifestyle.

A college friend of mine, Tom, was the son of a prominent businessman and was being groomed to take over the family business. As a child, he had been sent to the finest private schools and had been forced to work in his father's office during the summer rather than go to summer camp with his friends. This "training" continued through high school despite his best attempts to tell his father that he was not interested in the business world. Tom had developed a love of architecture and secretly pursued this interest through reading and attending lectures. Still unable to resist his father's control, Tom applied to and was accepted at an Ivy League university to study business.

Going away to school became the opportunity Tom needed to assert his independence. Without telling his father, Tom declared architecture as his major. He went home for holidays less and less and got a job so he would not be beholden to his father financially. Without his father's knowledge, Tom applied for and received a scholarship to a leading architecture school and transferred after his sophomore year.

Now, twenty years later, Tom is a successful and happy architect. Unfortunately, he still has almost no contact with his father.

RED FLAG #6: BEING FRIENDS WITH YOUR CHILD

Except in extreme cases of abuse, one is hard pressed to find a child who says that he does not love his parents. It just comes with the job of parenting—you do a decent job and your child loves you. But some parents want more. They also want to be "liked" by their child.

Parents have been led to believe that it is important to be "friends" with their children, and fear that being tough on them will undermine the growth of this friendship. This idea has caused far more harm than good. Whenever the parent of a client says to me that she and her daughter are best friends, a big red flag goes up. This is often the key to why I have been brought in. Simply put, parents and children should not be friends (in the traditional peer-to-peer sense of the word). Parents should have *adult* friends and children should have *peers* as friends.

You shouldn't be friends with your child because it places an unfair burden for your happiness and welfare on her shoulders. Friendships are based on mutual *and* equal concern between two people. Though your child should have some concern for your well-being, it should not be equal to yours for her. Your child lacks that maturity and the tools to assume that responsibility.

You should not be friends with your child for the same reason that bosses should not be friends with their employees: because sometimes you must say and do things to your child that friends would not say and do to friends. Friends do not give orders to friends, but you must periodically order your child to do something that she does not want to do. Friends also don't discipline friends, but you must sometimes discipline your child. I am not saying that you must be a mean-spirited, dictatorial ogre with your child. To the contrary, the approach that I advocate in this book will enable you and your child to develop the strongest, most loving, and most supportive relationship possible.

RED FLAG #7: TAKING ON YOUR CHILD'S RESPONSIBILITIES

The development of contingent children begins when you start to take on the responsibilities of your child. You may do this because you connect your own success as a parent—and your self-esteem—to your child's success. You may do it because you want to guarantee your child is successful to validate your own needs. Or you may be trying to ensure that your child—and, by extension, you—succeed.

If you are taking on your child's responsibilities, you may believe that your child is unwilling to assume them himself. If you perceive that your child is consciously neglecting his responsibilities, instead of considering why this might be happening, you might be using a negative form of pushing—constantly asking whether he has fulfilled his responsibilities or punishing him for not doing so—in an ultimately futile attempt to force your child to succeed. Invariably, this approach will reduce your child's ownership and motivation, and will foster anger and resentment toward you, thereby undermining the very thing that you wanted in the first place—greater achievement.

Regardless of the underlying reason, if you are assuming your child's responsibilities, you are communicating to her that you don't trust her or that you don't believe she is competent enough to adequately fulfill her own responsibilities. Your child will begin to internalize your lack of trust and may develop the belief that she is not trustworthy or competent. For many children, it opens the door to avoiding their responsibilities: "Heck, why should I do it if my parents will do it for me?"

A practical way for you to check whether you might be assuming your child's responsibilities is to ask yourself whether you "micromanage" his life. It is a fundamental responsibility for you to manage your child's life by instilling important values, providing guidance and direction, setting appropriate boundaries, and attaching consequences to his behavior. However, micromanaging your child's life means intruding on his responsibilities. It means getting involved in areas of his life that are not your responsibility. As a general rule, any action on your part that interferes with your child's ownership of an achievement activity, his sense of control over his participation, his ability to make choices, his learning the connection between effort and outcome, and his being held accountable for his actions can be considered micromanagement. Micromanagement involves taking over responsibility for the particular things your child needs to do in his achievement activity. For example, if you find yourself preparing your child's equipment, asking him daily if he has practiced, or doing his homework, it's time to back off.

Sonja wanted her son, Anthony, to get into a top school. No one in her family had ever gone to college and she decided it was her mission to ensure that he not only went to college, but that he graduate from one of the finest universities in the world. To make sure Anthony did everything he could to achieve this goal, Sonja was constantly asking him if he had done his homework (at first, he always did), she checked his work (even though she didn't know much about the subject), and pestered him to put in more time studying for his exams. Unfortunately, Sonja's efforts had the opposite of her desired effect. Anthony began to show little interest in subjects that he had previously enjoyed, put less and less effort into his studies, and his grades were slipping. Sonja was micromanaging her son's academic life. By not allowing

Anthony to assume his responsibilities, Sonja was taking away his ownership of his studies. Without this ownership, his interest, motivation, and performance declined too.

Concerned about Anthony's deteriorating grades, Sonja spoke to his school's counselor. He saw Sonja's anxiety and sensed that she was putting considerable pressure on Anthony. The counselor suggested to Sonja that she conduct an experiment in which, for two weeks, she wouldn't speak to Anthony about school, homework, or grades. Though Sonja didn't quite understand how this would help, she said she would try.

Early in the two-week period, Anthony came home expecting to be harassed by his mother as usual about his schoolwork, but was surprised when she didn't say anything. Though bewildered, he felt relieved and went about his business of studying throughout the week. Sonja noticed that Anthony was more relaxed and seemed to be getting his work done. She was also aware that they were getting along better.

The two weeks turned into three, then four, and midterm exams were approaching. Sonja was nervous about not being involved in Anthony's preparations, but things seemed to be going well, so she decided to continue the experiment until she received his midterm grades. Anthony came home with his midterm grades and a big smile on his face. His grades were back up to where they had been, with those in two subjects even having improved. Sonja was thrilled and called the school counselor to thank him.

The sad irony of the first part of this scenario is that when parents assume their child's responsibilities they actually guarantee the thing they fear most—failure in the achievement activity. If you take on your child's responsibilities on a regular basis, you will be defeating the long-term success of your child by regularly conveying your lack of trust and confidence.

RAISING AN INDEPENDENT CHILD

Independence is not something that your child can gain on her own. She has neither the perspective nor the experience to develop independence separately from you. Rather, it is a gift you give your child that she will cherish and benefit from her entire life. You can provide your child with several essential ingredients for gaining independence. You must give your child love and respect. These expressions give her the sense of security that allows her to explore and take risks. You must show confidence in your child's capabilities. She is then likely to internalize this faith you have in her and develop an enduring sense of competence for herself. You must teach her that she has control over her life. You need to provide her with guidance and then the freedom to make her own choices and decisions. Finally, you must show her what her responsibilities are, that she must accept these responsibilities, and then you must hold her accountable for her achievement efforts.

BE THE PARENT

One thing you absolutely must do that precedes almost everything in this book is *be the parent!* It's your job and it's your relationship with your child. If you assume your role as the parent, your child can more easily assume his role as the child. Being your child's friend—which isn't your job—can create additional dependence because he has the added responsibilities of having an "equal" relationship with you. Knowing that you are the parent and he is the child establishes clear boundaries, roles, and responsibilities that enable him to pursue his job—which is to progressively gain independence from you.

Your role as a parent involves, initially, providing structure for your child's life in the form of boundaries, expectations, and consequences. Then, as your child grows, the role changes to one of increasingly placing the onus for her life on her shoulders. This transition involves a shift from micromanaging (yes, you must micromanage your child's life until she has the experiences and skills to micromanage her own life) to managing to simply giving feedback to your child about her life. This evolution means giving your child more options and decisions, fewer boundaries, expectations, and consequences, and more freedom to determine the course of her life.

TEACH RESPONSIBILITY

One of your tasks as the parent is to teach your child about responsibility. The best way to ensure that you and your child assume the appropriate responsibilities is for each of you to know what your responsibilities are. If you and your child have a clear understanding of what is expected of each of you, then it will be easier to stay within the confines of those responsibilities. When your child begins an achievement activity, you should sit down with him or her and outline each of your responsibilities within age-appropriate boundaries.

Make a list of what you as a parent will be doing to help your child succeed. Be sure to solicit feedback from her about what she believes you can do to help her. Encourage your child to tell you if she thinks a particular responsibility should *not* be yours. When this occurs, be sure she offers adequate justification and shows you how she will assume that responsibility.

Then, make a list of what your child's responsibilities should be in her own efforts in the achievement activity. Before you share your thoughts with her, have her describe what she will need to do to succeed. If you feel your child has missed some important responsibilities, suggest them to her and see if she agrees.

Next, identify other individuals who will have responsibilities in your child's achievement activity, such as a teacher, instructor, or coach. List what responsibilities they should have (if possible, these people should take part in this process).

There should also be consequences for not fulfilling responsibilities. Ideally, there should be consequences for both your child and you, but it is probably unrealistic for your child to "punish" you in some way (though there are certainly some parents who could use a "time-out" every once in a while). The best consequences are those that remove something of importance to your child and give her the power to get it back by acting appropriately.

This process provides absolute clarity to both you and your child about what your "jobs" are. It also allows for no confusion at a later point when either of you steps over the line and assumes the other's responsibilities or neglects his or her own.

DEMAND ACCOUNTABILITY

Many parts of our culture send a message to children that *nothing is their fault.* Whether rationalizing criminal behavior as owing to a difficult upbringing, looking for scapegoats on which to blame misfortune, or faulting others for their failures, children are constantly told that they do not need to be responsible for their actions. Yet, the ability of children to hold themselves accountable for their actions is a critical part of becoming a successful achiever.

The reluctance of children to take responsibility for their actions is based on their desire to protect themselves from failure. By avoiding accountability, children protect their egos from having to accept that they failed because of something about themselves. By blaming outside factors, such as other people, bad luck, or unfairness, children can safeguard their egos from harm.

Some children may inconsistently take responsibility for their actions. I call this "selective accountability," which means that children are more likely to take responsibility when they succeed than when they fail. Avoiding or accepting responsibility has a trade-off: self-protection vs. self-enhancement. It's easy to take responsibility for success, but the difficulty is also being accountable for failure. But children must realize that they cannot have one without the other. They cannot truly have ownership of their successes without also accepting ownership of their failures.

Parents sometimes sabotage the opportunity for their children to learn accountability in the way they comfort their child after a failure. In attempting to relieve the disappointment that inevitably accompanies poor achievement, you might find yourself trying to placate your child by pointing out external reasons for her poor grade or goof in a recital. Though this might provide her with some temporary emotional relief, it prevents her from taking responsibility for her efforts. It also removes your child's ability to learn why she failed and to change her actions in the future. Says Allison Armstrong, a coauthor of *The Child and the Machine*, "Yet parents often feel they should try to spare their children disappointment. In the mistaken belief that the perfect childhood is obstacle-free, some parents unknowingly sabotage their child's progress toward growth and independence."

You can facilitate your child's accountability for her successes and failures by actively pointing out the connection between her actions and their outcomes. The worthwhile way to soothe your child's negative emotions is to show her how to produce a different, more positive outcome in the future. With this approach, your child has both the perception that she can effect a better result at the next opportunity and she possesses the specific means to do so. For example: A girl is disappointed and sad because she played poorly in an important tennis tournament and was beaten by several competitors. Instead of making excuses for her play, her father listens to her, empathizes with her feelings, and gently points out that she did not practice very hard the previous two weeks and passed up several opportunities to play some competitive practice matches. He also indicates that if she put in sufficient time and effort before the next tournament, she would play better and possibly beat the same opponents the next time. Thus, the girl's feelings of disappointment are acknowledged, she is held accountable for her achievement efforts, and she is given the means to change her performance in the future. More important, when she does succeed she will be completely entitled to own her triumph.

ENCOURAGE EXPLORATION

Early in your child's life, you need to keep him on a fairly short "leash" to ensure his safety. You always keep an eye on him when he is playing and you never allow him to wander too far away from you. This care builds your child's sense of security by teaching him that he has a safe place to which to return if he ventures too far and that you are there to protect him when needed.

There is, however, a fine line between a sense of security and a sense of dependence. When your child has established his sense of security, you must then encourage him to explore the world beyond the safety net that you provide. This "push out of the nest" allows your child to take the first steps of independence from you by enabling him to test his own capabilities in the "real world" and to find a sense of security within himself. With more experiences through exploration beyond your immediate grasp, your child will gain confidence in his internalized sense of security, which will further encourage him to explore more on his own, well beyond your safety net.

You can foster this exploration by actively encouraging your child to explore the unknown within age-appropriate limits. For example, you can ask your two-year-old to get a ball that you placed around the side of your house. You can have your seven-year-old ride her bike to her friend's house two blocks away. Or you can allow your fourteen-year-old to go on a camping trip in the mountains with several of her friends (assuming she has some camping experience). Encouraging these types of exploratory opportunities may make you uncomfortable, but they are essential experiences for your child's evolution to independence.

You can also identify situations that cause your child some fear and encourage him to face his fear and explore the situation. You can do this by talking to your child about the fear, providing another perspective that reduces the fear, and offering him some skills that might neutralize his fear. If needed, you can also accompany your child the first time he faces the situation and give him guidance on how to master the fear, then allow him to face the situation on his own in the future.

One way that parents inadvertently inhibit their child's sense of security and cause dependence is by expressing fear, anger, or hurt when their child begins to explore her environment. If you act angry or overly fearful when your child explores a little too far, it might be that your overreaction is due to your own fears about exploration and risk. If you overreact to your child's exploratory experiences, she may internalize this response and develop a belief that the world is a dangerous place that should not be explored. Learning to recognize your own fears and to keep them in check so you don't pass them on to your child is vital to the development of an independent child. If you think this might be you but aren't sure, get a second opinion from a professional or a trusted friend. (I add this only because people who are hyperfearful are often the last ones to know it—it's hard to see in oneself.)

You can also communicate positive messages about exploration. Whether visiting a museum, allowing your child to go to the park alone, or watching a scary movie, you can convey to your child that exploration is a fun and exciting experience that should be sought out and relished. If you express positive emotions about exploration with your child, he is more likely to adopt those same beliefs and emotions that will encourage him to further explore his world and his limits.

A final thought about encouraging exploration in your child: The reality is that the world has, in many ways, become an increasingly dangerous place to raise children. My recommendations for promoting exploration in your child are not intended to expose your child to undue risk. Rather, they are offered to help you understand what beliefs and emotions you have about exploration that may interfere with this process. I also offer recommendations to assist you in exposing your child to exploratory experiences that are essential for the development of independent children. As with all of my suggestions, you must use your best judgment to decide which explorations are too dangerous and which are in your child's best interests.

RESPOND TO EARLY WARNING SIGNS

The emergence of contingent children does not occur overnight. Rather, these problems develop over years of the children's exposure to unhealthy perspectives, attitudes, emotions, and behavior. Seeing early warning signs of one type of contingent child in your child should be a wake-up call that you need to make changes in how you are influencing your child. Persistent signs of perfectionism, harsh self-criticism, loss of motivation and enjoyment, performance anxiety, inappropriate emotions, and other behaviors described in the Red Flags sections of this book should all tell you that something is wrong and that your child might be heading down a unhealthy road. The earlier you can recognize these potential problems, the better chance you have to make changes and redirect the course that your child's life is taking.

You first need to examine your beliefs, emotions, and behavior with your child. What kind of love do you express to your child? What messages have you communicated to your child about success and failure? How invested are you in your child's achievement efforts? What are your expectations for your child? What emotions do you commonly show your child when she succeeds or fails? What attitudes are you modeling for your child? If early signs of a contingent child are becoming evident, you will need to examine your parenting approach. Just as you often ask your child to change, you must also change for the good of your child. This soul searching can be a difficult process. It demands that you take a close look at who you are, what you believe, and what you are communicating to your child. You may find it helpful to seek out the assistance of your spouse, a close friend, or a psychotherapist.

Once you identify how your beliefs, emotions, and behavior may be contributing to the development of a contingent child, you need to take action that communicates messages that will encourage your child to take a different road. Healthier messages may include giving value love, establishing clear boundaries, emphasizing effort rather than results, giving your child more responsibility in his achievement activities, responding differently emotionally to your child's successes and failures, or any of the many other recommendations made earlier. Most important, you must make these changes as soon as possible and communicate these new messages in a clear and consistent manner so that your child "gets it" and can respond to them in a way that will foster success and happiness.

Maybe this story will help. Eleven-year-old Chrissy was a spoiled child. Her parents hadn't received enough from their parents and compensated by heaping their love on Chrissy. Chrissy's parents set no boundaries for her and, though they didn't have much money, gave Chrissy everything they could afford regardless of what she did.

Her parents didn't realize their outpouring of love and unlimited freedom made Chrissy a scared little girl. Because her parents let her make all the decisions and allowed her to do whatever she wanted, Chrissy felt that her parents couldn't protect her. Chrissy expressed this fear as anger toward her parents and disruptiveness and low achievement at school. Chrissy was a disrespectful, lazy, and angry child who was on her way to becoming a Disappointer. Her parents saw Chrissy's difficulties, but were at a loss to understand why she misbehaved or how to help her.

The counselor at Chrissy's school saw her problems increasing, so she scheduled a meeting with her parents, who were desperate for help. After a lengthy discussion about Chrissy's behavior and home life, the counselor made the following suggestions: Chrissy's parents needed to set clear expectations about her behavior toward them, responsibilities around the house, schoolwork, and her time away from the house. They also needed to establish and administer consequences for when she did not live up to expectations.

Chrissy's parents sat down with her that evening and laid down "the new law of the land." They expressed their concerns about her, described their new expectations and consequences, and emphasized their love for her. As expected, after having free rein over her life for so long, Chrissy resisted mightily, challenging her parents every time they invoked the expectations and enforced a consequence for the new "laws." During the first month, her parents had doubts about whether their new approach was going to work. But they were committed to staying with the plan and, with their mutual support and continued guidance from the school counselor, they remained steadfast through Chrissy's temper tantrums and resistance.

Then something amazing started to happen. Chrissy's resistance to the new expectations began to diminish and she started to respond to the demands her parents placed on her. Chrissy became more respectful to her parents, assumed her household responsibilities—first with some prompting, then on her own—and began to apply herself in school.

When all these changes were occurring, Chrissy was confused. A part of her hated having limits placed on her after so many years of freedom, but another part of her begrudgingly liked her parents' being tough on her. Chrissy believed her parents were finally showing that they really loved her and that she could count on them to protect her from harm. Thanks to the courage and resoluteness of her parents, Chrissy was going to be okay.

LIFE LESSONS FOR OWNERSHIP

1. There is no free lunch. Don't feel entitled to anything you don't sweat and struggle for.
2. Set goals and work quietly and systematically toward them.
3. Assign yourself.
4. Don't be afraid of taking risks or of being criticized.
5. Never give up.

6. Be confident that you can make a difference.
7. Be a can-do, will-try person.
8. You are in charge of your own attitude.
9. Be reliable. Be faithful. Finish what you start.

Edelman, M. W. (1992). *The measure of our success: A letter to my children and yours.* Boston: Beacon Press

PART III

EMOTIONAL MASTERY

The emotions that children feel during their achievement experiences cover the spectrum from excitement and joy to frustration and anger. Whichever emotions are most powerful and prevalent will determine children's perceptions about achievement. Positive emotions about achievement—both success and failure—foster positive perceptions about achievement and encourage its pursuit. Children who have positive experiences come to associate achievement with emotions such as excitement, satisfaction and happiness. Though negative emotions such as frustration and disappointment are natural and healthy parts of trying to do something new or competing at a high level, excessively negative emotions, such as fear and despair, can cause children to connect their efforts with feeling bad, which will ultimately discourage their interest in pursuing their dreams. Unhealthy negative emotions are a child's greatest obstacles to achievement because the feelings are so forceful and immediate. Strong negative emotions affect children at many levels, undermining their confidence, blurring their focus, and sapping their motivation.

A child's emotional responses to their attempts to achieve develop as they accumulate experiences in their efforts. These emotional responses take shape as beliefs and attitudes that children hold about achievement. The negative emotions associated with these experiences and perceptions are commonly known as the "baggage" children develop and carry with them into adulthood. One of the most difficult aspects of unhealthy emotions is that they become ingrained, so they cause children to automatically respond with a particular preprogrammed emotional reaction to an achievement situation, even when that emotional response does more harm than good. For example: A child is constantly chastised by his father for getting low grades in school. In time, he comes to fear taking school tests because he knows that if he does poorly, his father will be angry with him. This fear causes him to do poorly on his tests, thereby producing the reaction from his father that he most fears.

The kinds of emotional reactions that children have in response to achievement depend on everything I have discussed to this point. What you do in the development of your child's self-esteem and feelings of ownership will determine the emotions he will experience in his achievement efforts. These emotions, in turn, will determine your child's motivation to pursue future achievement and to find happiness in those pursuits.

Children with high self-esteem believe in their ability to be successful. If your child's self-esteem is based on your approval of her efforts as opposed to your approval of how well she did, she will have a healthy perspective on success and failure. This wisdom will foster emotions that usually produce a self-fulfilling prophecy of success. Also, in response to failure, the negative emotions that your child experiences will not be debilitating or long lasting.

Children with low self-esteem don't have faith in their capabilities. They assume they will fail. Children with low self-esteem can become fearful of achievement because they were raised with love that was conditional on how they performed. This fearful environment triggers devastating negative emotions, which almost guarantee failure. When low self-esteem children do experience success, rather than feeling strong positive emotions, their only reward is the absence of negative emotions.

Children with ownership of their achievement feel strong emotions—both positive and negative—because achievement is important to them. At the same time, negative emotions in response to the occasional failure are not devastating because achievement is not overly connected to their self-esteem—even when they fail they still know they are lovable and competent people. Failure is not a terribly threatening experience and, because they believe they have control over their achievement, children believe that they can alter the outcome in the future. So negative emotions act to motivate children with ownership to overcome their failures and continue to achieve.

Children with no ownership—you, the parent has ownership—can experience strong and painful emotions. These children feel anger, resentment, sadness, and despair acutely because they have the burden of your emotions to deal with when they fail and, because they were raised with outcome love, failure is devastating to their self-esteem. They also feel helpless to change their circumstances, so they feel trapped and unable to escape the situation.

CHAPTER 7

Why Am I So Scared?
Threat vs. Challenge

If I could boil down everything I do with young successful achievers and sum up their emotional reactions to achievement, it would come down to one simple distinction—whether children view trying to achieve something as an emotional threat or as an emotional challenge. Gaining insight into the why, how, and what of this distinction is essential for helping your child develop healthy and constructive emotional reactions to his or her achievement efforts.

EMOTIONAL THREAT

Emotional threat lies at the heart of the negative emotional reactions that children have to their achievement efforts. This negative emotional response is grounded in a child's uncertainty about being loved by his parents and about being perceived as a competent person. It is the result of many parental miscalculations, including parental overinvestment, outcome love, bottom-line parenting, expecting perfection, and fostering a child's false self. Children are so terrified that they will fail and then not receive their parents' love that even the idea of putting themselves in a position where failure is possible is terrifying. Could there be anything more threatening to your child than the belief that you won't love him if he fails?

EMOTIONAL VICIOUS CYCLE

Paradoxically, the emotional threat reaction, although created by children to protect themselves, ensures a self-fulfilling prophecy of the very thing they fear the most—failure and the loss of their parents' love. If your child perceives taking a risk to be emotionally threatening, he will begin his achievement efforts from a position of weakness—inadequacy, doubt, and fear. From this unenviable position, an *emotional vicious cycle* begins, such that every psychological and emotional factor that affects achievement turns against your child.

The threat reaction suggests to your child that he isn't capable of overcoming the demands that are causing the threat—"I wouldn't feel this scared if I actually thought I could succeed." So your child's confidence declines and he is overwhelmed with negative and defeatist thoughts. These beliefs further contribute to an increasingly certain failure. This loss of confidence reduces motivation because your child will have little impetus to engage in an activity in which he believes he will fail. The threat reaction also causes anxiety and all of the negative physical symptoms associated with fear—muscle tension, butterflies, shortness of breath, and muscle tremors—which cause more discomfort and further raise the specter of failure (and, if the activity is physical in nature, this anxiety hurts performance directly). Because the threat reaction is so strong, the negative emotions, thoughts, and physical sensations draw your child's attention to all of the negative aspects of the achievement experience and he will have difficulty focusing on what will help him succeed. All of these negative manifestations of the threat reaction ultimately result in poor achievement and the realization of the very thing that he fears most—failure and the loss of his parents' love.

This dread then morphs into other, equally destructive emotions that drive children further from achievement. Each step downward in this vicious cycle separately and cumulatively makes children view achievement as a dangerous and frightening experience that they must avoid at all costs.

Sammy was terrified of an upcoming debate competition. In past competitions, when Sammy performed well, his mother, Joyce, smothered him with love and wanted to buy him things. But when he messed up, his mother became angry and distant. Sammy knew how important the state debate championships were to his mother. Joyce had been talking about them for weeks, making sure he practiced every day and telling him that she was going to put the trophy in the living room where everyone could see it.

Sammy barely slept the night before the competition. He envisioned the next day's terror again and again. All he could think about was stammering or forgetting his speech. Sammy thought that it would be great to get laryngitis so he wouldn't be able to compete. In the morning he felt worse. His heart was pounding and he felt like he was going to suffocate. Though he tried reviewing his speech, all he could focus on was his mother in the audience and how disappointed she would be if he choked. Sammy walked onstage feeling like a deer caught in a car's headlights. He was destined to fail!

Children are often in the difficult position of being afraid of achievement, yet do not have the option to avoid it. You, subtly or forcibly, can pressure your child into continuing her participation in an achievement activity despite her clear lack of interest or enjoyment. This coercion worsens the threat response because children feel powerless, trapped, and out of control.

When forced into an achievement activity, children may first transform their fear into frustration in an attempt to gain control of the situation. This frustration may act to motivate them to put in effort to gain control. Expression of this frustration may cause your child to exact a small amount of revenge on you, by breaking a golf club during a tournament or yelling at the conductor of the orchestra, for example. This frustration will continue to interfere with your child's efforts to succeed because he will be unable to think clearly or to focus effectively.

Unfortunately, with the presence of so great a threat, your child has little hope of success. Her frustration ultimately shifts to anger as she realizes she's stuck in a situation from which there is no apparent escape. This anger further motivates your child to try to extricate herself from this threatening situation. Unfortunately, the anger inhibits her ability to direct her energy toward success by clouding her thinking and causing more anxiety.

Invariably, children are not able to free themselves and the anger turns to panic as they see that they have no control over the situation and they have no way out. This panic usually results in a final, intensive—though frantic and undirected—effort to regain control, again, unfortunately, to no avail. Finally, despair sets in when children give up because they feel thoroughly helpless to avoid failure. Children simply accept it because they believe they have no other choice.

FEAR OF FAILURE

A negative emotional reaction is typically associated with a profound fear of failure in children. The Pennsylvania State University researcher David Conroy defines fear of failure as "a belief that a perceived failure will be followed by an aversive consequence," most commonly, upsetting important others, losing social influence, experiencing shame and embarrassment, devaluing oneself, and having an uncertain future. He further views fear of failure as a defensive reaction to learning that the love people desire is dependent on their success or that it will be withdrawn following failure.

Fear of failure among our youth is widespread and the toll it takes on children can be devastating. Two studies reported that 35 percent of college students indicated that fear of failure interfered with their academic achievements and their lives. Fear of failure has been associated with many achievement and psychological difficulties in school, artistic, and sports settings, including low self-esteem, decreased intrinsic motivation, lower grades, cheating, physical complaints, eating disorders, drug abuse, anxiety, and depression. It may also be more prevalent among gifted children.

Children usually develop a fear of failure from their parents and it arises most often between the ages of five and nine. One study found that mothers with a high fear of failure had daughters with a high fear of failure and high-fear-of-failure fathers had sons with a high fear of failure. Also, when mothers placed demands on their children which they were not yet capable of handling, the children learned to fear failure. Moreover, children with a high fear of failure tended to be raised in families with marital conflict, avoidance of communication, hostility, and power struggles.

Children with a fear of failure tend to believe that they are not adequately rewarded for their achievement successes and are punished severely for their achievement failures. Chances are that your child's primary achievement motivation is the desire to be praised. However, for children with a fear of failure, avoiding criticism becomes the more powerful motivation. This motivation tends to create children who are submissive and who remain dependent on their parents rather than becoming increasingly more self-reliant as they move through adolescence.

Children may seek to avoid failure by not engaging in the achievement activity in which failure can occur. If children don't try anything, they will be safe from failure. Getting injured or sick (or faking it), causing their equipment to become damaged, or forgetting or losing their materials are common ways that children can avoid engaging in an achievement activity.

Children may avoid failure by failing as quickly as possible in their activity, but having an excuse ready so that they don't have to take responsibility for the failure. By doing so, children are able to protect their self-esteem by not having to take the blame for having failed.

A fear-based response to achievement can also motivate some children to succeed. The goal of children who are threatened by achievement is to distance themselves sufficiently from failure, thereby removing its threat. For children who don't have the power to escape or excuse their achievement participation, the third way to avoid failure is to become successful. As long as these children are successful, they relieve the threat of failure by getting as far away from failure as possible.

As Dr. David Conroy concludes, "It appears that FF [fear of failure] may primarily be a defensive adaptation. . . . Ironically and tragically, this adaptation may not be adaptive at all as it presents a tremendous emotional burden that, at the very least, makes performance distressful and may even cause performance to deteriorate."

FEAR OF SUCCESS

"Fear of success? Why would anyone be afraid of becoming successful? Isn't that what everyone wants?" you might ask. Yet children who feel threatened by achievement often harbor a fear of success. This fear is not based on achieving success itself, but rather on the ramifications of success. As the opposite side of the fear-of-failure coin, Dr. David Conroy defines fear of success as "a belief that a perceived success will be followed by an aversive consequence," such as the pressure to constantly match or exceed previous achievements, unwanted attention and recognition, social and emotional isolation, and an overly rigid future.

In a sense, attaining success "raises the bar" for your child, creating greater expectations of success and more pressure to succeed. After success, you are going to expect your child to succeed more often. Your child's success also raises the level of achievement that is considered successful. You may assume that if your child attains one level of success, then he is expected to reach an even higher level the next time.

With each success and new expectation, the burden on your child can grow. Her fear of success worsens because each new level of success and heightened expectations diminishes your child's belief in her ability to succeed in the future. Her fear of success increases because she sees failure as more likely, more disappointing to others, and, ultimately, more devastating to her self-esteem.

Achieving success can also put your child in the spotlight, where he receives more attention from teachers, instructors, coaches, and peers. With this success and added recognition, your child now not only has to deal with his own expectations and yours, but he must also meet the perceived expectations of many others. Some children may not have a temperament that is suited to being on center stage. Children who are introverted, shy, insecure, or uncomfortable socially may develop a fear of success because of their discomfort with the attention. The fear of success enables them to avoid the spotlight, but, unfortunately, it also keeps them from fully achieving their goals.

Many people believe that the most successful people are also the most popular and well-accepted, such as the stereotypical starting quarterback and head cheerleader in high school. However, the popularity of children in school is often more associated with physical attractiveness and social skills than achievement—the stereotypical class nerd may be the most successful, but he is far from the most popular. Because peer acceptance is an important issue for children, a fear of success may arise from concerns related to jealousy, rivalry, and worries about becoming socially isolated. Dr. Mary Pipher speaks of the "dumbing down" of adolescent girls because they believe that if they appear smarter than boys, then the boys will find them less desirable.

One of the dangers of your child's early success in an achievement activity is being pushed onto a future life course to which she may not aspire. Showing promise in an academic area, performing art, or sport can cause you to see a bright future for your child in that area. You may then direct your child's life toward a predetermined future without asking her whether that life path is one that she wants to follow. Fear of success may arise out of the concern that she will be required to live a life for which she has little interest or motivation to pursue. The easiest way for your child to circumvent this overly rigid future is to avoid the success that will lead to that undesired future.

Kelly didn't know what to do. He had been playing basketball forever because his two older brothers played and his family's life basically revolved around the sport. Kelly's brothers were both high school stars and now played for major universities. Kelly seemed to be a pretty good player himself, but he knew he could never live up to everyone's expectations. In fact, the idea of "following in their footsteps" terrified him. Also, whereas his brothers were outgoing and boisterous, Kelly was rather shy and quiet. He didn't like being the center of attention and the idea of having the team, his family, and the town count on him to win a game, well, he couldn't think of anything worse. Kelly wanted to do his best, but he couldn't face the possibility of letting everyone down. He wanted to quit, but he couldn't because it would really disappoint people. So when Kelly got to high school, he developed a series of nagging, minor injuries that kept him from being able to play his best. Everyone was sympathetic and people said that he would have been just as good as his brothers if he wasn't so injury-prone.

EMOTIONAL CHALLENGE

Once you've pushed your little nestling out of the nest and she's flapped her wings a few times, you may see that she not only enjoys flying, but that she wants to get better at it. Your child has an innate desire to achieve excellence, to push herself beyond her perceived limits, to attain her goals, and to grow as an achiever and as a person. If you nurture your child with the kind of love that supports her efforts (as opposed to being dependent on how well she does), she will be secure in your love and, as a result, feel *challenged* rather than *threatened* by the process of trying to be really great at something. Then your child will be able to see herself as a competent person who has the capabilities to succeed. These two basic beliefs will enable your child to view the demands of achievement as a challenge worth pursuing—with a positive attitude, high expectations of success, and feelings of excitement and joy.

Children who respond to challenges with confidence instead of fear enjoy the process of their achievement activity regardless of whether they succeed or fail. The emphasis of emotional challenge is on children's having fun and seeing achievement as exciting and enriching. Achievement, when seen as a challenge, is an experience that is relished and sought out at every opportunity. Thus, the challenge reaction is highly motivating, to the point where children embrace rather than recoil from achievement.

EMOTIONAL UPWARD SPIRAL

If your child perceives achievement as an emotional challenge, she starts her achievement efforts from a position of strength—competence, purpose, and determination. This position of strength initiates an *emotional upward spiral* that literally propels her to success and happiness. Your child's goal is to achieve success and all of her efforts are directed toward pursuing the challenge that will lead to that goal.

The challenge reaction tells your child that he is capable and has a fundamental belief that if he works hard, he will be successful. This attitude gives your child the motivation and perseverance to continue his efforts in the face of setbacks and failure. This positive attitude allows your child to feel relaxed and energized instead of fearful and anxious. Because he is pursuing a goal that he really wants to achieve, your child can focus well on what will allow him to do his best. The challenge reaction also generates many positive emotions like excitement and contentment, which make the achievement experience enjoyable.

RED FLAGS

Is your child threatened by achievement? How can you tell if your child is overwhelmed by a fear of failure or success? How can you find out if your child has a positive emotional response to the demands of achievement? I describe below a number of clear signs for you to look for in your child that will tell you if she reacts to achievement negatively or positively.

RED FLAG #1: PERFORMANCE ANXIETY

Children naturally experience some nervousness before they audition, compete, perform in public, or take an exam. This increase in physiological activation is the human body's way of preparing itself for the demands that performing will place on it. Ideally, this physical activity enhances the body's and the mind's capabilities, allowing a child to perform at her highest level. However, when your child experiences debilitating performance anxiety—her reaction is more fear than excitement—she is sending a powerful message to you that she feels threatened.

Low self-esteem is often associated with performance anxiety. Because self-esteem is related to competence, a child with low self-esteem believes that he is unlikely to succeed because he lacks the capabilities to reach his goals. He is also afraid that his parents will not love him if he fails. These beliefs can cause him to fear engaging in an activity in which he believes he will fail. Performance anxiety also results from worry about parental expectations. If your child feels pressure from you, he will experience higher performance anxiety and perform poorly. Two common worries among young achievers are: "What will my parents think?" and "I will let my parents down."

Performance anxiety in your child is usually easy to spot. Your child will appear tense and distracted. His muscles may be tight and his breathing may be short and choppy. Your child may say defeatist things and show a reluctance about his upcoming performance. He may be distracted and have a hard time paying attention to you when you speak to him. Your child will be in a bad mood, noticeably on edge, and easily irritated or angered.

RED FLAG #2: PUNISHMENT EXCEEDS THE CRIME

One of the most common red flags that shows your child is threatened by achievement is if she expresses a negative emotional reaction that is disproportionate to the apparent severity of her failure. In effect, you are witnessing your child inflicting a punishment on herself that far exceeds the crime she believes she has committed, whether it was a missed putt in a golf tournament, a few mistakes in a recital, or some incorrect answers on a math test. For example, a ballet dancer I worked with would beat herself up emotionally for missing a single step in her choreography. Her level of performance would steadily decline and she would feel terrible about her dancing and about herself. By the end of rehearsal, she would be battered and bruised by her own emotions.

If you are a highly critical parent, your child may be learning to subject himself to extreme self-punishment because he has internalized your responses to his mistakes or failures. If you are harshly critical of even the smallest mistakes, you will communicate to your child that these flaws are unacceptable. If your child is a perfectionist, he will not tolerate any mistakes because they are a threat to his sense of competence and his ability to gain your love. To stop making mistakes, your child may believe that he must punish himself for his mistakes severely. Unfortunately, such self-castigation usually results in more miscues.

If you are unfairly demanding, this extreme self-punishment may also be a way for your child to protect herself from withdrawal of your love. Your child can expect to be chastised by you after a failure. By punishing herself even more harshly than you would, your child is, in a sense, beating you to it, which she hopes will show you that you don't need to punish her because she has suffered enough.

RED FLAG #3: SELF-DEFEATING BEHAVIOR

Self-defeating behavior is the most paradoxical red flag of achievement problems. Children who engage in self-defeating behavior act in ways that ensure they will fail, but that also provide them with an excuse for their failure. A typical self-defeating scenario goes like this: In order to please you, your son expresses a strong desire to succeed. Yet in pursuing a specific goal, he exerts little effort, thereby producing the inevitable failure. Your child then says, "I would have succeeded, but I didn't feel like trying."

This is the paradox of self-defeating behavior. Why would your child want to fail when, with even only moderate effort, the prospects of success are reasonably high? The answer to this question lies in a fundamental conflict. The primary motivation for your child if she is engaging in self-defeating behavior is to protect her self-esteem, but there are competing forces: your inappropriate pressure on your child to succeed and her fear of failure and not receiving your love. The fear of further hurting her self-esteem by failing far outweighs any perceived benefits to her self-esteem that might arise from a likely success. This need to protect your child's self-esteem predominates despite the fact that the objective likelihood of success is much greater that the chances of failure.

But the *realistic* likelihood of success and failure is not the issue here. Your child's *perceived* likelihood of success and failure is what matters. In most achievement activities, if your child works hard, he has a very good chance of achieving success and only a small chance of failure. If you put his chances on a scale, you would expect that the great likelihood of success would tip the scale toward success. But what makes your child's perceived chances so powerful is the immense emotional weight that he places on that small likelihood of failure. If you put your child's perceived chances of failure on the scale, its emotional weight would tip the scale heavily toward failure. You can see why your child would choose to avoid that seemingly minute—but emotionally heavy—chance of failure.

Children who engage in self-defeating behavior consider the likeli-hood of reaching a certain goal, make a pessimistic judgment, and then direct their efforts to avoid that expected negative outcome. Given this paradox and the power of some children's belief that they will fail, you can begin to understand how fragile a child's self-esteem can be and how enormous the threat of failure is to their self-esteem.

If your child's behavior is self-defeating, how it protects his self-esteem depends on how he assigns responsibility for his failures. If he blames failure on innate qualities by saying "I am stupid" or "I have no talent," he damages self-esteem most because it reflects directly on his competence (or lack of competence), which would make him feel unworthy of your love. Qualities such as intelligence or ability are also fixed and unchangeable, so your child would have little hope of gaining competence and your love in the future.

Your child can blame his failure on external influences and might say, "There wasn't enough time" or "The test was not fair." Blaming external factors protects your child's self-esteem by placing responsi-bility outside of himself: "Mom and Dad have to still love me because it wasn't my fault that I failed." Because these external causes of failure can change, your child can hope to have more time or have a more fair exam in the future. But it's often difficult to come up with acceptable external reasons for failure. "The dog ate my homework" or some var-iation of that excuse usually won't fly.

Your child needs to find a way to simultaneously accept and avoid responsibility for his failure, thereby getting himself off the hook with you and, at the same time, protecting his self-esteem. Your child needs to be able to take responsibility for his failure—thereby appeasing you and still receiving your love—and have the cause of his failure be some-thing about himself that he can change (for example, effort, study time)—thereby protecting his self-esteem. Saying he didn't try protects your child's self-esteem because he can accept responsibility for his failure ("I didn't try hard enough") and he can still be competent and capable of succeeding ("I would have done well otherwise"), ensuring that you will still love him. Your child seems to say, "It was me, but it really wasn't me." "Why not?" "Because I really wasn't trying. If I had tried, I would have succeeded."

Self-defeating behavior is rarely a game that your child will play consciously and it should not be trivialized. If your child uses these excuses on occasion, but usually gives her best effort and accepts responsibility for her actions, her behavior can be attributed to typical child irresponsibility and limit-testing. But if these behaviors occur more often than not, and are coupled with other signs of a negative emotional response, then you should take this self-defeating behavior seriously and explore why your child is acting in such an unhealthy way.

RED FLAG #4: SAFETY ZONE

One of the most fascinating and oddly adaptive ways I have found young achievers to avoid their fears of failure and of success is to stay in what I call the *safety zone*. This safety zone lies far from failure, but not too close to success. If your child is in the safety zone, he manages to consistently perform at up to 95 percent of his ability. He may finish in the top 10 to 20 percent in school, but is never at the very top of his class, or he may often place sixth through tenth in sports events, but never make it onto the podium. Is your child not even close to failing, but doesn't consider himself to be truly successful either? Is your child doing just fine but not fully realizing his ability?

If your child is in the safety zone, he works hard, but never quite hard enough. He never really lays it on the line and truly takes a risk to be his best. Your child does just enough to perform well above failure and to do "pretty darned well," but never enough to do "phenomenally well."

This safety zone protects your child from having to face the consequences of both failure and success. By performing at a level well above failure, your child can be sure that she won't disappoint her teachers, coaches, teammates, friends, and, most important, you. Your child is able to reduce her fear of failure and avoid the threat to her self-esteem that would accompany failure.

At the same time, the safety zone enables your child to escape the pressures of success. She does not have to deal with the increased expectations and pressures that accompany success. It also allows your child to reduce her fear of failure, which usually increases with success. As long as your child stays in the safety zone, few people will notice her and she can stay in a place that enables her to be reasonably successful and, at the same time, feel protected and unthreatened.

A question I am often asked is "How do you know if a child is in the safety zone or if he has simply reached the top end of his ability?" If your child is in the safety zone, he probably shows flashes of real success and real failure. Your child will periodically have a really good performance that is markedly above past performances, indicating that higher achievement is possible. Unfortunately, this good performance may raise your expectations for your child and cause him to feel added pressure to succeed. Your safety-zone child will also have a really poor performance—often shortly after the strong performance—which lowers your expectations and relieves the pressure he feels. These failures also help your child gauge where his safety zone lies and how much effort he needs to expend to maintain its protection and comfort. In contrast, if your child has attained his highest level of ability, his performance will be generally consistent and result in neither surprising successes nor dramatic failures.

If your child is in the safety zone, she remains there at a cost to her achievement and her happiness in her efforts. Your child will never fully realize her promise and will always be frustrated by never becoming truly successful. Your child will feel additional frustration because she has no idea why she can't fully reach her goals. Your child may sense that an obstacle is in her path, but she is unable to figure out what it is. As a result, your child, though she may achieve some degree of success, is never completely fulfilled in her efforts or satisfied with her achievements.

RED FLAG #5: UNHAPPY SUCCESS

Children who respond to feeling threatened by achievement by striving for success ensure that they will reach a high level of success because fear is a powerful motivator, but they pay a price for servitude to this demon that they call failure. As long as children remain far from failure—which success allows them to do—they will have reduced the fear they feel. However, whatever level of success these children achieve, they will never be truly happy because of this burden they carry. These children are *unhappy successes*.

If your child is an unhappy success, from a distant observer's perspective, he may seem to have it all. He may be successful in many avenues of his life. Your child may excel in school, where he achieves the highest grades, participates in student government, and is involved in many clubs and organizations. He may star in sports, captain a team, and provide inspirational leadership. Your child may show artistic talents in many areas, for example, play a musical instrument, edit the school newspaper, and act in the school repertory.

On top of these achievements, your child may also be socially popular and admired. In addition to being driven to success, your child may also be a Pleaser. To satisfy his need for success, he may be extremely giving, participating in food drives, tutoring or mentoring an underprivileged child, or giving of himself to family and friends.

But his internal experience is entirely different. He feels like he is hiding a deep, dark secret that no one can ever learn—*he is an imposter*—and that sooner or later people will figure out that he is really an incompetent person who is not worthy of anyone's love. This fear torments him and drives him harder to succeed.

Dartmouth student-athlete Sarah Devens appeared to have been such an unhappy success. Successful in school, a star in sports, popular and loved by all, she seemed to have it all. Yet her life became unbearable.

Most unhappy successes live with this threat for their entire lives. Others make peace with themselves at some point with the help of psychotherapy or other forms of internal exploration. Still others are less fortunate. The burden becomes intolerable and they begin to buckle under its weight. It may start with a drop in achievement accompanied by "reasonable" explanations that are accepted by all because these lapses are so totally uncharacteristic of them. As the decline in achievement becomes more persistent, it becomes clear that these children have a problem. Their emotional lives may then spiral down to complete avoidance of this fear, dropping out of activities that they previously had loved and excelled at. There may also be other signs of rebellion against their own lives—changes in dress and grooming, mistreatment of others, and unhealthy new habits, such as the use of alcohol or drugs. If this decline goes unchecked, the consequences may be dire and irreversible.

Developing Emotional Challenge

Every recommendation that I make in this book is directed toward helping your child develop a positive emotional response to achievement. The ability of your child to have a positive emotional response begins with a firm grounding in self-esteem based on your child's strong belief that you love her and that she is competent. A positive emotional reaction also comes from ownership of her achievement, so that she is driven to succeed by her own passion, motivation, and determination. Finally, your child will develop a positive emotional response when she has internalized the emotional tools she needs to respond positively to the inevitable obstacles and setbacks that she will experience as she pursues her achievement goals.

VALUE OF SUCCESS *AND* FAILURE

There are many misconceptions about both success and failure that can interfere with your child's efforts to become a successful achiever. One of the most damaging is the idea that successes never fail and failures always fail. Yet the reality is that "successes" fail much more often than "failures." People who are failures fail a few times and quit. But successes fail many times, learn from the failures, and begin to succeed because of what they learned. In time, the many failures and the lessons learned allow successes to succeed regularly. Writes the *Boston Globe* writer John Powers: "Failure can be a terrific motivator. Michael Jordan was cut from his high school basketball team. Thomas Edison was pulled out of school because his teacher thought he was 'addled.' . . . Germany and Japan, reduced to smoking rubble, signed an unconditional surrender in 1945. They didn't ask for runner-up trophies." *Learning to fail and learning from failure* are essential contributors to success and a perspective that will foster achievement.

Failure provides benefits such as information about your child's progress. Failure is the best means for your child to look in the mirror. It clearly and unambiguously shows your child the areas he needs to improve. Failure also indicates to your child what not to do in his efforts, which narrows down the possibilities of what he needs to do to be successful. Failure also teaches the essential lessons of perseverance and the ability to overcome adversity. Most fundamentally, as Dr. Wayne Dyer suggests, "Take the fear out of failure, and help children to understand the difference between failing at a task and being a failure as a person."

Experiencing failure alone, though, will not help your child achieve success. Too much failure and your child will become discouraged, lose confidence and motivation, and come to view achievement as an unpleasant experience to be avoided. Your child also needs to experience success because, if combined with a healthy perspective, success can provide invaluable lessons for your child's pursuit of lifelong success and happiness.

Success builds confidence and trust in your child, which helps him to overcome adversity, obstacles, and setbacks on the road to achievement. It validates the dedication, hard work, patience, and perseverance that your child devotes to an achievement activity. Success acts to motivate him to further achievement. Success also generates positive emotions, such as excitement, joy, pride, and happiness, which further reinforce your child's confidence, motivation, and passion for the achievement activity.

Interestingly, early and consistent success can present potential problems for children. Youthful prodigies who never realized their promise are commonplace. Success can breed complacency, because if children succeed early and easily they have little motivation to work hard and improve. Children with too much early success don't learn the importance of effort to gain achievement because they never had to work hard to succeed. Too much early success also doesn't encourage children to self-reflect and identify areas in need of improvement. Many children who succeed young become reluctant to look in the mirror for fear that they will see something that is inconsistent with their perceptions of themselves as successful. Too much success doesn't teach children how to constructively handle setbacks that they will inevitably encounter as they reach higher levels of performance. If you are the parent of a gifted child who has experienced considerable early success, you may need to find appropriate challenges for your child, either by raising the level of challenge in her primary achievement activity or by challenging her outside of the area of her talent. These new challenges will enable your child to develop the attitudes and skills that will prepare her for the serious tests that she can expect to face in her future achievement efforts.

With this perspective, success is not such an intoxicant that it inhibits further growth, and failure is not such a monumental loss that it diminishes the desire to pursue success. Rather, they are both inevitable and necessary parts of the process leading toward achievement and happiness.

RISK-TAKING

Taking risks is an essential part of your child's developing a positive emotional response to his achievement. Only if your child is unthreatened by failure will he be willing to take risks because, by their very nature, risks increase the likelihood of failure. If your child sees achievement as a challenge to pursue, he will understand that risks also provide the opportunity to achieve even greater success. Risk-taking will enable your child to move out of his comfort zone, test his capabilities, gain confidence in himself, and achieve new levels of success. When you look at great successes—Rosa Parks, Mahatma Gandhi, Boris Spassky, and Bill Gates—you also see great risk takers. These people knew that only by taking risks were great rewards possible. As the best-selling author Leo Buscaglia observed, "To try is to risk failure. But risks need to be taken, because the greatest hazard in life is to risk nothing. The person who risks nothing, does nothing, has nothing and is nothing. They may avoid suffering and sorrow, but they cannot learn, feel change, grow, love and live. Chained by their certitudes, they are a slave; they have forfeited their freedom. Only a person who risks is free."

Though there is evidence that inborn temperament affects risk-taking, you can influence the attitude that your child develops toward risk. How much your child is willing to risk is often dictated by your attitude and behavior toward risk. If you are reluctant to seek out risks and you shy away from risks when they present themselves, you are encouraging your child to do the same. Conversely, if you take risks in your life, and the risks are usually rewarded, then your child will likely learn the value and benefits of taking risks. But if you take risks that are reckless, potentially harmful, and aren't rewarded, then you may teach your child attitudes about risk that are no less detrimental than not taking risks at all.

You should actively teach your child about the value of risks and how taking risks can foster her success and happiness. You can help your child learn to recognize risks, judge whether risks are worth taking, and how best to act on risks. The first thing you need to do is tell your child what a risk is—to expose yourself to the chance of loss or injury without certainty of the outcome. You can also explain why people take risks—usually to gain some increased benefit that would not occur if the risk were not taken—and why people don't take risks—the costs of failure outweigh the benefits of success. Then, you can introduce your child to "calculated risks," in which you look at upsides and downsides of the risk and decide whether the risk is worthwhile. An important lesson you can teach your child is that risks in which you can accept failure without dire consequences—whose costs may be undesirable, but not devastating—and in which the benefits are highly attractive are worth taking. Conversely, risks that may result in loss or injury that is long-term or irreversible are generally not good risks to take. You can clarify your child's understanding of risks with examples from your own life, including experiences from school, work, sports, and other activities in which you have taken risks.

You can model risk-taking for your child with small risks, such as when playing a game, or big risks, such as deciding to change jobs. Your child's life is also rife with opportunities to teach her about risk-taking. Games provide a fun and stimulating setting in which you can create risky situations and both model risk-taking and guide your child in making good risk-taking decisions. Unfortunately, unlike earlier generations, which were raised with lots of unstructured games such as tag, kick the can, and hide and seek, your child probably participates primarily in organized games, though some still play variations of those old neighborhood games and others they make up.

School also presents great risk-taking opportunities, such as when your child chooses to raise her hand in class and answer a question, prepares a presentation for a class, or decides whether to try out for a school play. If your child participates in sports, she is constantly faced with risk-taking opportunities, such as whether to shoot the basketball in the closing seconds of a game, ski a black diamond trail, canter a horse, or learn a more difficult and dangerous gymnastics dismount. Life in general is also full of situations in which your child can take risks—climbing higher up the tree in the neighborhood park, facing the school bully, and inline skating down a hill, for example.

You can also point out risky situations that present themselves in life, whether on television, at the movies, in books, or on videos. Every experience in which you or your child can observe or take a risk is an opportunity for her to become more familiar and comfortable with taking risks. These opportunities can be "in the moment" lessons about risk when you share with your child how she can decide whether a risk is worth taking.

As your child's understanding of risks grows, you can encourage her to take risks, first, in relatively minor situations where the costs are minimal (as in a game), and, later, in more important situations where the stakes are higher (deciding whether to devote all her time to studying for one test rather than distributing her study time between two tests). In your child's early risk-taking experiences, you can guide her through the risk process and assist her—not direct her—in making the best choice of whether to take a risk.

You must understand that risk-taking is, by definition, potentially harmful to your child. Though I strongly advocate risk-taking, I do not encourage you to place your child in situations that are unsafe. You must use your best judgment in deciding what risks are healthy for your child and what risks are possibly dangerous. Early in your child's life, your most important role is to provide a safe and secure environment in which he can grow. As your child matures, you cede responsibility for his safety and security to him. Your ability to show your child how to make good risk-taking decisions can either propel him to new heights of success and happiness (for example, academic, artistic, or athletic achievement, healthy relationships) or endanger his health and future (for example, alcohol and drug use, sexual activity). By teaching your child how to make good decisions about risk-taking, you are giving him the power and the tools to balance his need for both safety and risk in a way that will promote his success and happiness.

PERSPECTIVE ON MISTAKES

How your child comes to understand the meaning of mistakes will have a dramatic effect on her ability to improve and achieve. As the poet Nikki Giovanni states, "Mistakes are a fact of life. It is the response to the mistakes that counts." Unfortunately, parents often communicate a very different message. What happens if you convey to your child that mistakes are bad and reflect poorly on her? You will be placing your child in the vise of being expected to pursue achievement—which inevitably involves making mistakes—but knowing that she will be criticized for her mistakes. Your child may then become fearful of making even the smallest mistakes and eventually come to believe that if she makes a mistake, she is an incompetent person who is not worthy of your love. Says Dr. John Gray: "To expect children not to make mistakes gives them a cruel and inaccurate message about life. It sets a standard that can never be lived up to."

Many parents and their children hold a negative perception about mistakes in spite of being able to see the world's greatest achievers make mistakes routinely. In every sporting event, dance performance, musical recital, and scientific inquiry, people at the top of their fields make mistakes on a regular basis. Because they do, it would seem not only expected but also acceptable that young achievers would too. What many people do not realize is that one of the things that makes the greatest achievers in the world so successful is not that they make no mistakes, but rather how they react to them. "Failure is an important part of the learning process. . . . There's truth to the clichés—'No pain, no gain,' 'You win some, you lose some.' . . . Experiencing failure helps kids become resilient and less frustrated by everyday setbacks," says Dr. Frank Vitro, a professor at Texas Women's University.

You need to communicate to your child that mistakes are a natural and necessary part of achievement. Your child must accept and learn from her mistakes. Mistakes are guides to what your child needs to work on to improve. Without them, betterment will be a random and undirected process. Mistakes can tell your child that she is taking risks and moving out of her comfort zone. If your child never makes mistakes, she is probably not pushing herself hard enough, she will not improve, and she will never become truly successful. You and your child need to learn that mistakes are failure only if she does not learn from them. "Loving and concerned parents who allow for failure wind up with kids who tend to choose success," say Dr. Foster Cline and Jim Fay.

RESPOND POSITIVELY TO ADVERSITY

The road to success is a bumpy one. It's filled with many barriers, setbacks, and struggles. Some of this adversity is external to your child—demanding academic requirements, complex information and skills, difficult conditions, and tough opposition. Internal obstacles exist too, including loss of motivation, decline in confidence, distractions, negative emotions, impatience, and the desire to give up. How your child responds to these demands will dictate the limits of achievement and happiness that he ultimately attains. "How can we grow without struggle and doubt and a misstep or two? If we spare our children that—or try to—we'll not be successful anyway; we'll end up prodding them toward other kinds of troubles, the kind we may not have anticipated," writes Robert Coles in his book *The Moral Intelligence of Children*. The distinction between feeling threatened and feeling challenged explains why children can approach the same demands and respond in diametrically opposed ways.

Children who experience the adversity of achievement as a threat do so because it heightens their fear of failure. Obstacles make achievement more difficult and success less likely, which triggers the threat reaction because the probability of failure grows. Paradoxically, children who respond negatively to adversity actually make the demands greater and harder to overcome, and failure more likely.

Children who see the adversity of achievement as a challenge do so because their self-esteem is connected to their efforts instead of to their successes and failures. Your child needs to see adversity as *achievement-within-achievement* activities. Adversity will be an opportunity to demonstrate her competence, validate her efforts, and gain even more satisfaction from her successes. Notes Dr. Frank Vitro: "Overcoming obstacles can boost your child's self-esteem even more than an easy triumph."

How your child learns to respond to adversity depends largely on how *you* respond to adversity, and the perspective you teach him about the inevitable setbacks he will experience in his achievement efforts. You should be keenly aware of your reactions to setbacks, whether in a relatively unimportant situation, such as having difficulty balancing your checkbook, or in a critical situation, such as losing out on a job promotion. If you show frustration, anger, or despair when you face obstacles, you will be modeling this behavior for your child.

Dr. Peter Goldenthal, the author of *Beyond Sibling Rivalry*, suggests the following ways to help children respond positively to adversity: First, put the situation in perspective. Show your child that a setback is not the end of the world. Second, don't rush to the rescue. Let your child try to solve the problem him- or herself. Third, play up the positive. Point out to your child all the good things that happened besides the obstacle. Fourth, suggest step-by-step success. Help your child set goals using the setback as useful information. Finally, admit your own mistakes. Share with your child difficulties that you had when you were young and how you overcame them.

LAST 5 PERCENT

Being able to make the transition from feeling threatened to feeling challenged will enable your child to access the last 5 percent of her ability. It is in this highest level of commitment that your child is able to set aside her fears of failure and success, move out of her safety zone, and experience true success and happiness. Being able to get within that last 5 percent is the difference between being pretty good and being exceptional. This last 5 percent involves your child's being willing to "lay it on the line," where the "it" is her self-esteem, and to find out what she is truly capable of.

But if your child views achievement as threatening, she will not be able to reach for that last 5 percent. With a fear of achievement, your child believes that failure with no excuses will cause you to see her as incompetent and to withdraw your love for her. The danger of reaching for that last 5 percent—and what will keep your child from striving for it—is that if she doesn't succeed after giving it her best effort, she will have no excuses and she must take full responsibility for her failure.

Only when your child sees achievement in a positive and challenging light—where her competence and your love are not at risk—and she is willing to lay her self-esteem on the line will she be comfortable going for that last 5 percent. An essential lesson that your child must learn is that *only by risking failure will your child achieve true success.*

So laying it on the line is a choice that your child must make for herself, when she is ready. Does your child play it safe and do just fine or does she push the envelope and find out how high she can really achieve? The ultimate benefit of being able to respond to an achievement opportunity as a challenge rather than as a threat is that your child will know that she has done everything possible to be her best and she will never have to ask the question, "I wonder what could have been?"

EMOTIONAL LESSONS FOR ACHIEVEMENT

1. Learn to cope with failure.
2. Develop a sense of commitment.

3. Handle fear.

4. Handle frustration.

5. Handle embarrassment.

6. Handle competition.

7. Handle adjustments.

Fine, A. H., & Sachs, M. L. (1997). *Total sports experience for kids: A parents' guide to success in youth sports.* South Bend, IN: Diamond Communications.

∞

CHAPTER 8

Will I Be a Child Forever?
Child vs. Adult

One of the most surprising and unfortunate observations I have made in my work with achieving children is that many of them have deferred emotional development. Many children who are highly committed to an achievement activity are from two to five years younger emotionally than they are chronologically. Though these children often exhibit substantial maturity in some areas—perhaps they are physically mature or ahead of their peers in their achievement activity—they have underdeveloped emotional capabilities. This slowed emotional growth appears to be related to the excessive investment their parents have made in their children's achievement efforts.

For parents who have a balanced perspective, achievement seems to foster their children's emotional development. These children often show emotional maturity beyond their years because their parents use achievement as an avenue for teaching their children about emotions. They provide their children with opportunities to learn about and gain mastery over their emotions. For instance, after a poor performance by your child, you need to allow him to feel the disappointment and hurt of failure. You can also acknowledge and affirm the emotions he is experiencing. Then you can offer your child a positive and healthy perspective on those feelings and show him how to deal with the emotions on his own.

Parents who use achievement as an avenue for emotional development nurture several essential qualities and skills that Dr. Daniel Goleman associates with emotional intelligence. Emotionally mature people possess awareness of their emotional states, control of their emotions, and empathy toward others' emotions. They are also skilled in listening, resolving conflict, and cooperation.

In contrast, the achievement efforts of children of overly invested parents appear to interfere with normal emotional development. These emotionally immature children often exhibit emotions that are inappropriate or disproportional to the situation. Overly invested parents protect their children from their own emotions in the mistaken belief that emotions will hurt their children's ultimate success. Because these children have not been allowed to experience emotions, they have little awareness or understanding of what they are feeling. Unless you can provide your child with emotional "training," your child will not be able to respond to the challenges of life in healthy and mature ways.

Until children become involved in an achievement activity, many parents devote most of their energy to their children's emotional development (in addition to their physical and intellectual development). Parents normally provide their children with opportunities that allow them to acquire experience with emotions and to gain emotional maturity. Returning to the person-as-house metaphor, these experiences enable children to build strong and resilient houses that can stand up to the most inclement weather.

However, parents who lose perspective on their child's achievement activities seem to abandon the construction of his emotional self. Parents can become so focused on facilitating their child's development in his achievement area that they stop paying attention to his emotional development. Their child's house is in danger of never being completed and their child will be unable to protect himself from life's elements. "As soon as the child is regarded as a possession for which one has a particular goal, as soon as one exerts control over him, his vital growth will be violently interrupted," observes Alice Miller.

The children of overinvested parents lack the basic tools of emotional life that will allow them to become professionally and socially successful and happy in adulthood. In a very real sense, they are children inside adult bodies and their lack of emotional maturity will inhibit all aspects of their adult lives.

RED FLAGS

Parents don't intentionally cause their children to remain emotionally immature. Parents' efforts that lead to emotional immaturity—though often misguided—are usually grounded in their love for their children and their desire for their children to be happy and pain-free. Parents are naturally motivated to protect their children from pain. Sheltering their children from emotional harm is an expression of this wish to safeguard them. When parents see their children in pain, they want to "kiss it and make it better." Unfortunately, parents don't realize that when it comes to emotional pain, they may actually be making it worse.

Parents want their children to become successful. By directing the energy they put into their children's development toward their achievement efforts, parents believe they are increasing their children's chances of success. But parents need to understand that by inhibiting their children's emotional experiences, they are neglecting an essential ingredient in their children's success.

Parents may also unwittingly encourage emotional immaturity with their own emotional reactions. As significant role models, how you respond to frustration and anger will influence how your child learns to react to his or her own emotions. When parents express their emotions in an unhealthy and destructive way, they are communicating to their children that that reaction is appropriate.

Parents may interfere with their children's emotional development because they have yet to come to grips with their own emotional lives. Having not yet understood their own emotions, they have difficulty responding to the emotions that their children experience. By protecting their children from emotions, some parents may also be protecting themselves.

Certainly, children are expected to act like children for much of their childhood. However, as they enter and move through adolescence, there should be a decrease in childish behavior and an increase in adult behavior. Children who continue to demonstrate childish attitudes, perceptions, reactions, and emotions are in danger of ingraining such behavior so deeply that they never replace it with appropriate adult behavior.

Much of childhood is devoted to preparing children for adulthood. A goal of childhood is to teach your child what he needs to know to be a successful and happy adult. To that end, you will need to clearly understand what separates children from adults so you can assist your child in making that transition as quickly and smoothly as possible.

RED FLAG #1: IMMATURE ATTITUDES

The life of a child is one of self-absorption and immediate gratification. From an early age, your child is the center of your universe and demands much of your attention so her needs can be met. If the constant attention you gave your child as an infant continues into early childhood, she may develop an *egocentrism*, believing that all of her needs will be satisfied on demand. Attitudes such as "The world revolves around me," "I want it," and "I want it NOW" will develop if you allow your child to believe that her needs and wishes take precedence over everyone else's needs. If you always respond to your child's demands without delay or thought, she will have a great deal of difficulty growing out of her "I am the center of the universe" attitude.

Does it appear that your child is always in control, that she, rather than you, runs the show? Does your child believe that she can always get what she wants? If your child cannot get something herself, do you give it to her immediately? If your child can't get it right away, will she do whatever she must to get it—complain, cry, or whine—until she wears you down and you give in?

Your child is driven to *receive love and approval* from you and others. To get the love she needs, your child may come to think that she "must please everyone" and that she "must be liked by everyone." By pleasing others, your child may believe that she will receive the love she needs to feel good about herself. Unfortunately, it is impossible to please everyone, so your child will never receive all the love she thinks she needs and will end up disappointed. "The need for universal acceptance is instilled in our children at an early age. This prevents them from forming their own concept of self-respect, and instead substitutes a fear of being unloved," notes Dr. Stanley Krippner.

If your child becomes overly dependent on others to have his needs met and to feel loved, he can develop unhealthy perceptions about the relationship between achievement and being loved. When attempting to succeed in his achievement activity, he will be hindered by the belief that "I must be successful or I won't be loved" or "If I fail, I am not worthy of love." These beliefs will inhibit his ability to achieve to his highest level, to find satisfaction in his efforts, and to be happy.

Absolutism is another common quality of emotionally immature children, in which they view the world as black and white: They are either having their needs met or not, they are being loved or not, they are perfect or not, they either succeed or they fail. For example, if your child wants a whole bag of cookies and refuses any when you offer him only a few. Your child has created an inflexible world that offers her little margin for error in any aspect of her life. This rigidity will limit your child in her options—she never has more than two—and will trap her in an internal world that conflicts with the uncertain and nuanced nature of the real world.

RED FLAG #2: IMMATURE REACTIONS TO
DISAPPOINTMENT

Disappointment is perhaps the most immediate negative emotion children experience after a perceived failure. Disappointment involves the
feelings of thwarted desire, loss, and discouragement when children fail
to fulfill their hopes and expectations—or those of others. Children are
going to feel disappointment when they don't achieve their goals or
believe they have let you down. Disappointment is a natural response
to failure, but emotionally immature children often react to their disappointment in ways that increase the likelihood of more failure and
disappointment. Immature children who are faced with disappointment reduce their effort, give up easily, or quit altogether. This reaction
to disappointment can cause them to feel incompetent and inadequate,
which, if persistent, will lower their self-esteem. Though some disappointment following failure is normal, emotionally immature children
mope around the house, look downtrodden, and feel sorry for themselves for far longer than they should.

Your natural tendency when you see your child feeling bad is to try
to make him feel better. Mollifying your child with excessive expressions of affection or by buying him gifts, though it may bring your
child some immediate relief and make you feel better, does more harm
than good. Writes Allison Armstrong: "Many parents today try too hard
to smooth away life's rough edges in the hopes of keeping disappointment at bay. . . . Often these children are in college before they suffer
a major disappointment. . . . Children with no experience solving life's
little setbacks have a much harder time when they're faced with the big
ones." Placating your child doesn't allow him to understand his disappointment and figure out how to put it behind him. Your child needs
to be able to just sit with his disappointment and ask "Why do I feel
so bad?" and "What can I do to get over feeling this way?" Pacifying
your child may also communicate to him that you don't think he is
capable of handling and overcoming the setback. Your reaction will

only interfere with your child's ability to surmount future obstacles and it will make disappointment more painful in the future.

RED FLAG #3: IMMATURE REACTIONS TO FRUSTRATION

One of the best ways to judge your child's emotional maturity is to see how she responds when she doesn't get her way. How does your young child behave when she experiences frustration, such as when she wants something to drink but you are talking on the telephone (for a reasonable interval) or when she is losing at a game with a friend. Red flags of children's reactions to frustration include impatience and temper tantrums if their needs aren't met immediately.

Emotionally immature children typically experience strong negative emotions—frustration and anger—when they don't get their way because they never learned to effectively handle not having their needs met. Immature children don't learn patience or alternative ways of managing their frustration or satisfying their needs. They react impulsively, striking out in anger at the person who is not satisfying their needs. Immature children often throw temper tantrums to release their anger. They also whine, cajole, nag, and needle in an attempt to manipulate their parents into giving them what they want.

If you are the parent of an emotionally immature child, the chances are you have already fallen into the trap of inadvertently keeping your child from learning to tolerate frustration. When you provide him with immediate gratification and give in to his needs and demands too quickly, your child won't be able to experience enough frustration to figure out what the feeling is, what causes it, and to begin to develop other solutions for his frustration: "I can ask someone else to get me a glass of water."

Without realizing it, this immaturity becomes ingrained as emotional reactions that will act as a significant obstacle to your child in adulthood. Those immature emotional reactions to frustration that might work in childhood—you give your child what she wants just to quiet her—will cause the opposite reaction in adulthood. Adults don't like to meet the needs of emotionally immature adults. Think of how an airline gate agent responds to an irate traveler as compared to a calm and cooperative flyer.

RED FLAG #4: IMMATURE ANGER

A noticeable way in which emotionally immature children distinguish themselves is how they deal with their anger. Their anger is usually inappropriate and out of proportion to the situation. At the heart of this anger lies a child's learned belief that he should get what he wants when he wants it. When this belief confronts reality, his frustration has no appropriate next place to go. Scream louder! No response? Scream even louder. Your child wants a snack before dinner, but you know that if you give it to him he won't want to eat his dinner. Your refusal frustrates him and then angers him because you won't relent and give in to his wants.

Expressing anger immaturely usually hurts a child When your child communicates with anger, the message that is conveyed is the negativity and intensity of the emotions. This message, not the real message, is the one which you will be reacting to. The actual message that your child is trying to communicate—that he's not getting his needs met—is lost in the anger and he is less likely to have you hear and respond to his true message.

The most common way emotionally immature children deal with their anger is by expressing it openly to you. This anger is typically uncontrolled, unfocused, and unrelenting. It acts as an immediate emotional release for pent-up frustration. Unfortunately, parents often react to their child's anger with anger of their own. When you model anger, your and your child's mutual expressions of anger feed on each other, creating a vicious cycle of conflict and ill feelings on both sides. For example: Your child gets angry at you for not giving him what he wants and then you lash out at him because he won't stop nagging you. The end result is that both you and your child feel bad, your feelings toward each other are diminished (at least temporarily), and you are unable to resolve the problem that led to your child's anger in the first place.

If a child's anger has been punished severely in the past, she may be afraid to express it openly and she may feel compelled to suppress it out of fear of reprisal. Children may turn that anger inward and punish themselves with low self-esteem, perfectionism, depression, or anxiety. They may also express their anger outwardly in subtle ways in the form of loss of motivation, self-defeating behavior, and passive-aggressive behavior as a way to get back at you for not responding to their needs.

Anger is a normal and healthy part of growing up and a necessary part of the separation process that occurs between you and your child. This anger is also an important part of the emotional maturation process. However, a child's persistent anger toward her parents, particularly when focused on one area, such as an achievement activity, can harm the parent-child relationship. For example: A child is angry at her parents for forcing her to take dance lessons because she wants to be with her friends playing soccer instead. To get back at her parents, she disrupts dance classes and intentionally forgets her choreography in the dance school's recital. Her parents express their embarrassment at her behavior with anger and distance. This response both hurts and angers her and further impels her to resist her parents, which hurts their relationship even more.

RED FLAG #5: EMOTIONAL OVERPROTECTION

One of the most common causes of emotional immaturity in children is parents' protecting their children from experiencing their own emotions. These parents do everything they can to make sure that their child doesn't feel emotions, especially so-called bad emotions, such as frustration, anger, and sadness. For example, after a poor grade on a test, a mother might do everything she can to placate, cover up, or distract her son from feeling bad in the misguided belief that it will make him happier.

Not only do some parents protect their children from potential emotional disturbance, but they also bend over backward to cater to their child's needs in the hopes of keeping him happy. They avoid situations that might cause their child to feel bad. Parents become slaves to their child's emotions.

But protecting your child from deeply experiencing her own emotions produces the opposite effect. Without experiencing and understanding her feelings, your child will never learn how to positively handle the many emotional challenges she will face as she progresses through childhood and into adulthood.

Another unintended consequence of emotional overprotection occurs if you give your child the message that he is too fragile to deal with problems on his own. "If children believe they can't manage setbacks, chances are they'll avoid striving for things they want," suggests family therapist Richard Sugarman. The inability to experience and understand negative emotions will make it impossible for your child to fully feel and appreciate positive emotions. Like two sides of the same coin, your child cannot experience one side of his emotions without also experiencing the other side.

RED FLAG #6: ASSUMING EMOTIONAL MATURITY

Assumptions that parents make about their children who are physically mature or far ahead of other children in their achievement activity can also lead to slowed emotional development. Some adolescents mature physically much earlier than their peers. These teenagers look and usually act very much like adults. Parents can easily forget that their child still experiences emotions as a child.

Similar assumptions can arise with children who are advanced in their achievement development. Parents may assume that because their child is so mature in her achievement activity—whether intellectual, technical, or physical—she must also be emotionally mature. Former tennis prodigy Jennifer Capriati exemplifies these kinds of assumptions. At thirteen years of age, Jennifer had the physical maturity of a young woman and was competing successfully against the best women tennis players in the world. Her parents, coaches, other players, and the media all assumed that she was also emotionally mature, even though she was only thirteen and had led a sheltered life. Because of this assumption, demands appropriate for an adult were placed on her, including high expectations of winning, making a great deal of money, supporting her family, making commercial endorsements, and shining in the spotlight of media attention.

Everyone, including perhaps Jennifer, assumed that she had the emotional tools to handle the pressures placed on her. Unfortunately, time and painful experience proved these assumptions to be wrong. Within a few years, Jennifer dropped out of tennis and had drug problems and encounters with the law. Fortunately, there appears to be a happy ending to this story, or at least a happy continuation. After several years away from the game and time for considerable introspection and growing up, Jennifer has returned to tennis a more mature and perhaps wary young woman with a healthier perspective on her life and tennis career. Also, the tremendous talent that she demonstrated ten years ago has reemerged, most recently with victories in the 2001 Australian and French Opens. "This time I'm going to know when it gets to be too much or when I don't feel comfortable. This time, I'm the one in control," says Capriati.

RED FLAG #7: NO EMOTIONS

I have worked with families in which normal expression of emotion was largely nonexistent. It's not that family members didn't just express negative emotions, it's that they didn't express *any* emotions. The parents in these families had often been raised in emotionally detached families themselves and never came to grips with their own emotional lives. They simply passed on this emotional detachment to their children without realizing it. John Gottman, Lynn Katz, and Carole Hooven, the authors of *Meta-Emotion*, call this "emotional dismissing," in which experiencing and discussing emotions are taboo within a family.

This absence of emotions in a family—whether anger, sadness, or joy—can be as harmful to a child as an overwhelming expression of negative emotions can be in other families. Without the expression of emotions, children will not feel loved—love must be clearly expressed— and many of the red flags that we have seen throughout this book will develop. If you are unable to clearly express your love for your child, he will never be able to experience true happiness. Your child will never learn the value and importance of happiness in his life. Without the opportunity to receive or express important emotions, your child will not have the opportunity to experience and develop his own emotional amplitude, and he will have no chance to reach emotional maturity.

Another painful by-product of children who grow up in a "cold" family is that they develop beliefs that emotions are not acceptable and, even worse, that emotions are signs of weakness. Your child will build up internal walls to keep her emotions in check; she simply will not express strong emotions of any kind. Unfortunately, even though a child might not express emotions, she still feels them, particularly negative emotions such as frustration, anger, and sadness. If you have a cold family, your child will have learned that every time she feels these emotions, she must push them down, but they will continue to boil inside of her unresolved. Children from cold families are often sullen, withdrawn, and depressed, and chances are that this depression will not be diagnosed or treated. These "cold" children grow up to be unhappy, "emotionally autistic" adults who struggle in every facet of their lives because they lack the capacity to feel and experience their emotions in a healthy way.

I worked with a young professional athlete, Kyra, who grew up in just such a family. Her parents showed no real love or affection for her. They provided her with every nonemotional kind of resource, and often said to Kyra, "Isn't that enough?" Whenever she reached out emotionally or tried to talk to them about what she was feeling, they would change the subject or end the conversation. Kyra learned to shut all of her emotions inside of her. She learned never to express emotions in front of her parents or to ask for emotions from them. This emotional habit transferred to all of her relationships. Kyra grew up to become a very successful athlete, but as she entered her early twenties she began to realize how truly unhappy she was. While recovering from an injury that kept her away from her sport for an extended period, Kyra was finally ready to face her pain. During one of our first sessions, she was describing how she never felt loved by her parents. I was struck by the absolute absence of emotions on her part as these difficult words came out. The disconnect between the emotions of her words and the lack of emotions behind her words was stunning. I asked her what she was feeling at the time and she said matter-of-factly, "I don't feel anything."

After several months of hard work on Kyra's part, I began to see cracks in her armor; watery eyes, sad face, signs of emotions that were consistent with her painful words. Then one day Kyra's emotional floodgates opened and, as she spoke about her parents, she cried, as she put it, "like I was releasing twenty years of pain." This experience was the turning point for Kyra as she has discovered her emotions and, with increasing frequency, her happiness.

EMOTIONAL MATURITY

You now have an understanding of some of the attitudes, perceptions, and reactions that are characteristic of emotionally immature children. You also now know what actions parents take that can slow down their children's emotional development. Now we can look at what qualities are associated with emotionally mature adults and what it takes to foster the development of these emotionally mature qualities in children.

MATURE ATTITUDES

The life of an adult is one of delayed gratification and awareness of others. As children mature emotionally, they need to understand that the world does not revolve around them and that their needs will not be met in the same way as when they were younger. You can show your child that others have needs too and that he has to take responsibility not only for himself, but also for others. For example, if you are helping one of your children and your other child wants something, you can point out that you are busy and that you will help him as soon as you are finished. To reduce his frustration and impatience, you can show him that he can use this waiting period by finding him something to do until you are free. "I'm going to give Billy a bath now. Would you like to make a beautiful picture for me? You have only fifteen minutes!"

Emotionally mature children lose their egocentrism and understand that their needs will not always be met and that they will not always get what they want. In a sense, adults develop a more realistic view of the world and their importance in it. For example, adults may want something, but if they have matured appropriately they will be able to say, "If I can't have it now, maybe I can get it later" and "I want it, but if I can't have it, I can accept that." As children assume these adult attitudes they learn to reduce their inevitable frustration when they don't receive immediate gratification. They will be learning how to respond more reasonably to the uncertainties of the adult world.

You can teach your child that she cannot always be in control and that there will be times when she can do nothing about her circumstances. She must simply *accept* them. Your child needs to learn that the only thing she can control is herself and, specifically, her attitude toward what life gives her. Guiding your child through these times by offering a positive and calming perspective can encourage this understanding. You can show your child what she can focus on and gain control of to improve her situation. For example, if your child is feeling frustrated and helpless in a class because she can't seem to figure out the subject matter, you can help her understand why she is having difficulties and assist her in finding a solution. You could encourage her to ask the teacher for help or you could guide her in solving the problem. If your child is able to do this successfully, she will have taken a great leap forward in learning how to resolve negative emotions and gain control of a situation.

Maturing children also learn that they will not always be able to count on you to meet their needs. Instead, they will need to take responsibility for their own needs. For example, instead of immediately helping your child with a computer problem, ask him to spend ten minutes looking for a solution on his own. You can remind him of the problem-solving tools you showed him before and have him try to break the problem down into smaller sections or to try a different approach. If the problem is to find the source of a famous quote on the Internet, you could suggest that he try a different search engine or type in different wording. If he is still unable to solve the problem, rather than fixing it yourself—which may be the fastest and easiest thing to do— ask him questions and guide him toward finding the answer himself. If you don't know the answer, explain to him your own step-by-step process as you try to solve the problem with him.

A fundamental change that separates adults from children and exemplifies emotional maturity is the ability to gain self-validation instead of being dependent on others for how they feel about themselves. For your child to make the healthy transition to emotional maturity, she needs to learn to give self-love and support her own sense of self-worth.

Of course, everyone needs some validation from others, but emotionally mature children discover that they don't need to gain love and affirmation from everyone. Rather, they can be more selective in whom they please and by whom they must be liked. They develop attitudes such as "I only need to please those people who are important to me" and "It's okay if not everyone likes me."

Unlike the rigid absolutism that is common with emotionally immature children, emotional maturity provides children with a world made up of many shades of gray. Your emotionally mature child can view the world in degrees—she can have some of her needs met, she can be liked to varying degrees by different people, she will make some mistakes, she will both succeed and fail along the path of achievement—and she can find satisfaction and happiness in these various shades of gray.

This "gray thinking" creates a fluid world that enables your child to choose from numerous options and gives him many opportunities to learn and grow. This flexibility enables your emotionally mature child to adapt to the uncertain, ambiguous, and ever-changing nature of the adult world. You can encourage gray thinking by looking for situations in which your child is seeing something in black and white and point out that more than two options exist from which he can choose. For example: Your child didn't make the "A" soccer team and wants to quit because she's not any good. You can point out that she did make the "B" team, which many girls didn't make, and that if she works hard to improve this year, maybe she can make the "A" team next year.

Emotionally mature children also have healthy attitudes about achievement. Because they have the ability to validate themselves, they are able to place success and failure in perspective and at a proper distance from a place in which failure might be a threat to their self-esteem. Attitudes such as "I want to do my best" and "It's okay for me to fail sometimes" allow children to see achievement as a challenge worth pursuing. Every recommendation in this book is aimed at developing this positive attitude toward achievement in your child.

MATURE REACTIONS TO DISAPPOINTMENT

Disappointment is a normal, though difficult, part of childhood. Your child will inevitably experience disappointment in school, sports, the arts, and friendships. How your child learns to respond to disappointment will determine its impact on her future achievement and happiness. You can teach your child to see stumbling blocks as opportunities to improve and grow. Offering your child a different perspective on her disappointment—"I know it feels bad right now, but what can you learn from it?"—gives her tools she can use to avoid or minimize her disappointment in the future, and to turn the obstacles to her advantage.

After "falling off the horse," your child will naturally feel a brief period of letdown, but then you must encourage her to pick herself up and get back on the horse. By staying positive and enthusiastic, you can show your child another, better way of feeling in response to failure and guide her in finding a way to overcome her setback and return to her path of achievement. Rather than the disappointment disheartening your child and causing her to feel bad about herself, you can help your child use the experience to affirm her capabilities by showing herself that she can conquer her past failures. For example, if your child isn't improving as fast as she wants on her musical instrument, you can tell her how common it is for musicians to reach plateaus in their playing and how these "flat spots" in their progress are necessary and usually a prelude to another period of improvement. You can also encourage her to keep working hard and express your confidence that her progress will continue.

Your attitude toward your child's inevitable disappointments will influence how he responds to life's obstacles. You should view your child's disappointments as training for adulthood. "Childhood disappointment is actually a practice lap on the course to adulthood. If you run interference whenever disappointment threatens, you're setting kids up to run a marathon without ever letting them train for it," adds Allison Armstrong. You must convey to your child that failure and disappointment are a part of life and what matters is how they react to them. You can also give your child a boost by showing him that you believe in him, that he should have faith in himself, and that if he keeps trying, he will probably reach his goals: "Life is full of setbacks and disappointment, but if you keep working hard, I know you can do it."

Allison Armstrong offers the following suggestions on how to respond to your child's disappointments: Don't distort the situation to make your child feel better. Allow her to express her feelings about the setback and offer a perspective that may give her another way of looking at it. Support your child, but don't give her a consolation prize. Be realistic about your child's capabilities. Give her feedback that considers her true abilities. Help your child find ways to surmount the causes of her difficulties. Finally, tell your child that she will survive these disappointments and will achieve her goals if she keeps trying hard.

MATURE REACTIONS TO FRUSTRATION

An emotionally mature child responds to frustration in ways that resolve the frustration and that will most likely lead to getting at least some of her needs met at some point. This maturity allows your child to step back from the immediate frustration at not getting what she wants and to think clearly about how she can best get her needs met.

Children who learn to delay gratification are confident, assertive, and capable of dealing constructively with frustration. They are also self-motivated, persist in the face of obstacles, and are less likely to crumble under the weight of stress. These children are also outstanding students who demonstrate the qualities associated with being a successful achiever.

How your child deals with frustration is influenced by how you react to it. If you model an unhealthy response to the frustration you experience in your life—with anger or impatience—your child may learn that this is an appropriate way to deal with frustration. If you are calm, positive, and look for solutions when you get frustrated, your child will likely adopt this approach to frustration.

How you respond to your child's frustration will also affect how she learns to deal with her frustration. If you become angry and direct your irritation at your child, her frustration may escalate and expand into other harmful emotions that further keep your child from getting her needs met. If you respond to your child's frustration by asking her in a soothing voice what she is frustrated about and discuss how you want to help her deal with it, then she will likely calm down and follow your lead in looking for a solution to her frustration.

This capacity starts with your child's developing a healthy perspective about his unmet needs. You can teach your child that whether his needs are satisfied or not is not a reflection of whether you love him or of his value as a person. Thus, your child's unmet needs do not pose a threat to him. An emotionally mature child perceives a failure as a challenge that he can overcome with patience and positive action, and enables him to respond to these situations in a more constructive way.

With the threat to his self-esteem removed, your emotionally mature child is able to accept the situation for what it is—he's not readily going to get what he wants—and he can then consider his options rather than dwelling on what he can't have. By doing so, your child lets go of those things over which he has no control and focuses on what he can do something about. Your emotionally mature child has learned to confront a situation, instead of treating it like a threat to be avoided. He also realizes that, if he is going to ultimately have his needs met, he will have to rely on himself for finding resolution to his needs.

You can teach your child to engage in a deliberate process in which her goal is to look for solutions to her present situation. If your child does experience some frustration and disappointment, she will have the maturity to talk herself out of her negative feelings and redirect her energy in a more positive way. Teaching your child to engage in gray thinking will allow her to consider varying degrees of getting what she wants rather than persisting futilely in trying to get all of her needs met. Emotionally mature children realize that if they persevere in their efforts, in time, they will achieve their goals and have their needs met. For example: Your child wants a new bike, but the one he has already is perfectly fine. You, reasonably, don't think it's appropriate to buy him a new bike at this time. To encourage his responding in a healthy way to the frustration at not getting what he wants, you can ask him to think of other ways that he can get a new bike if he really wants it that strongly. He responds with the idea that he could do extra work around the house and earn the money to buy the bike himself. To support and reward his initiative, you may even offer to split the cost with him. Or your child is frustrated and depressed because he didn't achieve his goal of finishing in the top three of a gymnastics competition and he says that he feels like a total loser. You can point out that his scores and placings were much improved over the same meet last year, that he nailed two skills with which he had been struggling, and that his coach said that if he continues to train hard, he is right on track for the upcoming state competition. In both instances, showing your child "gray" ways of looking at his experiences enable him to view his experiences more positively, and he sees that he has control over those experiences that previously seemed out of his control.

According to Ross W. Greene, the author of *The Explosive Child*, you can teach your child better ways of managing her frustration. You can reduce the conflict between yourself and your frustrated child. You can anticipate situations in which your child is likely to become frustrated. You can focus less on reward and punishment of behavior. Finally, you can emphasize communication and collaborative problem-solving.

MATURE ANGER

Of course, even emotionally mature people get angry. It's a normal and healthy part of being human. But what separates adults from children is how they react to their anger and how they express it. Emotionally immature children are consumed by and lose control of their anger. Emotionally mature children are able to maintain control of the anger and redirect the negative energy in a positive direction that provides resolution to the problem that led to the anger.

Research by Case Western Reserve University psychologists Diana

Tice and Roy Baumeister revealed that venting anger, contrary to dissipating it, actually heightens and prolongs it. They found that a much more effective approach was to calm down and then seek a solution with the person or situation that caused the anger. Notes Aristotle: "Anyone can become angry—that is easy. But to be angry with the right person, to the right degree, at the right time, for the right purpose, and in the right way—this is not easy."

Emotionally mature children's greatest asset when they experience anger is that they have the control to avoid being consumed by it. Instead, they are able to stay detached from it enough to direct it in a constructive way. Their overriding goal needs to be to find a solution that is in their best interests instead of just letting out their anger. Also, because they understand gray thinking, they're not compelled to try to "win" at all costs. Rather, they appreciate the value of compromise—it is better to have some of their needs met than none at all—and look for "win-win" results where they get some of their needs met and resolution occurs to the satisfaction of everyone involved.

Unlike childish anger, emotionally mature anger is appropriate to the magnitude of the perceived offense. Thus, the situation that causes the anger is kept in perspective by your child. Instead of reacting impulsively and often escalating the problem, your emotionally mature child is able to examine its cause, consider his options in how to react, and choose the best course of action. Emotionally mature children learn to express their emotions in ways that resolve their immediate emotional needs—communicate and relieve their anger—and that leads to a long-term solution of the cause of the anger.

You can help your child understand that the message she communicates by expressing her anger will determine the ultimate resolution of the cause of the anger. When, for example, your child is angry at you, she needs you to hear the substance of the message, not just the emotional content. By doing so, you will understand that your child is angry and why she is angry. With this information and the way it was conveyed, you will hear the message, be open to it, and want to respond positively to the message. Your response, in turn, encourages your child to express her anger in healthy and constructive ways.

You can also offer your child alternatives to venting when he gets angry. If you can stop your child's anger early, before it has reached "critical mass" and fully consumes him, you have a chance to redirect it in a healthier way. For example, you can teach your child the "count to ten" or "take a break" methods, where you ask him to go away for a short time and then return when he is more composed. When your child loses control—which is inevitable from time to time—you can show him that you are listening, want to help solve the problem, and have him tell you the problem. Your response will have a quieting effect on him and help him regain control of his anger. Your goal is to enable your child to internalize these tools of anger management so he doesn't need you to remind him:

"You seem awfully angry, Josh."

"I am."

"What can you do first?"

"Count to ten."

"Thanks. While you do that, I'll be waiting patiently."

EMOTIONALLY MATURE PARENTS

Many children are slow to develop emotionally because one or both of their parents are emotionally immature. For example, when a child throws a tantrum because he doesn't get what he wants, his emotionally immature father may react with a tantrum of his own. This vicious cycle soon escalates into an anger-filled shouting match that creates more anger in both the child and his father. This reaction not only doesn't solve the immediate problem, but it also teaches the child that emotionally immature anger is a way adults deal with conflict too, which validates his own use of anger.

Your child can learn her emotional habits from you by watching how you react in emotional situations. Yet you may have your own emotional habits that you learned as a child that may have persisted into your adult life. If you have unhealthy emotional habits, you will likely communicate those habits to your child either directly— "You can't trust anyone"—or indirectly, through modeling of your reactions to emotional situations. For example, if a child wanders a short way from her mother and her mother reacts with fear (because she grew up believing the world was a dangerous place), her daughter may also develop this belief. If her mother's reaction occurs often, her daughter may ingrain the same belief and develop a threat reaction to exploration and risk. This emotional habit may continue throughout her life and cause her to fear and avoid exploration and risk as an adult.

Emotionally mature children most often have emotionally mature parents. As the adult, you must act like one and show your child how to act like one as well. You need to stay calm, not express inappropriate anger at your child, set clear boundaries, and stand your ground. This response acts as a calming influence for your angry child and helps him to direct his anger in a more productive way. It also models a calm and composed approach to anger that your child can internalize and use to his benefit in the future.

Maintaining emotional control is not easy when raising a child. You will at times be tired and stressed, and your child's behavior—perhaps her incessant whining for something she wants—may cause you to become frustrated and react with anger. Occasional expressions of anger will do little harm. However, if your child is exposed to anger regularly—especially if the anger is directed toward her—the hurt your child feels from your anger and the "okayness" of using anger will be internalized and your child will learn to use casual and frequent anger herself.

Every time you or your child experiences emotions, particularly when they are negative, you have an opportunity to teach your child a valuable lesson. If you respond to your emotions in a constructive way or you help your child react to his emotions beneficially, the lesson will foster his emotional growth and his evolving emotional maturity will serve him well as he progresses toward adulthood. Dr. Wayne Dyer writes that "each person must learn from the very beginning that his inner world belongs to him only, and that everything he thinks, feels, and ultimately does as a human being is within his power to control. This is the ultimate freedom that you can give your children: *the knowledge and belief that they can control their own inner worlds.*"

DON'T FORGET THE POSITIVE EMOTIONS

While the majority of Part III focuses on negative emotions and how you can teach your child to overcome them, showing your child positive emotions and how they can contribute to success and happiness is also of great importance. An unfortunate aspect of parents who express strong negative emotions and parents who are unemotional is that they often don't express positive emotions. Expressing positive emotions is an incredible gift you can give your child. Seeing, feeling, and expressing positive emotions are important because they communicate to your child what to seek out and look forward to. Love, excitement, joy, enthusiasm, contentment, and happiness are the emotions your child deserves to experience and are the rewards for her efforts in all aspects of her life.

Children learn about positive emotions by seeing you express them and being allowed to feel positive emotions themselves. When you are happy, show it. When you are excited about something, share it with your child. When you thoroughly enjoy something you are doing, tell your child why. When you feel contented, describe the feeling to your child. Most important, when you are with your child, express your love in any way you can.

Just as experiencing and being guided through negative emotions helps your child gain emotional maturity, so too does feeling and learning about positive emotions. Whenever you are with your child, you have an opportunity to create positive emotions, express positive emotions, share positive emotions, and talk about the positive emotions that each of you feels. You can also help your child identify what experiences, activities, and people produce these emotions. These opportunities will guide your child in learning how to create positive emotions on her own.

KEYS TO EMOTIONAL MATURITY

1. *Confidence.* A sense of control and mastery of one's body, behavior, and world; the child's sense that he is more likely than not to succeed at what he undertakes, and that adults will be helpful.
2. *Curiosity.* The sense that finding out about things is positive and leads to pleasure.
3. *Intentionality.* The wish and capacity to have an impact, and to act upon that with persistence. This is related to a sense of competence, of being effective.
4. *Self-control.* The ability to modulate and control one's own actions in age-appropriate ways: a sense of inner control.
5. *Relatedness.* The ability to engage with others based on the sense of being understood by and understanding others.
6. *Capacity to communicate.* The wish and ability to verbally exchange ideas, feelings, and concepts with others. This is related to a sense of trust in others and of pleasure in engaging with others, including adults.
7. *Cooperativeness.* The ability to balance one's own needs with those of others in a group activity.

Goleman, D. (1995). *Emotional intelligence.* New York: Bantam.

CHAPTER 9

What Can I Do?
Victim vs. Master

Does your child seem to be at the mercy of her emotions? Does your child have the capacity to change her emotions when those emotions begin to interfere with achievement and her happiness? Is your child an emotional victim or an emotional master? The culmination of your work in guiding the essential development of your child as a successful achiever occurs in helping your child develop emotional mastery.

EMOTIONAL HABITS

Much of growing up involves your child's developing habits that he uses in school, other achievement efforts, extracurricular activities, and relationships as he proceeds through childhood and into adulthood. Emotional habits are learned ways of responding to situations emotionally. Habits that your child develops include characteristic ways in which he responds to the world, such as his motivation in school; how friendly he is to people; how he deals with family conflict; and the ways that he responds to situations that may cause disappointment, frustration, anger, sadness, and other emotions. These emotional habits develop through early experiences in situations that elicit emotional reactions. Most emotional responses can be categorized as either threat reactions or challenge reactions. For example: A boy is chastised by his mother for playing poorly in his Little League baseball games. He experiences anxiety every time he plays and this reaction becomes an emotional habit that is expressed whenever he feels pressure to succeed. Or a girl is supported and encouraged by her parents for her hard work before her monthly piano recitals, in which she usually performs well. Her parents share her excitement regardless of how she plays. She is always excited during the week before her recitals and this response becomes an emotional habit that generalizes to other pressure situations in her life.

Ideally, emotional habits should facilitate achievement and happiness, and enable your child to evolve into a mature adult. Positive emotional habits include responding well to adversity, being able to let go of disappointment and frustration, and the ability to manage anger and sadness constructively. You can foster the emergence of healthy emotional habits by exposing your child to situations that will produce emotional reactions, allow your child to experience the emotions, and then provide your child with the tools to master the situations and the accompanying emotions.

Children can develop unhealthy emotional habits that neither feel good nor help them achieve their goals. For example: A child feels that receiving love from his parents depends on how well he does in school. He develops a threat reaction to achievement. If this conditional love persists, he will develop an emotional habit of resentment and anger toward his parents and feel fear whenever he takes a test. This emotional habit then will emerge whenever he is faced with any situation in which he is being evaluated in the future. This threat reaction, though clearly not beneficial, will continue to hurt his achievement efforts and his happiness well into adulthood. Moreover, as this boy grows up and this emotional habit continues to arise, he will be at a loss to understand why he often feels so bad.

A question you may ask is "Why would my child adopt emotional habits that are unhealthy and that don't serve him well?" Children at an early age are not rational beings. They lack the cognitive capabilities, experience, and perspective to think through experiences and decide the best way to deal with them. Instead, children are intuitive beings whose primary drive is to protect themselves from harm. Because, at an early age, children lack the capacity to think deliberately, they are not yet capable of choosing how they should respond to an emotional situation. They simply react automatically in the way that will best protect them from the immediate perceived threat. Notes New York University neuroscientist Joseph LeDoux: "Some emotional reactions and emotional memories can be formed without any conscious, cognitive participation at all."

Emotional habits that develop at an early age are usually functional in some way at the time they are first experienced, having some protective value to children. For example: A mother was angry at her son when he did poorly on a school test. To reduce his worry that she would stay angry at him and wouldn't love him if he continued to do poorly, the boy worked extra hard on that subject before the next test. Now if he does poorly on a test, he berates himself to show his mother that he knows he is bad and that it won't happen again. This emotional response protects him from having to face his mother's anger and shields him from feeling fear of losing his mother's love. Because his mother's reaction to poor test scores persists, his emotional response will eventually become an emotional habit in response to the threat of disapproval and loss of his mother's love.

Unfortunately, many habits that at one time served a useful purpose—they can protect your child from some perceived threat—ultimately prove to inhibit her as she moves toward adulthood. These emotional habits, which were helpful to your child when she was young, will have the opposite effect later in life. Emotional habits learned in childhood are often no longer beneficial to adults, yet your child may continue to engage in these habits because they are so highly ingrained and practiced.

In the instance of the student just mentioned, his emotional habit extended beyond his school experiences and into his athletic efforts as well. He evolved into a perfectionist and a Pleaser who was driven to avoid failure and make his mother unhappy. Though he became quite successful in his professional life, he became an adult who was never truly happy because he would never allow himself to be satisfied with his achievement efforts. He created the same kind of Pleaser relationships with his girlfriends, in which he did everything he could to avoid disappointing and angering them.

EMOTIONAL VICTIMS

Many children grow up as *emotional victims*, believing that they have little control over their emotions and that they can't do anything to gain control. If their emotions hurt them, they just have to accept them because they don't believe they can change their emotions. They possess unhealthy and unproductive emotional habits, their emotions have control over them, and their emotions interfere with their achievement and happiness.

Children who are emotional victims are immature; overly dependent on adults; and feel incompetent, helpless, and generally threatened by the outside world. They are at the mercy of themselves rather than being in their own command. They do not believe they can control or change their inner worlds, so they have no sense of ownership or responsibility for their emotions. Emotional victims do not believe they can control their thoughts, emotions, or actions. They are controlled by whatever emotional habits they developed early in their lives and often act as their own worst enemies by thinking, feeling, and behaving in ways that produce negative emotions and that hinder their achievement and happiness.

Emotional victims are often not "in touch" with their emotional lives. They experience and act on their emotions without a clear sense of what they feel or what is compelling them. For example: A young girl feels anger toward her parents and expresses that anger directly and uncontrollably. What she is really trying to express is that she feels hurt and sad because she believes that her parents don't really love her. Emotional victims come to fear all emotions because they are usually uncomfortable. Emotional victims prefer to lead lives that are safe, predictable, and free of any emotion. Unfortunately, because they avoid negative emotions, they are also not able to fully experience positive emotions, such as excitement, joy, and happiness. So emotional victims become prisoners of their emotions and are unable to escape from their confines.

Emotional victims struggle in their achievement efforts because they view trying to achieve anything as an endeavor that is likely to cause them pain. This threat reaction causes a self-fulfilling prophecy: They expect to fail, they perform poorly, and their failure causes even more pain.

Emotional victims also have difficulties in their relationships. Because they are most concerned with being hurt by others, emotional victims are loath to make themselves vulnerable to the possibility of disappointment and heartbreak. They shut themselves off from all of their emotions, including positive ones such as love, respect, and caring for others. Others sense the emotional inaccessibility of emotional victims and are unwilling to open themselves up to someone who seems to be incapable of reciprocating.

EMOTIONAL MASTERS

If you raise your child to be an emotional master, she will learn that she is in command of her emotions. Your child will be keenly aware of her emotions and will be comfortable experiencing the complete spectrum of emotions, from anger and sadness to excitement and joy. Your child will develop healthy and productive emotional habits that foster her achievement and her happiness. Qualities that Dr. Daniel Goleman associates with emotional mastery include the ability to stay motivated and persist in the face of frustration, to control urges and the need for immediate gratification, to be able to adjust mood, and to keep negative emotions from interfering with the ability to think clearly and act appropriately.

You can develop emotional mastery in your child by encouraging him to experience and understand his emotional life. Your child will learn to recognize what emotions he feels and why he feels them. As your child grows, he will get in touch with and embrace his emotions—both positive and negative—because he knows that his emotions provide richness and depth to his life. Most essential, as an emotional master, your child will learn that he has the ability to alter his emotions in ways that foster his achievement and happiness.

Attributes found in emotional masters include maturity, competence, responsibility, and feeling effectual and challenged. Though children who are emotional masters may realize that they have little control of much in their lives, they believe that they have control over their emotions. This sense of control of their emotions frees emotional masters to take risks, face the inevitable failures of achievement, and experience all that life has to offer.

All of these assets converge to enable emotional masters to be their own best allies. These emotionally mature children have the ability to ensure that the energy that they put into their achievement efforts—and the positive and negative emotions they feel as part of those efforts—help them progress toward their goals. Emotional masters not only reach a high level of achievement, but they also find happiness in the effort itself. They keep their failures in perspective and derive great satisfaction and joy from their pursuit of success.

If you raise your child to be an emotional master, you are giving your child a gift for life that will help her reap immeasurable benefits in all aspects of her life. By being able to fully and accurately experience and express her emotions comfortably and appropriately, your child can embrace an achievement activity with passion and energy. Because an emotional master views achievement as a challenge rather than a threat, your child can respond positively to the numerous obstacles she will face in her achievement efforts and she can use her emotions as tools to reach her achievement goals.

Emotional masters are also capable of developing rich and meaningful relationships because they are confident and at ease with themselves. They are capable of becoming emotionally vulnerable and communicating their emotions to others in a healthy way. Others sense this emotional availability and feel comfortable reciprocating those feelings. Experiencing success in their achievement activities and social lives enables emotional masters to experience the gratification of emotionally enriching lives.

RED FLAGS

Most of the red flags that are described in this book are warning signs of children becoming emotional victims. All of these red flags share a common element: Children are doing things that are not in their own best interests. The most serious red flag of all is when your child thinks, feels, and acts in ways that interfere with her achievement and happiness. Any time your child does things that actually impede rather than foster the attainment of her goals, you should see a large red flag going up the flagpole in your mind, signaling that there may be a problem that needs to be addressed.

A common occurrence for emotional victims is having trouble putting their achievement difficulties behind them and letting go of negative emotions. You should take particular note when your child's negative emotions begin to influence other parts of her life, such as her health, daily habits, relationships, and other achievement activities. For example: Days after a poor flute recital, Denise was still talking about her failure, continually expressing her disappointment. She dwelt on her perceived failure, her negative emotions persisted, and eventually she began to play poorly during her lessons and practice. She began to lose sleep, neglect her appearance, and skip her homework. This inability to leave the past behind has caused Denise to associate playing her flute with feeling bad. This unhealthy attitude has created a fear-based response that has interfered with her subsequent achievement efforts and happiness.

Perhaps the most significant red flag that you should look for in your child is the persistent occurrence of a emotional vicious cycle like the one the flute player got into. This downward spiral of negative emotions—from frustration to anger to panic to despair—is the hallmark of an emotional victim. Once she has experienced the first negative emotions in her achievement efforts, an emotional victim will lack the ability to consciously alter her emotions and stop her destructive descent. Instead, these unhealthy emotional habits can drive an emotional victim into an emotional tailspin that ensures failure in all of her efforts.

RAISING AN EMOTIONAL MASTER

Emotions play perhaps the ultimate role in your child's becoming a successful achiever. Achievement and happiness develop when your child can express every ounce of ability that he possesses in his achievement activity and find the utmost joy in his participation. To commit his fullest ability, your child must first commit himself emotionally. This emotional commitment means risking how he feels about himself—his self-esteem—by accepting the possibility and consequences of failure. If your child can make that commitment, accept failure, and take that risk, he frees himself emotionally from the burden of a fear-based response and allows himself to fully express his ability and seek out success and happiness.

When your child strives to become a successful achiever, she must actually participate in two "games." The *achievement game* is against the achievement activity itself—an academic exam, a chess match, a musical recital, a sports competition—in which your child needs to perform her best to be successful. But in order to win the achievement game, your child must first win the *mental game.* This "game between the ears" can be won only by an emotional master.

PARENTS AS EMOTIONAL MASTERS

A consistent theme of this book is that you are largely responsible for whether your child becomes a successful achiever. You must ensure that you support her development into an emotional master. You need to examine the impact you have on your child—both positive and negative—and identify what you need to change to foster her growth. For example, if you are micromanaging your child's sports participation—reminding her to practice, packing her equipment—you need to step back and allow your child to take on these responsibilities, even if she doesn't always fulfill her own responsibilities. If you are double checking and correcting your child's homework, you should let her double check and correct her own homework. If you are an overly involved parent who is willing to make these changes, by being less intrusive and allowing your child to gain ownership of her achievement efforts, she will likely be more successful and happier, thus meeting your needs as well as her own.

The development of successful achievers is greatly facilitated when you possess the qualities that your child needs to learn. This is no less true for emotional mastery. Your child will learn his most basic emotional habits from you through observation and modeling. If you are an emotional victim, it is likely that, unless your child has other strong role models to influence him, he too will become an emotional victim.

If you as a parent are an emotional master, you have a good start on instilling these positive habits in your child.

Parents who are emotional masters are less likely to become overly invested in their child's achievement activity because they are emotionally mature and can maintain a positive perspective on their child's achievement efforts. Emotionally mature parents are more likely to be aware of their own needs and have the capacity to set them aside from time to time in the best interests of their child. Parents who are emotional masters will not be working at odds with their child's needs, but rather their goals and efforts will be congruent with those of their child. As a result, there won't be a battle of wills over whose needs get satisfied and whose goals get achieved.

Parents who are emotional masters will, from the start, teach their children healthy emotional habits that will foster their growth as successful achievers. These parents will not only "talk the talk" on emotional mastery, but they will also "walk the walk"—they will act as positive role models of what emotional habits their child should learn to become an emotional master and a successful achiever.

One of the strongest recommendations I can make to you to both prevent problems from arising with your child and to respond to difficulties that do occur is to see a psychotherapist. I do not make this suggestion because I think that most parents have significant psychological problems. To the contrary, I have found the vast majority of parents to be mentally healthy and generally positive influences on their children. At the same time, most parents—like most people—carry with them emotional habits from childhood that can interfere with their best-intentioned child-rearing practices.

You may be thinking, "Does everyone need to see a psychotherapist?" Probably not, but a reasonable threshold would be if anything you or your child is doing is hurting your child's achievement efforts, relationships, or happiness. If these red flags describe how you often are with your child, and also remind you of how you were raised, maybe you should get some outside help to make sure they're resolved.

I believe that the primary role of a psychotherapist is to provide understanding and perspective, and to help people remove obstacles that may be getting in their way. A psychotherapist can assist you by offering insights into how you are influencing your child. He or she can examine what emotional habits you are expressing that may be hindering your child's development. The psychotherapist can clarify your investment in your child's achievement activity. Finally, he or she can work with you to remove the barriers that keep you from doing what is best for your child.

PERSPECTIVE OF EMOTIONAL MASTERS

By gaining a healthy perspective on achievement, you are less likely to become overly invested in your child's achievement activities and your self-esteem—and hers—is not likely to become too connected with her successes and failures. This positive perspective can act as the foundation for your child's emotional mastery. Free from the pressures that an emotionally immature parent can place on her, your child will see that a rich emotional life is an essential part of achievement.

You and your child should *care about his achievement efforts*. Some level of ego investment in an achievement activity is normal, healthy, and necessary. Why should your child work hard to reach his goals if he doesn't really care about the activity? With this healthy investment, your child will give his best effort even when things get difficult. When he doesn't achieve what he had hoped, he will naturally be disappointed, but he will not be devastated.

Unfortunately, many parents go beyond this healthy level of caring and raise their child with an unhealthy perspective that emphasizes a simple three-letter word—"too." Any time you and your child care *too* much, the activity has become *too* important, and your child is trying *too* hard, it is a clear sign that your own self-esteem and that of your child are *too* connected to your child's achievement activities.

Emotional masters understand that *ups and downs* are a natural part of the achievement process. This attitude enables emotional masters to stay positive and motivated and keeps them from getting overly upset when they go through a down period. Emotional masters stay focused on giving their best effort and never give up, no matter how bad it gets. They look for the cause of their decline and then find a solution. With this perspective, emotional masters respond positively to down periods by halting the emotional vicious cycle, minimizing the length and depth of the low point, and are able to swing back up to a high point sooner.

Emotional masters understand that *achievement is about love.* The relationship between achievement and love starts with loving your child for what she is trying to do, not love that's based on how it turns out. This love enables your child to feel loved and competent and allows her to then love herself in the same way. Your love for your child and her own self-love remove any threat to her self-esteem in the risks that she's going to take to reach her achievement goals. This love frees your child to love the achievement activity itself—not just the success—unconditionally and through all of its vicissitudes. Your child's love of herself and her achievement activity strengthens your child's love for you by providing the opportunity to have such an enriching experience and allowing her to find such joy and satisfaction in her participation.

CHOOSING TO BE AN EMOTIONAL MASTER

Becoming an emotional master involves your child's developing the ability to make a choice about what emotions he feels and how he will react to those emotions. Your child can easily enjoy positive emotions—happiness, joy, serenity—and act on them. The difficulty for him is to experience negative emotions—frustration, anger, sadness—and to re-act in a way that encourages rather than detracts from his achievement and happiness.

How your child learns to respond to emotions is a *simple, but not easy, choice.* How your child reacts to his emotions is a simple choice because if your child has the option to feel bad and perform poorly or feel good and perform well, he will certainly choose the latter options. However, how your child responds to his emotions is not an easy choice because unhealthy emotional habits that your child may have learned can compel him to respond in ways that interfere with his achievement and happiness. Because of these emotional habits, your child may feel forced to take a road against his will.

Your child's ability to make this choice can develop in two ways. Ideally, you want to raise your child to be an emotional master. If you raise your child as an emotional master, she will learn healthy emotional habits that enable her to choose the path that guides her to success and happiness. Your child will not be in an internal struggle between bad emotional habits and immediate goals and healthy needs. She will naturally follow the road that leads her to becoming a successful achiever.

However, your child may develop some unhealthy emotional habits that keep her from seeing that she has choices about how she can respond to her emotions. You need to help your child see that she can make a choice: She can either continue down the road she is currently taking—as an emotional victim—or she can choose to take another route, one that will lead to emotional mastery. You can help your child to make this simple, but not easy, choice by making changes that will encourage her to adopt new and healthier emotional habits, which allow her to choose the path that will lead her to success and happiness.

DEVELOPING EMOTIONAL MASTERY

You need to guide your child in making several observations to begin the process of developing emotional mastery. Your child can learn to recognize when her emotions are not serving her well. She can come to understand that she will continue to feel bad and perform poorly if she allows her current negative emotional state to persist. Your child can come to realize that she needs to do something differently to reverse the negative trend.

You need to then allow your child to become familiar with her emotions by having her learn to recognize what emotions she is experiencing. You can ask your child, "What is this feeling you have?" Children can easily separate negative from positive emotions, but only with experience can they learn the differences between negative emotions. When your child feels bad, she needs to be able to distinguish whether she is, for example, fearful, angry, frustrated, sad, or disappointed. "This awareness of emotions is the fundamental emotional competence on which others, such as emotional self-control, build," notes Dr. Daniel Goleman.

You can facilitate your child's understanding by identifying situations as they happen as opportunities for your child to learn about her emotions, such as hurt feelings over a disappointing performance or anger over a conflict with a friend. You can encourage her to articulate precisely what she is feeling. You can describe different ways a person might feel in that situation and compare those feelings to what she is feeling at the moment.

Authors Gottman, Katz, and Hooven call this "emotional coaching," in which you guide your child in the exploration of her emotional world. They further note that emotional coaching is essential to a child's cognitive, social, and emotional development, and that it may act as a buffer against a variety of psychological problems. Children who are coached emotionally focus more effectively, are better learners, and do better in school.

Your child can get so wrapped up in the negative emotions of an achievement experience that she is unable to step back and see that her reactions are not serving her well and that she needs to change them. This is a point at which you can intervene, acting as a *temporary emotional manager*. For example, I worked with a young athlete who had a history of losing control of her emotions and seeing her performances deteriorate during practices and competitions. As soon as I saw the vicious emotional cycle begin in practice, I would step in and ask several questions (and get the following responses): "What emotions are you feeling right now?" ("I'm frustrated and really mad at myself.") "Are these emotions helping or hurting you?" ("They're hurting me.") "If you continue to feel this way, will your play get better or worse?" ("I'll play worse.") "Do you want to continue to play poorly or do you want to turn it around?" ("I want to turn it around.") And finally, "What do you need to do to turn it around?" ("I need to take some deep breaths, relax, and focus on what I need to do to play better.")

With your help both as a role model and with direct intervention as a temporary emotional manager, your child can learn to recognize, label, and understand her emotions. Your child can then search herself and her environment for possible causes of her emotional reactions. Seeing the reasons for her feelings provides your child with further information about the emotional experience and gives her greater understanding and control over what she feels. This process also encourages your child to "step back" from her emotions, which offers her a different perspective on them and often lessens their intensity and impact. This approach also acts to interrupt the emotional vicious cycle and provides your child with the opportunity to reverse its course.

With this more detached and better understood outlook on the situation, your child can then consider courses of action that will serve her best and choose the path that feels better and that will lead to success. These options can include different ways of thinking (for example, being positive, motivated, focusing on the process rather than on the outcome), feeling (for example, feeling excited, being psyched up), and acting (for example, having more energy, putting in greater effort). Finally, your child can choose and commit to a positive course of action directed at altering her current emotional state. The ultimate goal of this emotional mastery process is for your child to have the ability to choose an emotional path that will assist her in her pursuit of success and happiness.

Oscar was a high school senior who was becoming scared and depressed before taking the S.A.T.s. Oscar was avoiding studying and tried to convince himself that how he did on the S.A.T.s didn't matter. Oscar asked his mother for help in getting out of this hole he had dug himself. With his mother's help, Oscar examined how he felt and realized he was feeling so scared because he was worried about hurting his chances of getting into a good college. He also told her that he didn't want to disappoint her and his father. These feelings caused him to avoid studying (and the bad emotions), which made him even more scared and depressed because he knew he wouldn't be prepared to take the S.A.T.s and he would confirm his greatest fear by getting a really low score on the test.

Oscar's mother told him that she and his father loved him very much, would support his efforts in any way they could, and would be proud of him for doing his best no matter what he scored on the S.A.T.s. She pointed out to Oscar that this fear and worry was making it more likely that his fear would be realized. She asked him if that is what he wanted. Oscar replied emphatically, "No!" His mother asked him what would enable Oscar to keep this from happening. Oscar said, "I need to face my fear and focus on positive things that will help me be prepared for the S.A.T.s." With this new understanding of what he was feeling and the encouragement he received from his mother, Oscar was ready to take the good fork in the road. He made himself feel better by imagining that taking the S.A.T.s was one step toward reaching his dream of becoming a doctor and that it would feel great to achieve his goals. Finally, he laid out a plan of studying and taking practice tests in the month leading up to the S.A.T.s.

Oscar noticed several things after he chose to be an emotional master. He felt a lot less anxious about taking the S.A.T.s. Oscar also found that he was more productive in his studying. This raised his confidence, which generated positive emotions that replaced his previous apprehension. Oscar felt like he was caught in an upward spiral of positive thinking, emotions, and productivity, each of which fed on the others. Oscar approached the S.A.T.s feeling confident and prepared to do his best and, on receiving his results, he exceeded his expectations. And that felt really good!

EMOTIONAL MASTERY IS A PROCESS

Developing mastery in school or skills in sports or the arts takes many years of determination, patience, and persistence—remember the "10 years, 10,000 hours" rule. Helping your child become an emotional master is no different; it is an ongoing process to which your child needs to devote time and effort and you need to provide emotional coaching on a daily basis.

In the early stages of developing emotional mastery, your child will struggle with learning to control his emotions because emotions are powerful and unconscious forces that can seem out of his control. Your child may decide to make the right choice, but unhealthy emotions will still emerge and compel him down the unhealthy path. These setbacks should not discourage you or your child, or cause you to think that your emotional coaching isn't working. I have worked with clients for several years who during the first year just didn't get it. They weren't adopting the skills I was trying to teach and they were not improving. Their inability to learn these skills was both bewildering and frustrating. But I have learned that change takes time—a lot of time, of which children have plenty—and that just because children aren't changing doesn't mean they aren't listening and it is not sinking in. In most instances, these "slow" learners are not slow at all; they are just not ready to act on what they have learned. Then, what seems like out of the blue some time later—as much as a year or more—they start thinking, feeling, and acting in the ways I had suggested to them long before and they finally were able to make the big step to becoming emotional masters and successful achievers.

You shouldn't realistically expect your child to just break her unhealthy emotional habits and stop all of her negative emotions and replace them with positive ones immediately. Instead, your initial goal should be to *balance the scales*. As an emotional victim, your child's "emotional scales" have been tipped heavily toward negative emotions. As your child gains emotional mastery, she can strive to reduce her negative emotions and increase her positive emotions so that they are at least in balance. In time, as your child becomes more emotionally skilled, she can take the next step of weighting her emotional scales toward positive emotions. Your child will find a new sense of happiness and well-being when the scale has tipped in favor of positive emotions.

Making the healthy choice and following through will take considerable determination, focus, and effort. But each time your child makes the right choice, he is making it easier to choose the next time. The great thing about emotional mastery is that it is self-rewarding. When your child makes the correct choice, he not only feels better, he also performs better. Like Oscar, your child can experience the upward spiral of positive emotions and achievement. He will come to see that emotional mastery is a much better road to take. With each positive choice, your child slowly trains his emotional habits until, in time, negative emotional habits arise infrequently and, when they do, he has the skills to reassert his positive emotional habits. These healthy emotional habits enable your child to become a successful achiever.

Emotional mastery is a skill that is acquired with awareness, control, and practice. You can facilitate the development of emotional mastery by guiding your child through the emotional mastery process. You should look for less dramatic situations in which your child may experience some minor upset—for example, playing a game—and then guide her through emotional mastery. With experience in mastering minor emotional difficulties, your child can use these skills in increasingly more emotionally demanding situations—school exams, artistic performances, sports competitions—until she is able to demonstrate emotional mastery in achievement activities in which she is more invested.

With time and practice, these emotional mastery skills will be internalized and your child can gain access to them on his own. Additionally, your child can learn to use emotional mastery preventively. Your child can come to recognize common situations in which negative emotions arise and initiate the emotional mastery process before they appear, thereby stopping the vicious cycle before it starts and allowing himself to continue his journey to success and happiness.

SKILLS FOR EMOTIONAL MASTERY

EMOTIONAL SKILLS

1. Identifying and labeling feelings.
2. Expressing feelings.
3. Assessing the intensity of feelings.
4. Managing feelings.
5. Delaying gratification.
6. Controlling impulses.
7. Reducing stress.
8. Knowing the difference between feelings and actions.

COGNITIVE SKILLS

1. Self-talk—conducting an "inner dialogue" as a way to cope with a topic or challenge or reinforce one's own behavior.
2. Reading and interpreting social cues—for example, recognizing social influences on behavior and seeing oneself in the perspective of the larger community.
3. Using steps for problem-solving and decision-making—for instance, controlling impulses, setting goals, identifying alternative actions, anticipating consequences.
4. Understanding the perspective of others.
5. Understanding behavioral norms (what is and what is not acceptable behavior).

6. A positive attitude toward life.

7. Self-awareness—for example, developing realistic expectations about oneself.

BEHAVIORAL SKILLS

1. Nonverbal—communicating through eye contact, facial expressiveness, tone of voice, gestures, and so on.

2. Verbal—making clear requests, responding effectively to criticism, resisting negative influences, listening to others, helping others, participating in peer groups.

Goleman, D. (1995). *Emotional intelligence*. New York: Bantam.

Afterword

Giving your child a fundamental belief in him- or herself. Allowing your child to gain ownership of his or her achievements and life. Teaching your child to be an emotional master. Raising your child to be a successful achiever. These are the greatest gifts that you can give your child. Yet they are also the most difficult gifts to give.

You face an uphill battle in which you must struggle against formidable adversaries to deliver these gifts to your child. You must face your child's own inertia, which impels him or her to stay in one place rather than progress and grow. You need to combat unhealthy messages with which your child is bombarded by our superficial, image-oriented, and media-driven culture. Lastly, you must confront the biggest obstacle to raising a successful achiever—yourself. You need to face your own demons—your past baggage, emotional habits, and needs—that may interfere with your acting in the best interests of your child.

Because of this struggle, I have come to believe that *courage and commitment* are the two most important qualities you must have to raise a successful achiever. You need the courage to face the demons that may cause you to put your needs ahead of those of your child. You must have the fortitude to identify and change unhealthy emotional habits that may hurt your child. You must have the courage to make the right choice with every fork in the road you come to, with every decision that will either help or hurt your child's achievement and happiness.

You must also commit to the process of raising your child the very best you can. Child-rearing is not a part-time job. Raising your child is not an effort that can occur at your convenience. Rather, it is your daily obligation to do what is in the best interests of your child. This commitment makes you understand that every experience that your child has is an opportunity for success and happiness or another step down a road toward mediocrity and unhappiness. Commitment ensures that you make the right choice every day to have a positive impact on your child's life.

I hope that this book has provided you with the insights and tools to help you positively push your child to become a successful achiever. The responsibility to use them is yours. You are now at a fork in the road that will influence your child and your relationship with him or her for the rest of your lives. You can be a well-intentioned but passive or intrusive parent, or you can be a conscious, active, and positive force in your child's journey toward adulthood.

Which road do you choose?

Jim Taylor, Ph.D.
April 2002

BIBLIOGRAPHY

Adderholdt-Elliott, M. (1991). Perfectionism and the gifted adolescent. In M. Bireley and J. Genshaft (eds.), *Understanding the gifted adolescent: Educational, developmental, and multicultural issues.* Education and psychology of the gifted series (pp. 65–75). New York: Teachers College Press.

Anshel, M. H. (1991). Causes for drug abuse in sport: A survey of intercollegiate athletes. *Journal of Sport Behavior* 14, 283–307.

Antony, M. M., and Swinson, R. P. (1998). *When perfect isn't good enough: Strategies for coping with perfectionism.* Oakland, CA: New Harbinger Publications.

Armstrong, A. J. (July 2001). Dealing with disappointment. *Hemispheres,* 102–105.

Azar, B. (June 1997). Consistent parenting helps children regulate emotions. *APA Monitor,* 17.

Bakker, F. C. (1988). Personality differences between young dancers and non-dancers. *Personality and Individual Differences* 9, 121–131.

———. (1991). Development of personality in dancers: A longitudinal study. *Personality and Individual Differences* 12, 671–681.

Bishop, J. B., Bauer, K. W., and Becker, E. T. (1998). A survey of counseling needs of male and female college students. *Journal of College Student Development* 39, 205–210.

Bloom, B. S. (1985). *Developing talent in young people.* New York: Ballantine.

Bohnert, C. (Sept./Oct. 1999). Float like a butterfly, soar like an eagle. *Olympian,* 27–28.

Bradley, B. (April 2000). The game of life. *Parents,* 37–39.

Brazelton, T. B. (1987). *What every baby knows.* New York: Addison-Wesley.

Buri, J. R. (1988). The nature of humankind, authoritarianism, and self-esteem. *Journal of Psychology and Christianity* 7, 32–38.

Burke Mountain Academy. (December 18, 1998). *Newsletter #4.*

Burns, D. (1980). The perfectionist's script for self-defeat. *Psychology Today*, 34–51.

Callahan, G., and Steptoe, S. (July 24, 1995). An end too soon. *Sports Illustrated*, 33–36.

Clarke, J. I. (1978). *Self-esteem: A family affair*. Minneapolis: Winston Press.

Cline, F. W., and Fay, J. (1990). *Parenting with love and logic*. Colorado Springs: Pinon.

Coles, R. (1998). *The moral intelligence of children*. New York: Plume.

Conroy, D. E. Developing a multidimensional measure of fear of failure appraisals: The performance failure appraisal inventory. Paper presented at the annual meetings of the Association for the Advancement of Applied Sport Psychology, Nashville, TN, October 20, 2000.

———. (in press). Fear of failure: An exemplar of social development research in sport. *Quest*.

Conroy, D. E., Poczwardowski, A., and Henschen, K. P. (2000). Evaluative criteria and consequences associated with failure and success for elite athletes and performing artists. Manuscript submitted for publication.

Coopersmith, S. (1967). *The antecedents of self-esteem*. San Francisco: Freeman.

Csikszentmihalyi, M. (1975). *Beyond boredom and anxiety*. San Francisco: Jossey-Bass.

Deci, E. L., Koestner, R., and Ryan, R. M. (1999). A meta-analytic review of experiments examining the effects of extrinsic rewards on intrinsic motivation. *American Psychologist* 125, 627–668.

Dinkmeyer, D., and McKay, G. D. (1982). *Raising a responsible child: Practical steps to successful family relationships*. New York: Fireside.

Dobson, J. C. (1987). *Parenting isn't for cowards: Dealing confidently with the frustrations of child-rearing*. Waco, TX: World Books.

Dyer, W. W. (1985). *What do you really want for your children?* New York: William Morrow.

Edelman, M. W. (1992). *The measure of our success: A letter to my children and yours*. Boston: Beacon Press.

Elliot, A. J., and Church, M. A. (1997). A hierarchical model of approach and avoidance achievement motivation. *Journal of Personality and Social Psychology* 72, 218–232.

Elliot, A. J., & Sheldon, K. M. (1997). Avoidance achievement motivation: A personal goals analysis. *Journal of Personality and Social Psychology* 73, 171–185.

———. (1998). Avoidance personal goals and the personality-illness relationship. *Journal of Personality and Social Psychology* 75, 1282–1299.

Ericsson, K. A., and Charness, N. (1994). Expert performance: Its structure and acquisition. *American Psychologist* 49, 725–747.

Evitt, M. F. (March 2000). Raise a can-do kid. *Parents*, 199–200.

Felson, R. B., and Reed, M. (1986). The effects of parents on the self-appraisals of children. *Social Psychology Quarterly* 49, 302–308.

Ferrari, J. R. (1992). Procrastinators and perfect behavior: An exploratory factor analysis of self-presentation, self-awareness, and self-handicapping components. *Journal of Research in Personality* 26, 75–84.

Fine, A. H., and Sachs, M. L. (1997). *Total sports experience for kids: A parents' guide to success in youth sports*. South Bend, IN: Diamond Communications.

Flett, G. L., Hewitt, P. L., Blankstein, K. R., and Mosher, S. W. (1991). Perfectionism, self-actualization, and personal adjustment. *Journal of Social Behavior and Personality* 6, 147–160.

Flett, G. L., Hewitt, P. L., Endler, N. S., and Tassone, C. (1994). Perfectionism and components of state and trait anxiety. *Current Psychological Research and Reviews* 13, 326–350.

Forehand, R., and McKinney, B. (1993). Historical overview of child discipline in the United States: Implications for mental health clinicians and researchers. *Journal of Child & Family Studies* 2, 221–228.

Frome, P. M., & Fuchs, J. M. (1998). Parents' influence on children's achievement-related perceptions. *Journal of Personality and Social Psychology* 74, 435–452.

Frost, R. O., and Henderson, K. J. (1991). Perfectionism and reactions to athletic competition. *Journal of Sport and Exercise Psychology* 13, 323–335.

Frost, R. O., Marten, P. A., Lahart, C., and Rosenblate, R. (1990). The dimensions of perfectionism. *Cognitive Therapy and Research* 14, 449–468.

Gleick, E. (April 22, 1996). Every kid a star. *Time*, 39–40.

Goldenthal, P. (1999). *Beyond sibling rivalry: How to help your child become cooperative, caring, and compassionate*. New York: Henry Holt.

Goleman, D. (1995). *Emotional intelligence.* New York: Bantam.

Gottman, J. M., Katz, L. F., and Hooven, C. (1997). *Meta-emotion: How families communicate emotionally.* Mahwah, NJ: Lawrence Erlbaum.

Gould, S. (1977). *Teenagers: The continuing challenge.* New York: Hawthorn.

Gray, J. (1999). *Children are from heaven: Positive parenting skills for raising cooperative, confident, and compassionate children.* New York: HarperCollins.

Greene, L. J. (1995). *The life-smart kid: Teaching your child to use good judgment in every situation.* Rocklin, CA: Prima.

Greene, R. W. (1998). *The explosive child: A new approach to understanding and parenting easily frustrated, "chronically inflexible" children.* New York: HarperCollins.

Hamilton, L. H. (1999). A psychological profile of the adolescent dancer. *Journal of Dance Medicine and Science* 3, 48–50.

Harter, S. (1978). Effectance motivation reconsidered. *Human Development* 21, 34–64.

———. (1983). Developmental perspectives on self-esteem. In E. M. Hetherington (ed.), *Handbook on child psychology, socialization, personality, and development change* (pp. 275–385). New York: Wiley.

Harter, S., Marold, D. B., Whitesell, N. R., and Cobbs, G. A. model of the effects of perceived parent and peer support on adolescent false self behavior. *Child Development* 67, 360–374.

Hewitt, P. L., and Flett, G. L. (1990). Perfectionism and depression: A multidimensional analysis. *Journal of Social Behavior and Personality* 5, 423–438.

———. (1991). Perfectionism in the self and social contexts: Conceptualization, assessment, and association with psychopathology. *Journal of Personality and Social Psychology* 60, 456–470.

Hewitt, P. L., Flett, G. L., and Endler, N. S. (1995). Perfectionism, coping, and depression symptomatology in a clinical sample. *Clinical Psychology and Psychotherapy* 2, 47–58.

Hill, K. T. (1972). Anxiety in the evaluative context. In W. W. Hartup (ed.), *The young child* (vol. 2, pp. 225–263). Washington, DC: National Association for the Education of Young Children.

Juster, H. R., Heimberg, R. G., Frost, R. O., Holt, C. S., Mattia, J. I., and Faccenda, K. (1996). Social phobia and perfectionism. *Personality and Individual Differences* 21, 403–410.

Kabat-Zinn, M., and Kabat-Zinn, J. (1997). *Everyday blessings: The inner work of mindful parenting.* New York: Hyperion.

Kamins, M. L., and Dweck, C. S. (1999). Person versus process praise and criticism: Implications for contingent self-worth and coping. *Developmental Psychology* 35, 835–847.

Kimura, N. (December 1998). Quotation on child rearing. [Online.] Available: http://unr.edu/homepage/kimura/child.html.

Krippner, S. (1967). Ten commandments that block creativity. Presented at the annual meetings of the National Association for Gifted Children, Hartford, Connecticut, May, 1967.

Lee, B. P. H., Caputi, P., Anshel, M. H., and Walker, B. M. Perfectionism in sport: Relationship with sport-specific psychological skills. Presented at the Association for the Advancement of Applied Sport Psychology annual meetings, Banff, Alberta, Canada, September 25, 1999.

Lenning, D. J. (1999). Motivation and future temporal orientation: A test of the self-handicapping hypothesis. *Psychological Reports* 84, 1070–1072.

Love, III, D. (1997). *Every shot I take: Lessons learned about golf, life, and a father's love.* New York: Simon & Schuster.

Masten, A. S., and Coatsworth, J. D. (1998). The development of competence in favorable and unfavorable environments: Lessons from research on successful children. *American Psychologist* 53, 205–220.

McCann, N., and Oliver, R. (1988). Problems in families with gifted children: Implications for counselors. *Journal of Counseling and Development* 66, 275–278.

McClelland, D. C. (1958). Risk taking in children with high and low need for achievement. In J. W. Atkinson (ed.), *Motives in fantasy, action, and society* (pp. 306–321). Princeton, NJ: Van Nostrand.

McClelland, D. C., Atkinson, J. W., Clark, R. A., & Lowell, E. L. (1953). *The achievement motive.* New York: Irvington.

Miller, A. (1981). *The drama of the gifted child.* New York: Basic.

———. (1986). *Prisoner of Childhood.* New York: Basic.

Mueller, C. M., and Dweck, C. S. (1998). Praise for intelligence can undermine children's motivation and performance. *Journal of Personality and Social Psychology* 75, 33–52.

Murray, B. (June 1997). Verbal praise may be the best motivator of all. *APA Monitor*, 26.

Nevius, C. W. (September 1, 2001). Too good to be true. *San Francisco Chronicle*, A1, A8.

Nuttall, E. V., and Nuttall, R. L. (1976). Parent-child relationship and effective academic motivation. *Journal of Psychology* 94, 127–133.

Parke, R. D., MacDonald, K. B., Beitel, A., and Bhavnagri, N. (1988). The role of the family in the development of peer relationships. In R. Peters and R. J. McMahan (eds.), *Social learning systems: Approaches to marriage and the family* (pp. 17–44). New York: Brunner-Mazel.

Paterson, J. (May 2000). Try, try again. *Parents*, 221–222.

Pipher, M. (1994). *Reviving Ophelia: Saving the lives of adolescent girls*. New York: Ballantine.

Powers, J. (March 18, 1993). Feeling good (for nothing). *The Stowe Reporter*, 4–5.

Rimm, S. (1997). *Dr. Sylvia Rimm's Smart Parenting: How to Parent So Children Will Learn*. New York: Crown.

Rosemond, J. (September 1998). Crime and punishment: When only big consequences will do. *Hemispheres*, 99–101.

———. (November 1998). Parenting myths debunked. *Hemispheres*, 120–124.

Rotella, R. J., and Bunker, L. K. (1987). *Parenting your superstar: How to help your child get the most out of sports*. Champaign, IL: Leisure.

Rubenstein, C. (1997). *The sacrificial mother: Escaping the trap of self-denial*. New York: Hyperion.

Sarason, S. B., Davidson, K. S., Lighthall, F. F., Waite, R. R., and Ruebush, B. K. (1960). *Anxiety in elementary school children*. New York: Wiley.

Scanlon, T. K., and Lewthwaite, R. (1984). Social psychological aspects of competition for male youth sport participants. I: Predictors of competitive stress. *Journal of Sport Psychology* 6, 208–226.

Scanlon, T. K., and Passer, M. W. (1978). Factors related to competitive stress among male youth sport participants. *Medicine and Science in Sports* 10, 103–108.

———. (1979). Sources of competitive stress in young female athletes. *Journal of Sport Psychology* 1, 151–159.

Schmalt, H. D. (1982). Two concepts of fear of failure motivation. In R. Schwarzer, H. M. van der Ploeg, and C. D. Spielberger (eds.), *Advances in test anxiety research* (vol. 1, pp. 45–52). Lisse, The Netherlands: Swets & Zeitlinger.

Sheldon, K. M., Elliot, A. J., Kim, Y., and Kasser, T. (2001). What is satisfying about satisfying event: Testing 10 candidate psychological needs. *Journal of Personality and Social Psychology* 80, 325–339.

Shoda, Y., Mischel, W., and Peake, P. K. (1990). Predicting adolescent cognitive and self-regulatory competences from preschool delay of gratification. *Developmental Psychology* 26, 978–986.

Singh, S. (1992). Hostile press measure of fear of failure and its relation to child-rearing attitudes and behavior problems. *Journal of Social Psychology* 132, 397–399.

Smoll, F. (1997). Improving the quality of coach-parent relationships in youth sports. In J. M. Williams (ed.), *Applied sport psychology: Personal growth to peak performance* (3rd ed., pp. 63–73). Mountain View, CA: Mayfield.

Spear, N. (August 19, 2001). Adulthood 101. *San Francisco Chronicle*, B5.

Stipek, D., and Gralinski, J. H. (1996). Children's beliefs about intelligence and school performance. *Journal of Educational Psychology* 88, 397–407.

Strang, R. (1960). *Helping your gifted child.* New York: E. P. Dutton.

Taffel, R. (April 2000). Tune in to your child's true nature. *Parents*, 127–133.

Teevan, R. C. (1983). Childhood development of fear of failure motivation: A replication. *Psychological Reports* 53, 506.

Teevan, R. C., and McGhee, G. (1972). Childhood development of fear of failure motivation. *Journal of Personality and Social Psychology* 21, 345–348.

Tice, D., and Baumeister, R. F. (1993). Controlling anger: Self-induced emotional change. In D. Wegner and J. Pennebaker (eds.), *Handbook of mental control.* Englewood Cliffs, NJ: Prentice-Hall.

Treffert, D. A. (Fall 1975). Happiness is . . . the American dream. *Inspection News* 6, 23.

Trillin, C. (1996). *Messages from my father.* New York: Farrar, Straus & Giroux.

Vanderkam, L. (July 27, 2001). Hookups starve the soul. *USA Today,* 7A.

Vuko, E. P. (November 29, 1999). Unmotivated kids can change, if parents do. *The Hartford Courant,* D1–2.

Warren, L. (January 2000). After the fall. *Good Housekeeping,* 20–21.

Weeda, M., Winny, L., and Drop, M. J. (1985). The discriminative value of psychological characteristics in anorexia nervosa: Clinical and psychometric comparison between anorexia nervosa patients, ballet dancers and controls. *Journal of Psychiatric Research* 19, 285–290.

Weiss, M. R., Weise, D. M., and Klint, K. A. (1989). Head over heels with success: The relationship between self-efficacy and performance in competitive youth gymnastics. *Journal of Sport and Exercise Psychology* 11, 444–451.

Wertheim, L. J. (February 5, 2000). Jenny come lately. *Sports Illustrated,* 54–58.

Woodhouse, L. D. (1990). An exploratory study of the use of life history methods to determine treatment needs for female substance abusers. *Response to the Victimization of Women and Children* 13, 12–15.

Woods, E. (1992). *Playing through: Straight talk on hard work, big dreams and adventures with Tiger.* New York: HarperCollins.

Young, J. A., and Hipple, J. (1996). Social/emotional problems of university music students seeking assistance at a student counseling center. *Medical Problems of Performing Artists* 11, 123–126.

Zinsser, N., Bunker, L., and Williams, J. M. (1998). Cognitive techniques for building confidence and enhancing performance. *Applied sport psychology: Personal growth to peak performance* (pp. 270–295). Mountain View, CA: Mayfield.

INDEX

About the Author

Jim Taylor, Ph.D., has worked with young achievers and their parents in sports, the performing arts, and education for over sixteen years. He has provided children with the skills they need to become successful and happy. Dr. Taylor has helped parents understand how to best raise their children and has taught parents the tools they need to be conscious, positive, and active forces in their child's life.

Dr. Taylor has been a consultant for the United States and Japanese Ski Teams and the United States Tennis Association, and has worked with many athletes of all levels of ability in many sports. He has also worked with the Miami City Ballet, the Hartford Ballet Company, and the DanceAspen Summer School.

Dr. Taylor received his bachelor's degree from Middlebury College and earned his master's degree and Ph.D. in psychology from the University of Colorado. He is a former associate professor in the School of Psychology at Nova University in Ft. Lauderdale.

A former alpine ski racer who competed internationally, Dr. Taylor lived the life of a young achiever and learned firsthand about the challenges of achievement. He is also a United States Professional Tennis Association certified teaching professional, a second degree black belt and certified instructor in karate, and a sub-three-hour marathon runner.

Dr. Taylor has authored *Psychology of Dance, Psychological Approaches to Sports Injury Rehabilitation*, and *Comprehensive Sports Injury Management*. He has published more than 250 articles in scholarly and popular publications and has given more than 350 workshops and presentations throughout North America and Europe.

Dr. Taylor has appeared on the major television network affiliates in South Florida and on *ABC's World News This Weekend*. He has participated in many radio shows. His research has been the subject of syndicated sports columns that have appeared in dozens of newspapers across the country. Dr. Taylor has been a columnist for *The Denver Post* and *Ski Racing*. He has been interviewed for articles that have appeared in *The Miami Herald, The Ft. Lauderdale Sun-Sentinel, The Baltimore Sun, The Denver Post*, and many other newspapers and magazines.